ALL STRAC
ARE COU

Memoirs

ALL STRACHEYS ARE COUSINS

Memoirs

Amabel Williams-Ellis

WEIDENFELD AND NICOLSON
LONDON

First published in Great Britain by
George Weidenfeld & Nicolson Limited
91 Clapham High Street, London sw4 7ta
1983

ISBN 0 297 78208 8

Typeset by Deltatype, Ellesmere Port
Printed in Great Britain by
Butler & Tanner Limited
Frome and London

CONTENTS

ILLUSTRATIONS

AUTHOR'S NOTE

'What the soldier said isn't evidence,' said the Judge reprovingly to Sam Weller.

Since this book is intended as a case history, I – unlike Sam Weller – have tried to avoid secondary sources and to keep hindsight in its place. Thus I have left in the evidence errors of memory that combine to make up what I am. Some, or all, such errors may be significant.

In a case history, the evidence isn't about facts but about the impact of the environment, and is progressively felt and interpreted by a particular person.

One more point. This is not the tale of someone with an important speaking part in the long soap opera that we call History, or who was any kind of expert. In our culture it is from such non-experts, members of a jury or of a nation's voters that the experts demand opinions.

Amabel Williams-Ellis

One

LITTLE GIRL

I am between four and five years old, and sitting on the floor with my back to a pleasant coal fire. I know that my name is Amabel Strachey. I am nursing a doll and am waiting for something to happen that I believe will be of great consequence. The time of year is winter, and the place my Simpson grandparents' tall solid house in Kensington. There is a winter fog outside, not a bad one, but even so, down here in the library the gas-lights look a little dim and the room smells slightly of sulphur. The door at the far end of the room opens and in the doorway stands a figure, a woman, shortish and wearing some kind of uniform.

I am told, or I already know, that this is my new Nanny. I don't say anything, but I know and tell myself that a great deal depends on what she is like. For me she is Fate in a bonnet and cloak.

I am quite passive, for I feel – I am sure – that I have no choice. This seems so true that I do not believe that anything could be otherwise, or could be wrong. I can't see her distinctly, for the gas-jets do not throw their light very far through the dusk of London, and I am as mute as a fish. A child will make a resounding fuss over a trifle, but tell adults far too little about what affects it deeply.

So there I sit on a winter afternoon, nursing my doll and as mute as a fish.

Much later my mother told me that she had found out that another nurse had been unkind; I remember nothing of it.

This time my mother's choice was fortunate. With Nanny Holland there was neither neglect nor unkindness, but a just, loyal, often rough cherishing and support. On this support I and, three or four years later, my younger brother John came to feel that we could depend absolutely. Once, when we were both grown up, he said, speaking with vehemence and with an exaggeration that I thought at the time puzzling, yet somehow excusable: 'If it hadn't been for Nanny, you and I would both have died!'

We shouldn't, of course, have died. But at last I think that I know what he meant: she was important because we could turn to her when we wanted a square and bracing deal. Our difficulties were, by any standard, not formidable. Our circumstances were comfortable and we were surrounded by a number of adults, none of whom were hostile or malicious.

But my brother was a turbulent little boy and, looking back, it seems that something quite real prompted that odd grown-up remark. Turbulent children, up to four or five, can be terrified of their own violence. What John felt so grateful for was, I expect, the support of Nanny's outspoken dispensing of justice, and the efficacy of her restraining presence. Perhaps children may be even more grateful for such a guard against panic than for the love and indulgence that they also need. With Nanny we felt protected from 'going too far' – a state which is dreadful to a child and alarmingly easy to slip into.

Panic came to me mostly when I couldn't stop crying, or couldn't say I was sorry; a child can suffer despair when it can't stop being naughty. Pity the child in a temper-tantrum! He or she is desperate, suffering one of Milton's torments of the damned.

> Me, miserable, which way should I fly?
> Which way I fly is Hell, Myself am Hell!

Less turbulent than my younger brother, I had, by the time I can remember, passions that were easier to control, but even so I was sometimes thankful to cling to Nanny's safety barrier against that terrifying 'going too far'. She could also protect us both against discouragement and attacks of apparently causeless, or anyhow unidentified, misery.

I have crept under the nursery table, which has a long, fringed tablecloth. This is my refuge. Here it is warm and almost dark. After a while a grown-up hand lets in a little yellow lamplight and a voice says: 'Come out, Amabel. Come out you little pink and white monkey! Come and eat your tea. If you don't feel well you can go to bed. Don't hang about suffering.'

There always seemed to be such a table of refuge, whether at home or when, with Nanny and later also with a nursery-maid and my baby brother John, we found ourselves in the houses of one or other of our grandparents. Each place, though, had its own character.

No. 14 Cornwall Gardens in Kensington comes back most as a series of interiors – high darkish rooms with less resonance than most because of velvet *portières* to doors as well as windows; flights and flights of stairs took us away from these high dark rooms up to the less high, less dark nursery, where there waited a horse-on-wheels covered in real skin and about the size of a St Bernard dog. He was called John Balliol and had, I fancy, originally been given to my brother Tom, my elder by five years. Anyhow, he wasn't my horse, nor John's either; he was himself. Goodness knows why he was called John Balliol.

My Strachey grandfather and Sutton Court in Somerset, on the other hand, bring back outdoor recollections, but now I find some of them pretty dubious. Here is one, distinct but odd.

I am now five years old and am being driven with Nanny in a hansom cab. If the scene were London there would be nothing remarkable about it. But this is not London, and the drive is from Temple Meads station in Bristol to Sutton Court, an ancient manor house which is still the Strachey ancestral home. Not quite a stately home – it isn't big enough and is too informal – but it does have a medieval tower with a winding stair, gables and battlements.

A hansom cab is a most eccentric vehicle, so balanced that on the flat the horse is almost suspended on its belly-band, while the driver is perched up above a roof behind his passengers. Did this horse and driver really forsake the urban scene, the forecourt of Temple Meads station, forsake it for the winding, deep, up and down country roads whose hedges were just then white with dust and hawthorn blossom? It was some kind of a cab, I am sure of that; it wasn't the brougham-shaped four-wheeler called a growler. I am sure because what is distinct after more than eighty years is that the view out of it, during a drive which must have lasted more than an hour, is to the front – not the side as in a growler or a railway-carriage. In a brougham or growler, the coachman's back, as he sits high on his box, whip in hand, blocks the front view. But I could also see sideways and thus see the hedges, also the horse's ears and the white country road ahead. The road was narrow and it wound up the hills and down again. I think I must have been sitting on Nanny's knee and I know that I was still small.

Another memory of Sutton is also dubious in a different way.

Nanny and I are going back to London after a visit. This time crocuses, not white hawthorn, are the flowers that I see. They are yellow crocuses round a big tree and surrounded by mown grass.

But when I went back to Sutton half a century later to show my

cousin Charles O'Hagan the setting, I was at fault. There never seems
to have been such a tree in the place where memory says it stood. There
is no stump, nothing even to show its place. And yet the picture is
sharp.

I am holding Nanny's hand and looking back at the bent figure
of my Strachey grandfather, a small man with a trim white beard.
He is leaning on two sticks, and the memory of what I am thinking
is as clear as the tree or the colour of the crocuses. I am thinking:
how will grandpapa manage to walk back to the house if he hasn't
got me to lean on? But again I am fatalistic, just as I had been
about the arrival of Nanny.

How excellent this grandfather must have been to have convinced
such a little girl that she really was useful to him.

One more very early island of memory seems worth recording because
it is an instance of an unusual human quality sometimes known as
charisma and because it left a permanent impression on me. This one
has obviously a large admixture of those excellent but tricky ingredients, family tradition and myth.

I am by now five or six years old and am sitting with my mother
on a sofa, or rather I am scrambling about on the back of the sofa
on which she is sitting. From this sofa-back I can look out of the
window. It is the country, in Surrey; we are in our house, Little
Newlands, and I have a view of the rough gravel drive that leads to
it. I am alert because I have heard the clop-clop of a horse and the
rattle and scrunch of iron-rimmed wheels. It is the baker's cart,
usual on that day of the week. It is a high, two-wheeled cart, the
whole of its back forming a large box for the loaves. Today the cart
looks different because sitting very upright beside the driver on his
box is a thin lady in a black bonnet tied with ribbons under her
chin. She is holding on her lap a black leather bag.

I gesture to my mother that she should also look out of the
window. She does so.

'Good gracious!' she exclaims, jumping up, 'It must be Miss
Kingsley.'

It was indeed Mary Kingsley, the African explorer, or rather
anthropologist, and my mother's added conjecture that she has come to
stay turns out to be true.

Of all my parents' grown-up visitors, many of them then just as
renowned, Mary Kingsley is the one who produced the only really

brilliant early impression on me. She did indeed, for me, become a culture hero. I don't think she took any particular notice of me, as I undoubtedly did of her, nor was she the only explorer that I recall. Later there was the famous Gertrude Bell and also one Frank T. Bullen, a whaler and missionary. Anyhow, when I first saw the thin lady on the baker's cart, I was too young to be aware of the adventures and perils commonly suffered by explorers, or even to understand the funny stories that she apparently told as compellingly as she later wrote them.

No, the shining quality of which I was so much aware was something else; the grown-ups felt it too. I remember my sense of her presence as a sort of tingling. A sense of restrained vitality, was it? Like the luminous shine in the eyes of one of the great cats. A leopard, perhaps. There was certainly nothing shining – not in the conventional way – about the baker's-cart lady. The black bonnet, the long, full black skirt, the high-necked blouse and the ramrod back were as incongruous as they were deceptive on a woman not yet out of her thirties. This intrepid young explorer dressed like an old lady in Surrey, in London and in the African bush. So then she came into the house and took off her bonnet, and I saw that she wore her very fair hair flat on her head in two wings. Her face was rather long and her eyes piercingly blue. She was disciplined in her movements, very controlled, and as unselfish and as ungrasping as a nun.

I think our family tradition of two of her tales and sayings came from an aspect of her character that had nothing to do with Africa. And the strength of her charisma illustrates what made perfectly explicable her African exploits and the pleasant relations with two or three savage tribes. These two stories are concerned with Victorian London, for which she had as uninhibited a relish as she had for swamps and forests. My mother, an excellent story-teller, used to repeat some of her sayings. For instance this jingle:

> 'If I'd a five pound note,'
>   Said the cat's meat man,
> 'I'd marry you tomorrow,'
>   Said the cat's meat man.
> She expressed her approbation
>   Of his admirable plan,
> And she gave a five pound note
>   To the cat's meat man.

Cultivated as well as brave and learned, Miss Kingsley could not however pronounce the letter 'H' – not, that is, as it is sounded in

English. My mother, on request, would imitate Miss Kingsley describing how, on one of her returns from Africa, she had gone to visit a family of old London friends. The daughter of the house presently said:

'"Do come up and see my new 'at – do! Please, Miss Kingsley."'

'Now she knew quite well that I wasn't really a judge of an 'at. As soon as we were upstairs and the bedroom door was shut, she turned to me and she said: "Oh, Miss Kingsley, whatever shall I do? 'Arry's 'iding among the chimney pots." 'Arry was 'er young man, of course.'

At that stage in the story, when my mother told it to us, I always wanted to know what happened next – sure, however, that no situation could ever be too much for Miss Kingsley. What answer did I get? As usual when I – little bore that I must have been – wanted to go beyond the story-teller's 'curtain line', the answer was: 'Then the band played and the bricks fell down.' Infuriating! This is a reply I often received as an enquiring child.

One very natural question whose answer would have conveyed nothing whatever, never once occurred to me – not as a little girl. The question that could have been asked was why did Mary Kingsley and the often eminent and powerful people who will appear in the next few chapters, why did they frequent my parents? The answer to such a question I should obviously then not have understood.

Mary Kingsley was thus the first truly interesting person I recall appearing in our house, the first person of whom (till I was seven or so) I took the slightest notice and one of the few whose image is still vivid. Eminences came and then disappeared; they disappeared into the African bush with its dark faces, its juju and its talking drums, or, like Frank Bullen, they were rowed out to board some tossing ship on the Atlantic, or, like Gertrude Bell, to a white tent alongside the black tents of Arab nomads. But, for all that any little girl would know or care, these grown-ups were mostly and less dramatically off to an embassy, a residency, a vice-regal palace, or perhaps the White House.

There seem to have been a great many of these notables – diplomats, millionaires, politicians and so on. There were also a few writers – Rudyard Kipling and Lytton Strachey, for example, but, as far as I can recall, not a single scientist, few if any musicians, no one from the theatre, and of painters only Simon Bussy and Duncan Grant and my own Uncle Harry but, like Lytton and James Strachey, they didn't count, for they were kinsmen. For a long time, who the others all were and that some of them seemed to have wives or husbands and some did not, that some appeared at dinner parties – extraordinarily – in other than the usual white tie and tails, all this interested me not at all, not even that one weekend in somewhat of a whirl Mr Winston Churchill managed to bring along a lady called Clementine.

However, as I got a little older – nine or so – someone called Lord Cromer emerged and I began rather to like this Lord Cromer, who would arrive from India or our war in Afghanistan, or was it already from Egypt, where he was so concerned with trying to get General Gordon out of Khartoum. I dare say that by then he may have been ruling Egypt, to the annoyance of the French. He was large and impressive and, when he was Sir Evelyn Baring, had been unkindly nicknamed Over Baring. I liked him well enough because, coming often to stay, he would sit down and play chess with me. He always seemed to win. This I put down at the time to the fact that, as we played, he would usually be smoking Egyptian cigarettes and the smoke went in my eyes. Looking back, I suspect that, in truth, Lord Cromer was the better chess player.

Rudyard Kipling I took to rather more quickly – before, that is, I was up to chess. This was because he would often sit me on his knee and tell me one of his *Just So Stories*. These were not yet printed, nor could I have read them if they had been for, disgracefully, I couldn't read till I turned nine. He told the stories dramatically, often making me jump. The sing-song of some passage such as 'Then ran Dingo – Yellow Dog Dingo' would have lulled me just before the well-engineered jump came.

All the same I had mixed feelings about this Mr Kipling. On the good side was that I had been told, and what is more knew, that it was only right to be as kind as possible to him because, not so long ago, his little girl called Josephine had died. I really did feel sympathy: 'There runs a road by Merrow Down' – I thought that this poem was about her and that she must have been about my age too. His excellent stories and feeling sorry for him made me like him. On the other hand, he didn't like cats, which I held to be wrong and undiscerning of him. Also, instead of a little fair or reddish down on the backs of his hands and wrists, like my father and my cherished Uncle Harry, he had black hairs, hairs as black as his moustache.

Lord Northcliffe, then still Alfred Harmsworth, was by this time past the weekly *Tit-Bits* phase but not yet a press baron. All the same, when John and I were children, he had established himself in a grand and beautiful house which we often visited. Then there was Andrew Carnegie, the oil millionaire, who often came to our house.

Of others who came and went there was Arthur Balfour, who seemed languid, but to whom the others seemed to listen and who was apparently nearly always at least in the Cabinet and who was sometimes Prime Minister. He was one of the few of the grown-ups of whose manners the small observant child was critical. Suffering as he did, I now suppose, from some breathing difficulty such as asthma, I watched Arthur Balfour take an inhaler out of his pocket. So far so good; but, when he had done with it, I saw that he put it, not back into his pocket, but on to our elaborately adorned lunch table. Silent, of course, I reflected that if I had done such a thing it would have been very much disapproved of. But I already knew enough to be sure that nothing would be said in reproof, not to this Mr Balfour.

Of Rufus Isaacs, later Lord Reading and Viceroy of India, I don't remember much except that I didn't know what to say to him, or he to me, when chance left us for a few minutes alone. Child and man were both dumb.

There were many other eminences, some flamboyant, some grey. For instance, two who seemed faintly mysterious: one, so I heard someone say, was Secretary to the Cabinet. What could that mean? Another, an American, was said to be Secretary of State and to advise the President of the United States, who was called Mr Theodore Roosevelt, and whom, it seemed, my parents had visited at the White House.

In general, my impression as a child was that if you happened to go to the United States of America, you would naturally visit the President, or in Egypt the Residency, just as in a fairy-tale you naturally made for the palace of some king or caliph; also that grown-up men – not women of course – were usually MPs and in the Cabinet. This curious impression was reinforced year after year while I was a child. In later life, it affected the way in which both my brother John and I severally reacted to the pressures of grown-up life. The usual, regular thing, so we innocently supposed, was to be in the Cabinet or on the Opposition Front Bench, or in general to be some sort of an eminence. I don't know whether this was a good thing or not.

In the London streets, that is in the streets around Hyde Park and Kensington Gardens, there was, when I was still only about six years old, something new. I gathered that this remarkable thing was sometimes to be seen making its way among the familiar traffic of clip-clopping growlers and hansoms, the drays and jingling omnibuses, the elegant, gleaming victorias and the rubber-tyred, discreet broughams of the fashionable streets. This is how the scene comes back to me:

'But what is it, Nanny?'

'You'll see if you're lucky.'

'But tell me!'

So she tried. It was, Nanny said, a carriage that went without horses. It didn't go smoothly and quietly like a real carriage, it was noisy and it snorted and rattled.

At night in bed, in my mind's eye – in my child's eye – I saw something splendid. It would pull, I supposed, so it might be something like a railway engine, but it wouldn't surely look like one? No, because it was 'instead of' horses. It would surely look like what I had seen on a roundabout at a fair, only much bigger: a pair of splendid mechanical horses. Their legs would go trampling, their coats would shine with varnish, their red nostrils would steam, their manes would fly.

And then I saw! Misery!

These first motor cars looked to me (and still look to me on their museum stands) no better than old dog-carts with their shafts cut off – four-wheeled dog-carts that is. Certainly these new things went of themselves, but what of that?

But we weren't always in London. We were down at Little Newlands, picking primroses in the hazel copse with their catkins, and I was half listening to my father, who was murmuring to himself: 'Oh, spread again your leaves and flowers/Lonesome woodlands, sunny woodlands.'

Daddy, I thought censoriously, doesn't give his mind to picking.

Autumn again, London again. Leaving Hyde Park with Nanny, going back to tea – a clear impression again:

'What were all those men round the statue? One had a collecting box.'

'The Achilles statue? Those were the unemployed.'

It seemed from what she said that the men had no work and, because of that, no money.

'Not to buy their food?'

'No.'

This seemed to me dreadful (and it still does). I don't know what answer I received then, but I think that, at some point, grown-ups, to comfort me, said that there were workhouses and also that the men need not starve because they could volunteer for the army – and ought to do so.

Another clear picture. It's still autumn and therefore still London; it is about three o'clock in the afternoon, and so we are in the Park.

Horses – bays, greys and chestnuts trotting or cantering along Rotten Row; galloping isn't allowed. Suddenly they all slow down to a walk and then stop. The men take their hats off.

'Look, Amabel! No. Further away, over there. Try to remember.'

So I look and suppose that what I see ought to be interesting and important. Far away I can just see a very small old lady in an open landau carriage. She seems to have on a black bonnet. I'm told that the little old lady is Queen Victoria, so I suppose it's important and that this is why all the riders have stopped and why the men have taken their hats off – even if she is so far away that she couldn't know.

'We saw the Queen,' reports Nanny later to my mother, 'in the park, rather a long way off. I told Amabel to try to remember.'

It's the same day but later, after tea, 'the children's hour'. My mother tells me about her mother:

'My Granny?' I ask.

'Yes. Well, when she was a little girl, about your age, she had a dog, a big dog with a rough coat, and one day in Kensington Gardens this dog rushed into the Round Pond, swam about, came running out, and shook himself all over another little girl. She turned out to be little Princess Victoria.'

I listen, doubting. Children don't really believe that people who are unquestionably old were once children. So all I think is that my Granny is probably a nicer old lady than this Queen Victoria. I liked Granny.

But all that autumn it was my hoop that mattered most when I, as my grandmother and mother had done, went to walk in Kensington Gardens. I had a wooden hoop, a nice big one, but what I wanted was an iron hoop. Other children, especially boys, had iron hoops. Already it was boys' things that I liked. With iron hoops and hooked sticks you could make more noise. But in wild hands the iron kind were said to be dangerous to pedestrians on the Broad Walk.

Going home there was another possibility, but this meant eluding Nanny, whose vigilance was sometimes hampered by her walking with some other Nanny with a big pram. Going home you could, even with only a wooden hoop-stick, make quite a loud and satisfactory rattling noise by running fast as you drew the stick along the area railings. But an iron one was even better.

Looking down into the areas of the tall houses was also enjoyable. You might see a cook with a saucepan in her hand, or else a parlourmaid in a black dress with a white cap and apron might be standing on the area steps for a breath of air. But such pleasures meant that, on crowded pavements, you might lag behind and this was to be avoided, for to be alone like that was to feel desolate and abandoned; that was the worst of dawdling.

'Wait for me. Oh, wait for me.' But the best that grown-ups generally did was to slow down and to call back impatiently. Why did they have to go so fast? By not looking about them the two nannies missed so much!

A winter Sunday. We are in Kensington. Dusk is falling. I and a young nursery-maid are listening at the high-up nursery window for the sound of the muffin man's bell. Slowly it comes nearer down the street. If I am lucky, I am given some money and allowed to gallop down the endless flights of stairs. There, under the stucco-pillared porch, stands the muffin man. He sets down his bell, takes the big tray with its cover of green baize from his head, and brings out the warm muffins. He counts out the money, says, 'Thank you, little missie,' and, tray on head again and bell ringing once more, goes on further, several doors down the street to where someone, afraid of missing him, has thrown pennies ringing from a top window.

Spring again and we are at Newlands, and again picking primroses among the hazel catkins. Again I hear my father murmuring, 'Oh, spread again your leaves and flowers/Lonesome woodlands, sunny woodlands,' and I again think he doesn't pick as quickly as I do. Then I ask him to help with my damp, sweet-smelling bunch. The thin stalks, pale pink and tender, the close-packed flowers, rayed with leaves, must be tied with fine wool, darning wool. String would cut them. Should I give my father some of my bunches for the drawing-room? Spouting poetry like that, he hasn't picked many, hadn't been attending half the time.

'And there's beauty alive when the fairest is dead/And Zummer will always have maaids out afore/Their doors vor to chatty/And zee folk go by.'

We don't live in a village; Newlands is up on the Downs, so I imagine the maids in the poem as the pretty parlourmaid half-way up the area steps in Kensington, taking a breath of air and seeing folk go by.

My brother John was born when I was seven. He became rather, but by
no means exactly, the sort of man I had so often as a child seen through
the mists or over the banisters – an MP and a Minister. To me, then, he
was something very different: a longed-for 'little-brother-or-sister' for
whom (under instruction?) I had prayed every night, kneeling by my
bed.

I am standing by my father in his dressing-room as he shaves.
'Here a little child I stand, heaving up my either hand . . .'
'But, Daddy, that's wrong. I don't stand up to say my prayers.'
(The very idea!) But father just went on quoting as usual, 'Cold as
paddocks though they be . . .'
'What's paddocks?'
'Toads.'
I agree that toads feel cold. I tell Daddy so and remark that I
like them. He quotes again, but my thoughts go off after toads.
You pick them up, cup them in your hands, but not tight because
you are afraid of hurting them. Their throats throb – you are afraid
to hold tight for fear of hurting them – you don't really have them
properly fast, and they would jump, wildly. Their eyes being at the
top of their head means they cannot see where they jump, and
you are afraid that they will hurt themselves. You have no faith at
all in the ability of wild creatures to know what is good for them.

Practical answers to prayers are said by the pious to be a disappointment and a disillusionment. The answer to my prayer for a little
brother or sister was not a disappointment.
In that summer, now at Little Newlands, I loved and rejoiced and
was extra happy. This was, for one thing, because of pride, because of a
deep satisfaction, a fulfilment and also because of something trivial that
Nanny had said at the ceremony, the solemn rite of Baby's Bath. Any
self-respecting mother or nanny, at the century's beginning, laid out
everything ready beforehand for the rite.
The baby's bath was as elaborate as a Japanese tea ceremony. There
stood by a tin bath, on a bath-mat, a jug of very hot water and a jug of
cold. A sleeve was rolled up high, for only an elbow can be trusted to
test the temperature of the mixture. In our nursery a flounced, open
baby-basket on legs stood by the bath; in the basket were many things,
including powder, a big swansdown puff and a flannel binder with two
safety pins. On the nursery fireguard hung a garment twice as long as
the baby, made of flannel, not hemmed but bound with ribbon, plus an
equally long petticoat, nappies and their pins, a very fine knitted vest, a

crisp, clean, tucked and flounced cambric robe, and a fine Shetland shawl. Such were the appurtenances. 'Long tails' we called young babies. When they could sit up and then crawl, they were 'shortened'. This was definitely what anthropologists call a 'rite of passage'. 'We shortened him/her last week,' you would hear a mother or nanny say, looking proudly under the hood of a pram.

But that summer my little brother was still a 'long tail', that morning when the comment was made that so set me up. At the bath ceremony, Nanny had asked me for something (the powder-puff charged with orris-root powder perhaps) and had then said to a confidential onlooker to whom she had been telling about the nursery-maid, 'Little Amabel here, though she's not eight yet, is far more use than that girl.'

So I was of use! The great judge of such things had said it. Months after, back in London, going to sleep at night with the nursery fire winking on the ceiling, I felt fulfilled.

John, as I have said, was not my only brother. There was also Tom – a glorious being, five years older than me and then at Eton.

Sometimes, in the holidays, Tom would condescend for a while to play with his little sister. What did we play at? Something improving? Did he try to teach me? Don't you believe it! We played, as often as not, at torturing dolls – small twopenny dolls bought for the purpose. They had china or 'composition' heads, arms and legs, with calico bodies stuffed with sawdust. What or whom the dolls symbolized I don't know, nor do I know which of us proposed a game that I now look back on with trepidation – a trepidation that little Amabel didn't in the least feel.

Once, at Easter, this big brother brought to stay two equally glorious Etonian friends, one of whom left a cage of white rats in my care.

That summer was a time when having the baby made all sorts of excellent differences. He was declared to be delicate. For me the interesting consequence was that at Newlands we began to keep goats, which I sometimes milked and constantly studied. I studied them and their kids – I don't mean their health, but their temperaments. Observing them, as I somehow guessed even then, taught me more about our own species than could be learned from the horses, or from Jenny the donkey, or even from my delightful and affectionate tabby and her many families of kittens.

Goats are a social species but, more like cats – more like solitary creatures – they have wayward ways and are anarchists. The attitude of our goats to the hay that was made on the premises is just what you'd expect. One summer, as often in small-scale haymaking, a little stack of dubious hay was made. Many thistles were in it and it had been brought in after laying out in a long wet spell. This little stack stood, forlorn, in a corner of a field. Some was put into the goat-shed; the goats wouldn't touch it. So out in the field it stood, with an inadequate fence round it. Presently the four nannies and their kids were let into this field. The fence might be inadequate but, to the goats, its purpose was clear. Nannies and kids at once began to rear up, reach out, clamber and push. After a week the rejected hay had all been slyly, joyfully, surreptitiously munched, with the sideways motion of the jaws that, with an equally sideways look from yellow slit eyes, always seems so agreeably furtive. Taught by the goats, I still have a sneaking liking for the defiance and delinquency that I have alas so seldom practised.

I suppose I was mainly a good, conscientious girl. I didn't deliberately torment my governess, and I had a proper respect for the small girl called Melia in the farm next to Little Newlands. She was a year or two older and went to school (which seemed so much grander than having a governess!). I really didn't wonder that Melia didn't always want to play with me. In fact my childhood passed so calmly that now I can remember only one childish wound and two reprehensible acts. Of one of the scandals I am now ashamed, but I glory to remember the other.

Some grown-ups have come to visit my parents and have brought along a little girl. I am told to 'play with' this child, who is younger than I am. I know that decent feeling, hospitable ritual, the usual proper chivalrous children's code, mean that I have to 'be nice' to her – all afternoon. But, after a short effort, I decide that she is a milk-sop and a nit-wit and that it will be unbearable to spend the whole of that fine afternoon in her company instead of on my swing as planned. Little savage that I am, I tie her to a tree, leave her there and go off to my swing, whistling delinquently. The search-party that found her, weeping, also found me and I was, quite rightly, sent straight off to bed. I wonder what my shame-faced parents found to say to hers?

The other outrage was different and its technique was modern and effective, being as it was a splendid anticipation of the hostage-taking tactics of the 1970s and 1980s.

The scene is a low, thatched potato house at Newlands – big Newlands now. I am sitting triumphantly on its straw roof, not caring if the straw is scratching my bare legs and sandalled heels, and not caring that below me stands our gardener Mr Tann. His red moustache is bristling with irritation, his blue baize apron is heaving with his violent feelings. He is shouting up to me that I 'know perfectly well' that I mustn't climb and kick about like that – not on a thatch. I do 'know perfectly well' but don't speak, just stare down at him with what used to be called dumb insolence. He is furious, says he will come up and fetch me down.

'No, you won't.' say I, knowing 'perfectly well' that the thatch itself is in fact my hostage – fetching me down would damage it far more than my (really quite careful) climb up had done. So he, classically, threatens to tell my father, and I say, 'Father's in London.' He pretends to make for the tree by which I got up. I laugh and tell him he'd better not. The end of it is that angry Mr Tann goes away fuming and I feel – rightly or wrongly – that I have defeated a bully and a tyrant, one from whose cross ways my ally, plump, amiable Flora, the kitchen-maid, has lately smarted, I believe.

Of the wounding I should say at once that I believe it was not intended and that it happened before the time of Miss Green, my governess.

My mother has been giving me a reading lesson and it has been, as often, a failure. I am flustered, but convinced that I really did try, but it seems that she is convinced of the contrary. I am going away and, as I shut the door, the handle being still in my hand, I hear her voice: 'Little devil! Little fiend!'

I never told her or anyone that I had heard. The reason is, I suppose, that I had already half-understood a sad fact that cast a lifelong shadow for both of us: we seemed to be unable to love one another. I tried and pretended very hard, I know, and she did a great deal for me. She played the piano for me, saw to it that I learned early to enjoy reading and speaking French, kept Nanny with us though they didn't get on, and later in life did a great deal for me and her grandchildren. These were things that, with her temperament, must have cost her quite a lot of irritation and discomfort. She didn't seem jealous of my father's and my easy affection for each other, and later showed me that she could be fond of young things and of teenagers, as she did a great deal for one of our daughters.

I don't remember her ever taking me on her knee when she was reading to me (as she often did), or hugging and kissing me, or coming up to the nursery (as was, after all, the custom among Society mothers), coming in evening finery to bend over the bed and kiss a sleepy little girl goodnight. Was the shadow something to do with the fact that, as far as

I remember, she never did any of these small things, and does this letter of hers that *The Times* printed in 1906, when I was in my teens, throw any light on what we both missed? The letter certainly throws a curious light on what were sound Establishment views on women's place in the community just after the turn of the century. With one part of her letter I still heartily agree. A decline in the birth-rate now seems a curious matter for regret. Can Sidney Webb really have wanted it higher? Or were both he and my mother really regretting the then immensely high infant mortality figures?

May I suggest to Mr Sidney Webb as an educationist that in looking for remedies for the decline of the birth-rate, he should consider the question whether the present education of girls does or does not teach them that the highest duty of women to the State is the duty of motherhood? Intelligent and successful motherhood is of all professions the most necessary to the well-being of the nation. It is also the most exacting of all professions (it may certainly be scheduled as a 'dangerous trade'), and it calls for infinite daily and hourly self-sacrifice. Yet, except in a few special schools, from the beginning to the end of their education, not one serious word is taught on the subject to the girls who are to be the mothers of the next generation. Even our schools of domestic economy . . . aim at making the girls good housewives, but never teach plainly that the girl who wishes to do her duty as a 'citizen' must fit herself physically and mentally to be a good mother . . . They should be clearly taught that the highest service which women can perform for the State is to help in the care and bringing up of children – either their own or those of their neighbour.

I am, Sir, your obedient servant,

Amy Strachey[1]

Later, however, my mother was to pioneer the admirable child guidance movement, organizing, raising money and convincing sceptical and reluctant local authorities. We owe the existence of the profession of psychiatric social worker chiefly to her efforts.

Two

POWER OF THE PRESS

My father must have wanted to found a dynasty. Certainly he and my mother watched with pride and hope the development of their elder son, Tom, by now an undergraduate at Oxford. I was a girl of twelve when the blow fell.

Quite suddenly Tom, to me the glorious visitant from Eton and then the even more splendid undergraduate, died of pneumonia. When the first news of his illness came, I could tell that something very grave was threatened. Then, on the second day, the grown-up people said that Tom was 'in danger'. But I reassured myself; that he should die was impossible, it was something that could not be imagined, and that thus could not happen.

But it did happen.

My inexperienced sense of unreality, this conviction that something couldn't happen, often (so I hope) makes some sort of shield for children. A sense of unreality always obtrudes upon grief and the trivial commonly intrudes as well, and when we are grown up we feel shame that this should be so. I had a new jacket and skirt, bright blue, that I had worn only once. Would it be given away, I wondered, or would Nanny send it to be dyed? And then how strange it seemed that it would be no good to try to tell my little brother John anything about Tom having died. John was too young – only six – he wouldn't understand.

As for understanding, I didn't come anywhere near to knowing what it was that had happened. Not even the simple, inevitable part. This was fortunate. I am, it seems, a slow learner, so that it took two world wars and a quarter of a century of time and the loss of my own son – killed in action at about Tom's age – it took all that to make me understand. I do know now, however, that for normal affectionate parents, the loss of a child has something of the dreadful quality that is said to be part of the shock and even panic of an earthquake. An inadmissible reversal of the natural order has happened, we feel; we experience a shocking biological affront.

Even my own personal experience failed for a long time to make me realize that, for my poor parents, ambition had given to Tom's death an added source of pain. To this pain some few years later, John and I felt, alas, that we could not help but add. It was something in one of my

mother's books which I read many years after she had written it that
taught me what this added pain had been. Taking up her *St Loe Strachey
and His Paper*,[1] I read in it at random and saw that in 1928, many years
after my brother's death, she had, poor soul, still felt not only the
inevitable natural basic sorrow, but also the peculiar smart of a
thwarted ambition. He had been the one who could have followed on.
He had seemed so fit to inherit all that my father had built up. He could
have gone on with my father's 'championing of truth and justice' as my
parents felt it; with him the future of the *Spectator* would have been
assured. I think that my mother had loved Tom, not just done her duty
by him.

In 1907 this weekly paper's success was not a trivial thing, nor to
them a personal one, nor just a financial one either, though these things
must have come into it. My cousin James Strachey (brother to Lytton)
writing in 1964 about the *Spectator* commented: 'It was at that time far
the most widely read of the political weeklies, with a circulation in
the neighbourhood of twenty thousand copies, almost three times as
large as that of any of its rivals.'[2]

The curiously intricate details of British politics between 1900 and
1914 accounted, of course, for quite a lot of happenings in my family:
the increasing prestige of the *Spectator*, for instance, and for the number
of eminent persons who frequented my parents' London and country
houses. Many of them had to do with world affairs. The British Empire
was then at its zenith. As was continually emphasised on our maps, half
the habitable world was coloured red. It was ruled, that is, from
London and formed sometimes an easy, and sometimes an uneasy, part
of power in the world. It can well be realized that such a fact added to
the importance of home politics. The stakes were high, since they were
for this unstable but magnificent prize, for this rule by oligarchy, this
unmatched power to dominate. It was for this almost unparalleled
degree of power which Conservatives and Liberals contended.

The details really were of a fascinating intricacy because, though
Britain certainly was effectively an oligarchy, and though the British
Empire depended mainly on the decisions reached by those who
controlled one or other of the two main parties, there were, as always in
British history, also third and fourth forces at work. The radical left,
soon to put on flesh, if not muscle, as the Labour party, was of course
already a minor force. But there was also another – a fourth, un-
organized force. I repeat, even then we were not a total oligarchy.

To some extent people like my father remained descendants, not of
the Levellers, but of Cromwell's Ironsides, so that each of the main
oligarchic contenders for power had behind them obstinate and not

unintelligent supporters who had to be persuaded. The trade unions and the workers were in eclipse, not as much a force as in the days of the Chartists, but there were other radicals, to be found on the whole in universities. The term 'squire-radical' had a meaning too, as Robert Louis Stevenson observed. The Tories had their undisciplined 'citizen army' as well. These might be philanthropists, or were to be found in boardrooms, universities and rectories. As far as our family and the Press in general were concerned, the relevant point here is that all these undisciplined opinion-makers read the newspapers. People indeed liked to call the Press 'the Fourth Estate'.

Of the Press of the period, *The Times* seemed, no doubt, the leading power, but it also seemed predictable and its editor Doge-like. Two other powerful papers were the *Observer* published on Sunday, and the *Spectator* reaching its subscribers a day earlier, either on Friday or Saturday. There was also Massingham to the left of the Liberals with a smaller readership. Garvin on the *Observer* I believe, and my father on the *Spectator* I know, each controlled quite personally and independently these two widely read papers. They were the two independent unpredictables.

Until my father took it over, the *Spectator* had been merely another off-centre organ of opinion, but it had said the sorts of things that he believed needed to be said, and now it was triumphantly clear that he was really being listened to. His integrity was real. He believed that it was good that in London, in this power-house from which half the world was being ruled, the opinions that he represented should be heard, and he had wanted passionately that there should be a prospect of continuity.

These opinions of his, I repeat, were never quite predictable Conservative values. The paper was by no means as orthodox as *The Times*. True, he believed that we had a right to rule India, true that a best-selling book whose reputation he made was called *Deeds That Won The Empire*, true that he opposed Home Rule for Ireland, and that he held that women should not have votes. But he also believed in free trade and in the great value to the world of American democracy.

Professor Hugh Thomas, writing in 1973 a life of my brother John,[3] decided that my father, whom he never knew, must have been 'worldly, confident and dashing': 'From 1898 onward he had issued to the world an unending stream of orthodox, though vigorous, editorials providing intelligent rationalizations for conservative attitudes to the Empire . . . He made a success of the *Spectator* and became quite rich in consequence.'

But Hugh Thomas is wrong in one particular. My father and the

Spectator were not as orthodox as this suggests. What proper Conservative would have written a sentence like this in a long article in the *National Review* (in 1893) about the idea of a referendum? 'The unanswerable case in favour of correcting the faults of representation is by reposing a right of veto in the people.' He suggested plebiscites as a means by which the House of Lords might successfully continue to meet the charge of being against 'the people'. He even sketched out a referendum ballot-paper.

His views on the past also even made orthodoxy uneasy (he had taken a First in History at Oxford), for he believed and taught me to believe that the Roundheads had been in the right. And what about Diggers and Levellers? 'Inopportune and unrealistic' as Cromwell and my father felt. So what about Lloyd George's radical Liberals? Or did he favour the Asquithian Liberals? The awkward fact was, as good party men felt, that he could never be counted upon as either sort of Liberal. More than his feelings against Home Rule for Ireland prevented that. 'The Irish question' was as contentious as ever.

However, to his younger contemporaries he did, without doubt, seem a reactionary. James and Lytton Strachey – 'the Lancaster Gate Stracheys' as we called them – utterly dismissed all his ideas and were far from respectful in the way they did it: 'The younger members of our own family applied the term "Spectatorial" to any particularly pompous and respectable pronouncement. At the same time we were very fond of St Loe, who was the kindest of friends and a most entertaining companion, and was in many ways far from "Spectatorial" in real life. He had, in particular, a highly romantic admiration for the Strachey family.'[4]

The fact was that much of father's curious political effectiveness came from his unorthodoxy, and the situation was that father on Saturday and Mr Garvin in the *Observer* on Sunday were both vigorously promoting the party political see-saw and commenting with slight alarm on Lloyd George's trickle of benefits that became first Beveridge and then the Welfare State.

They had an influence that it is hard to credit today. Father and his paper were much noticed in popular as well as powerful and sophisticated circles. The *Daily Mail* published an article on his taking over of the paper, and called my father 'one of the great Anglo-Indian Stracheys and still [in 1899] a young man who belongs rather to the new than to the dying century'. The policy of the *Spectator* was said to be independent Liberalism. There followed an almost wistful comment on the limitations of a 'popular' newspaper with a vast circulation, the *Daily Mail* itself being, of course, one of the first and for years a dominant example: 'Mr Strachey and the *Spectator* serve a small public whose demands it is not irksome to obey and they have been able to defy the shocks of change and chance. They have been able to remain themselves because they are sure of their public.'

I did not know for many years that father's take-over of the *Spectator* had been on borrowed money and had depended in part on a loan from his younger, unworldly brother, the Uncle Harry of whom I was so fond. To him my parents felt lasting gratitude. I have heard my mother say that he was 'a saint', adding 'with a dash of cayenne pepper'. Fortunately the excellent saint lived on to help to civilize not only me but also my children. Unambitious he may have been, but never insipid. A musician and a painter, Uncle Harry perhaps rightly did not think much of his own aesthetic achievements, but his taste and his effect on us all had a luminous quality. He was the third son, and I often came to think of him as like the third son in a fairy tale, the simple straightforward one who, when the two older, more capable-seeming brothers have been defeated, gets the better of the Dark Powers.

These details about bygone take-overs and party politics are relevant to my own smaller affairs and to my parents' and brother John's larger ones, but also because they give clues to my father's standard of values and to those foreign and imperial persons with whom I was, as a little girl, so incongruously brought into contact. Yet it would, I fancy, be an over-simplification to think that all this was because my father was sole editor and proprietor of what he had made into a powerful organ of opinion. The important people that the red-haired girl observed with so little enthusiasm came, I think, also because, as James Strachey noticed, my father was such a pleasant creature. He was confident, casual, honest, unpompous and warm – unusual qualities in that Philistine epoch. Also my mother was a skilful hostess.

So, with a host who was cultivated and conversable and my mother to back him up, they came to enjoy the company. My mother, though rather shy sometimes and thus occasionally angular and abrupt, was really accomplished as a hostess, trained in the art by her mother. She was also an excellent, if domineering, domestic organizer and saw to it that the food was delicious. She was a tall, handsome woman, well read and accustomed to distinguished company both in London and Paris. Her father (my shy, retiring Simpson grandfather) had been an eminent lawyer, while her grandfather had been the Nassau Senior of the famous nineteenth-century Poor Law Acts at which Carlyle had so rightly stormed.

As for the history of the paper itself, father had had to act boldly in actually buying control. Mr Harmsworth, as Lord Northcliffe then was, had once offered for it, and I believe that it was only by quick borrowing that my father had managed to evade this particular take-over. The transactions were widely publicized so everybody knew that he had become not only an editor but also a proprietor.

This dashing side of his very active career made a lot of dull people uneasy, especially since his incongruous sincerity, too, gradually became well known. It was soon rightly believed that the offer of any sort of inducement such as money or honours or even flattery was likely to prove violently counter-productive. Thus it was that the rising or insecure statesman liked to keep in touch with him. Puzzled place men, too, liked to peer at him, and wondered how to make the next set of leading articles less abrasive to their chiefs.

Quotations from his leading articles went the rounds of London dinner parties. When Lord Rosebery became Prime Minister, he suggested in his leader that there were at least seven Lord Roseberys, one of them a racing man and the six others standing 'at all points of the political compass'. He also compared a proposed party rallying cry to 'a voice from the middle of a damp haystack'. In general, his ability to speak his mind in a way that forced people to listen, made the professionals, the bureaucrats and the faceless apparatus-men of both parties feel most uncomfortable.

While the small Parliamentary Labour Party was as yet only in the wings, 'socialism' was already a word that alarmed the Establishment and something that my father could not as yet countenance, so that it was only partly in fun that he would quote a current jingle:

> What is a Socialist? One who has yearnings
> For equal division of unequal earnings.
> Dreamer or idler or worse, he is willing
> To put down his penny and pocket my shilling.

After the searing misfortune of Tom's death, my poor parents had only vague suppositions for carrying on what my father felt was his contribution to the welfare of his country and to right thinking. The vague suppositions were that some day my schoolboy brother John and I might prove fit to inherit. My own later tentative apprenticeship on the literary side of the paper may have been a forlorn attempt at a salvage operation after the end of their original hopes.

Three

OVER THE BANISTERS

It did not surprise me (though it might have done) that a few months after Tom's death family life seemed to go on much as usual. I didn't realize how it affected my parents. Here my imaginative powers seem to have stopped, and the immediate consequences to me were minimal.

Miss Green, my governess, looked after my education, though Nanny Holland still looked after me. Miss Green was a tall, dark, handsome woman, very quiet in her ways, and with beautiful hands. She didn't live with us but a couple of miles away when we were at Newlands. Where she lived when we were in London, I don't remember, or even whether she came there with us, but I do remember going to tea with her at the Onslow Arms in Clandon, where my parents had billeted her. I already had that feeling of unreality about my surroundings which besets so many children as they begin to grow up; thus it seemed to me that her little bed-sitting room at this inn and the buttered toast she gave me at a fireside tea were much more real and in some way authentic than anything I saw, heard or ate at home.

In London I had several occasional teachers. One, a dusty German lady who came to the house purported to teach me the piano. She had had installed what I still think of as a really devilish instrument – a portable thing called a *Stum-Klavier*, a dumb piano, which had an ordinary keyboard but when you struck the notes they made no sound. Also your teacher could adjust it so as to make the touch hard or easy. I liked singing when my mother played, but, oh, the *Stum-Klavier*! I didn't like it at all.

And I didn't like my drawing class either. We had to do something called 'brushwork' in water-colours. Large carrots we drew with one stroke of the brush, and then for flowers several such strokes with another smaller brush loaded with other colours – one stroke each for pointed flower petals. I used to say that 'brushwork' gave me stomach-ache. However M. Bouvier and my French class I did like: '*Mignonne! Allons voir si la rose . . .*'

So I was being educated, but for what? Osbert Sitwell was clear and also indignant about the answer. Writing of his sister Edith (whose poetry I later often had the pleasure of publishing in the *Spectator*), he declares that Edith was being educated especially to please young men.

He observed:

My mother insisted that Edith should have the usual 'advantages' or what would people say? . . . It was decided that, after the manner of a Geisha, she must learn to charm by means of esoteric accomplishments . . . scarf-dancing, water-colours, recitation, small talk . . . In conversation she should be capable of an endless flow of remarks to which the young men need pay no attention unless they wished, that was what men liked . . . It kept the ball rolling . . .[1]

'You must never let a man be bored,' my grandmother said to me. 'Talk to him, talk about a leg of mutton if you can't think of anything better.' Simone de Beauvoir's memoirs emphasize the same sort of story. Her mother told her a moral tale about an eligible young man. When a very accomplished young lady was proposed by his family for his bride, the young man was told that she could play the piano and knew several foreign languages. But this particular young man had other ideas about eligible young ladies. His remark was, 'But can she sew?' It was best to be on the safe side, so Madame de Beauvoir's mother told her. She comments that she didn't like the idea of being prepared 'to meet the hypothetical tastes of an unknown and hypothetical young man'.[2]

Up to about twenty years ago, I used to feel full of indignation about such answers to the question of what a young lady was being educated for. Now I am not quite so clear. Obviously, if anybody is going to be educated to be an ornament to society, this should apply to boys also, just as it did in the eighteenth century in France and England. Knowing something about ritual behaviour makes the first chilly feeling, the shiveriness of the shy person introduced to new company, less alarming. Of all unlikely people, Leonard Woolf, that sterling character, notes in his reminiscences that, having learned on board ship to mix with people other than academics, he found his official work in Ceylon less frightening. We are necessarily a social species, so that ritual matters. Thus I hold that it is no kindness to let our children grow up either dowdies or so strange that they antagonize everybody in their circle.

Meantime there were other sides to my education. At Big New-lands – Little Newlands much enlarged – my parents had built a large room with huge rows of bookshelves – a book-wall really, a wall from floor to ceiling. In my innocence I vowed to read every single book, but I soon began to wilt. I couldn't go back on the vow. At fifteen I had a conscience. But, my conscience inquired, did this vow include every volume of the *Dictionary of National Biography* and the *Encyclopaedia Britannica*? I concluded with a sigh that it did. But then, as I have so

often done, I hedged and substituted 'Take down and *read in*' for 'read'.
So I fulfilled the vow in its amended form.

Another civilizing and enlightening process was going out with my
father: now it was riding, rather than picking primroses – riding over
the Surrey downs at all times of the year. Father's quotations, as they
had been during primrose-picking, were often just ordinarily appropriate to the weather or the changes of season; they were by no means
monotonous, also they had other changes, verbal changes. That is to
say, they often got polished or sometimes a trifle damaged and, in the
long pocket of my father's memory, they sometimes altered year after
succeeding year. The autumn in my father's version wouldn't always
be:

> Ye storm winds of Autumn
>> That rush by, that shake
> My window and ruffle
>> The gleam lighted lake
> Then pass to the hillside
>> Thin scattered with farms
> Where the scant trees shake sadly
>> Their yellowing arms.

The months pass and it's winter:

> Deep in the earth and fourteen wild Decembers
>> On those brown hills had vanished into Spring
> Faithful indeed is the spirit that remembers
>> After such years of pain and suffering.

The weeks pass:

> When the hounds of Spring are on Winter's traces
> And the mother of months in meadow and lane . . .

And now it's summer:

> Do not fear to put thy feet
> Naked in the river sweet
>> Think not newt nor asp nor toad
>> Will bite thy foot where thou hast trod
> Nor let the waters rising high
> As thou wadest in make thee cry
>> And sob but ever live with me
>> And not a wave shall trouble thee.

But summer passes:

>   And the sedge is withered from the lake
>   And no birds sing . . .

Sometimes people used to think ill of my father's habit of quoting. I did wonder sometimes myself why he didn't make up what he wanted to say, but I gradually learned better. He, like every writer, wanted the right word; we all want the right word or musical note or line, because we write or paint or compose partly to pay homage (that is in celebration) and partly to communicate. We try to match the word or the line to the thing or the thought or the feeling. But that isn't easy; even the great masters often muff it. Writers find that words wear out just as our bodies do.

I think my father put me on to the track of finding the answer to his quoting habit when he asked (apropos a particular poem) if I had noticed that the first lines of lyric poems were often the best. Once he quoted; 'Love still has something of the sea/From which his mother rose', and said that the rest of the poem wasn't particularly good, but that this really said something.

I practised writing (sketching in words) year after year, watching, noticing things, or the changing light, and tried to get the right words down on the paper. When I worked away at this, I realised how tricky it was. Sometimes I used to sigh and think it was like the feeling when I was small and tried to catch butterflies or shrimps: you thought you'd got the creature; you peered into your net but, alas, there was nothing there but a scrap of grass or a little sand. And then I thought again that such a simple simile didn't really fit the disappointment because, with this word-matching, it wasn't that you wanted to catch something – well, in a way you wanted to catch it – but the difficulty was to get it down on paper. Yes, it wasn't only the seeing, but the getting it down on paper.

Much later, I went out of politeness to a lecture and demonstration by a Master Gilder, who showed a film of the long business of beating out a lump of gold into thinner and thinner sheets, beating it, beating it, beating it until it was almost impalpable, and then he showed us that the difficulty was to get this gold leaf down on to the thing you wanted to gild. This might be an inn sign or the fascia of a shop, or it might be the initial of an illuminated manuscript. He said when your thin gold is ready, if you breathe too hard or the wind blows or somebody interrupts you, a single gold leaf is so fine that it blows away; you don't get it down on to the surface you are trying to gild.

And that's why my father quoted. When he quoted he was taking pleasure in an instance of the poet having triumphed, having in fact managed to get his scrap of almost impalpable gold leaf down where he meant it to be.

My father would often misquote on purpose:

> Timon hath made his everlasting mansion
> Upon the beached verge of the salt flood
> That *twice a day* with their embossed froth
> The turbulent waves shall cover.

'*Once a day!*' he would mutter, 'the accepted text, it's wrong as any sea-minded person like Shakespeare knows, the tides rise twice in the twenty-four hours.'

It wasn't just lyric poetry that my father quoted; he liked an aphorism as well as anybody. I rather think the same sort of thing – the gold-leaf analogy – is also true of the absurd or the satiric. In a joke or an epigram you've got to be agile to get the thing down on paper and sometimes it won't stick, and the scrap of gold leaf vanishes.

I think of a fresh epigram occasionally, but seldom manage to get the frail thing down into its place. At this moment the only aphorism of my own that I can think of is one that I don't like at all. It's this: 'We only know one thing about being alive: it's a capital offence.' Not usually my attitude.

Sometimes other riders joined us. I hated this. I should like to think that I hated it because these other riders were usually people who brought out the extrovert, worldly, almost role-playing side of my father's quick nature. I felt that this was not quite real; it was this other part of him, the part that the poets had nourished that I felt to be the true part. But I wonder if I was merely jealous.

Another more formal kind of instruction turned out also to have a lifelong effect. In the country, when the season allowed, Miss Green would take me Botanising. We worked on a system which sounds, looking back, as off-putting as the detested *Stum Klavier*. But no, it had opposite consequences. Gathering a few wild flowers, say Lesser Speedwell, Rest Harrow, Pimpernel or one or two of the puzzling umbelliferae or the geranium, back in the school-room we sat down to fill in forms which she called, I think, schedules. What had to be entered were the particulars of our plants: 'Stem?' Round or square, hairy or smooth. 'Leaves?' . . . 'Borne in opposite pairs?' 'Roots?' and so on. Then to counting carpels, petals and stamens, and to categorizing pistils. The result was that you made a definite identification. Your plant really was that particular kind of, say, Speedwell or Stitchwort or Herb Robert.

This dry-sounding bit of taxonomy did, as I say, contribute lifelong results. Here was firm ground, here was some sort of achievement.

Four

OTHER KINDS OF STRACHEYS

'Our lives are made up of Memory and Oblivion,' says Sir Thomas Browne. One of the things that oblivion has swallowed is the reason why John didn't come with me more often when, as a small child, I made these recurring visits to Sutton Court. The fact gave him less of the 'highly romantic regard' for our Strachey ancestors and traditions that Lytton and James note as characterizing father and Uncle Harry, and that I, rather uncharacteristically, retain.

My grandfather was dead by the time I was twelve or so; the circumstances of his death oblivion has also swallowed. I don't know when he died, but I do know that after this I still went often to Somerset, chiefly I think to see my Uncle Harry. He was quick moving, medium tall, red-haired, like a squirrel. My mother, writing about the Strachey family in general, paid tribute to his peculiar goodness and sweetness of character. All the things that I loved so much in my father also came out in this uncle, but with a few important differences: it wasn't poetry with him, but music and painting; nor was he ambitious, for the worldly side that my father showed was missing altogether, as it was in their only sister, my gentle, unobtrusive Aunt Frances.

About my Uncle Eddie, a taller, smoother version of the red-haired Stracheys, and about his wife, my Aunt Constance, I felt very differently. Not only was he the one thoroughly uncongenial member of the family but, though no doubt he had enough interest in politics to get himself elected as a Liberal Member of Parliament and then be made a peer by an Asquith administration, he had no interest in the things that sweetened the lives of his two brothers and that of their sister too – history and the arts. Yet I think that Aunt Constance – that odd, scatty woman with her hat always askew – must have been nice to me, though she obviously did not get on particularly well with my parents. At least she was spontaneous in her eccentric way.

One good thing about her from my point of view was that when I was about fourteen or so, she kept a squirrel at Sutton, a red squirrel, which lived in a big cage outside. She edited several volumes of Lear's letters and a couple of his nonsense books, and she was a natural Mrs Malaprop. The advertisement that she put in *The Times* was much appreciated: 'Lady Strachie (*sic*) strongly recommends her excellent caretaker and husband', on which *Punch* commented: 'Lord Strachie must be a proud man this day.'

Among the attractions of staying at Sutton, now that I was older, was the Black Walk – haunted of course. It was dark and overgrown and frequented by me because it was the short cut through the small park if you wanted to go to the village of Stowey, which I often did, for it was there that my Uncle Harry lived, in a house called Stowey Mead. Stowey Mead had light rooms, unlike Sutton itself, which was and is darkly Victorian and straight Gothick. Stowey Mead wasn't ancient or mysterious, and it smelt of Uncle Harry's oil paints. He had a housekeeper who looked after him and who made delicious scones. The story was that he had been early crossed in love and so had never married. I knew the lady of this legend and thought her horrid – a bully. This uncle had always been my best source of fairy-tales. He didn't tell or read them dramatically, not at all; he told them in a rather flat, unobtrusive way which left the words plain. In fact he trusted the story to tell itself; with him the words had a chance. I still, to this day, like under-telling rather than over-telling, and when I was a regular drama critic I used to plead passionately for the author's words.

My uncle would tell West Country/Somerset tales and ballads but also sometimes used to read from what still seem to me absolutely incomparable collections of traditional stories. These were J. J. Jacobs's versions of *Old English Fairy Tales, Celtic Fairy Tales* and so on, four or five volumes. I believe Jacobs was Jewish, certainly a learned academic, and as certainly he came from Australia. What a tale-teller he was! How such a man managed to convey, in print, fine shades of English dialect, distinguishing (say) Yorkshire from Lincolnshire, and that from Somerset or Dorset, is beyond conjecture. The Andrew Lang versions, the Coloured Fairy Books, are not a patch on Jacobs's.

I can't remember at what point I began greatly to admire another member of the family, Mim – my cousin Frances, daughter of the disliked Uncle Eddie and of the tolerable Aunt Constance. Mim turned out to be important in the family history. Tall, blonde, blue-eyed and with a complexion like a white tulip – not too white, for the satiny white of her complexion was tinged with colour. I think of her as altogether beautiful and already 'out' – a deb. Her graceful beauty counted with me, of course, but what I admired even more was that she had a workshop with a proper carpenter's bench. She was, in fact, an excellent carpenter and joiner. Kind and condescending to me, she once made a small four-legged table for me, square, strong, all properly professional, of seasoned wood, with joints mitred – no nails, only screws or wedges. It was quite low and she painted it green and it even had a drawer that never stuck. I had it for many many years, and my children had it when young.

Teddy, her brother, also fair and outstandingly good-looking, I don't remember at all at this period. I think he was away trying to be a Guards officer, poor soul.

I learned a lot on these visits. I was impressed, and still am, by Uncle Harry's large, bold wall-paintings, especially in Stowey Church. There is a fresco which I still like very well (I don't know what other people think of it): it shows, among other figures, a dark angel with spread wings which broods over the altar of the little church.

Another attraction at Sutton was gossip – some, but not all, about the gentry. There had been people who lived in a manor house second only to Sutton Court that stands next to Stowey Church who were known as 'the last of the Joneses' (which made my Welsh husband laugh when I first innocently began telling him family anecdotes). 'Yes, these new people,' went local gossip, 'I hear the very worst accounts of them. They sit all day in the parlour, burning two candles and ringing the bell.' This was apparently considered the height of hedonistic behaviour.

It was quite usual, when my father and uncles were boys, for the squirearchy to have local accents. My grandfather used to tell of a great-aunt who, in discussing a neighbour, asked: 'Edward don't despise 'um, do 'ee?' A younger generation could talk broad too, if so minded. I can still hear Uncle Harry begging a waggoner in a narrow lane that got wider later on, please to 'Take that gurt cart up the rhoad' or repeating a local saying, 'What we want is fewer o' they black parsons and more o' they black pigs.'

But the best stories were of my great-uncle William. I must actually have seen this legendary character for he came, as a photograph proves, to my Aunt Frances's wedding in Chew Magna church and I was, as I well remember, one of her bridesmaids. He was one of the most elusive of all the Stracheys, so it is just possible that I may not have seen him even if, as the photograph shows, he really was at that wedding. He had been, like so many other Stracheys of the period, for some years an official in India. This was, so I was told, during one of the times when his political patron, Lord Palmerston, was in office. He is said never to have altered his watch from Calcutta time, and in England always to have worn galoshes out of doors. Before he went to India he had been a man about town, so even when either 'Calcutta time' or just inability to make up his mind had grown upon him, he yet remained the man of the world. The tradition of what follows is vivid to me.

My father is a little boy and he and my Grandpapa are in London. They've gone to Garland's Hotel (or Brown's Hotel, I'm not sure which). The occasion is a visit to the dentist, the little boy – my father – being the patient. They have come down to dinner in the hotel Coffee Room. Next to their table is one incongruously laid for breakfast with toast-rack, an egg-cup, and a cup and saucer, indeed all the usual apparatus of a Victorian breakfast. 'Look, St Loe,' says my Grandpapa, pointing to the table. 'That must be for your Uncle William!'

And sure enough it was. Years earlier, Uncle William had come home on furlough with his valet Joseph, and they had gravitated to this small, elegant hotel. Uncle William had, it seems, said to his valet, 'Don't take the trunks upstairs, Joseph, I shall only stay here for a few days.' In fact he stayed there on and off for thirty years, somehow never going back to India, and the trunks were always kept downstairs. Year after year Joseph had, I suppose, brought up to his employer's room a coat, a pair of trousers, a top hat or whatever Uncle William needed, the trunks remaining below.

Not only had he been uncertain about how long he meant to stay but his days, having grown peculiar, had come full circle; that is to say, his breakfast was regularly served at half-past eight, but not at the conventional half-past eight!

Being a man of the world, Uncle William naturally used to go visiting, and also naturally he went to visit his older brother, my grandfather, at Sutton Court, arriving without notice (no telephones) and driving from Temple Meads station in a four-wheeler just like anyone else, except that the time might be unlikely. But, if he was going out to dinner, as well he might, there was the matter of evening dress, for he would of course have come down in the train in day clothes. Thus he would have to change in the four-wheeler. Consequently, anybody who noticed a four-wheeler with the blinds down proceeding from Bristol to Sutton, or to wherever he was dining, could be pretty sure, just as my grandfather had been, that this must be old Mr William Strachey. The popular opinion was that he kept strange hours because he was an astronomer or, better, an astrologer.

Not only the Strachey side of my family produced vintage uncles. My mother, not to be outdone, used to tell of some most supportive sayings uttered by her own rather more urban but also splendidly and independently Victorian uncles. 'My dear Amy! Remember there never can be a day so disagreeable that it wouldn't make a capital good night. The thing is to draw the blinds and light the gas.' Also, 'No one but a fool or a pauper is ever cold.' Or again, 'Last summer? Ah! That was on a Thursday as I seem to remember.'

Sutton and the whole Somerset connection has gone on intermittently affecting the rest of us to this day, sometimes only as a faint background sound, sometimes like a continuo on a harpsichord, and occasionally (but usually for other members of the family) as an important solo instrument in a concerto.

In a chapter on Stracheys, it seems in order temporarily to abandon chronology and to give an account of the strange story of what has happened to Sutton over the years. The story has some psychological interest, entails some melodrama and, indeed, may be held to throw some light on tribe formation and how family traditions come about. The tale, then, is principally of how the old house and its estate came to belong to its present diligent inheritor, my cousin Charles O'Hagan.

The saga really began, and was shrouded at first in confidentiality, when my brother John joined the Labour Party in the 1920s. This seems to have outraged and incensed our Uncle Eddie (though we knew nothing about his feelings), who thought it foul scorn that a wicked Socialist should have either a house or estates. Also, this devious uncle thought perhaps that it would be nice to keep all the inheritance tightly to his own immediate descendants. Who knows? Anyhow, the disaster of John inheriting seemed to our uncle quite likely to happen. The difficulty was that, though he had a son called Teddy, who could immediately inherit, this son seemed unlikely to marry so that John would become the heir. But Uncle Eddie also had this daughter Mim, or Frances, the blonde beauty whom I had admired so much. She could not inherit the peerage but she had married a peer, Lord O'Hagan, and they had a son who was as handsome as his mother was beautiful and who, in turn, had married and had a male heir.

So, as wicked uncles do in melodramas, Uncle Eddie set to work, persuaded Mim's O'Hagan descendants to help him save Sutton from my brother John, who by then had further appalled Uncle Eddie by parting from his American wife and marrying again. Sutton must of course go to a Strachey, explained our uncle to them, but names, said he, can after all be changed by deed-poll, O'Hagans could become Stracheys. They could keep the O'Hagan peerage just the same and also have Sutton and the estate to which, after all, they had a perfect right by kinship. A female link was surely perfectly valid. But he emphasised that there was a condition: he would only make such a will if they would agree to change their name.

Uncle Eddie made out a good case, so thought the adults in the O'Hagan-Towneley family; they were persuaded. It wasn't till some time later that some of the newly grown-up members began to have doubts about the ethics and the curious secrecy of the pact and the name-change.

Neither my father, nor Uncle Harry, nor my brother John seem at the time to have known anything about all this. I certainly did not. And now, with hindsight, I personally think none the better of our Wicked Uncle to be sure, but being a believer in Women's Lib (even if a mildish one), I can see no harm in it all. The beautiful Mim, already untimely dead alas, had surely given as good an heir as possible to Sutton, about whose shrine-like function I unreasonably care.

John, as has already been said, had been little at Sutton as a child and, being more rational, didn't share my sentimental, paradoxically strong but nonsensical feeling about the family shrines. Nor was his inheriting wealth easily compatible with socialist principles. For a Minister in a Labour Government, house and estate would have been a serious political liability. And then to him the names – Norton Malreward, Pensford, Stowey and Compton Dando – were less magical than they were to me.

But there supervened a further irony. As it all turned out, our cousin Teddy lived to be a supine and careless recluse of ninety, and outlived my brother. In his long years of living there as a solitary, the fabric of the house almost succumbed to neglect. His housekeeper Sarah Pritchard's splendid cleaning and polishing of a few rooms could not halt the massive attacks of dry rot to the principal timbers. When other parts of the house were more carefully examined, rot was found to lurk and drip in a dozen dark corners.

There is a moral here which I shall not try to decipher. The older generation, my father and Uncle Harry, didn't live long enough to know anything about this strange, protracted episode in the history of the house. Now, in the 1980s, the burden of renovation and reconstruction seems likely to be completed by Charles O'Hagan, who lives there with his wife and young daughter.

Five

THE RITUAL CHANGE

It was an odd world into which I 'Came Out', making one of the important ritual changes. The young girl, all of a sudden, no longer has to look over the banisters but joins the couples going down arm-in-arm to dinner. This change of status was important then for the young females of our sub-tribe and is still much regarded in many simpler communities both for males and females.

Such rites may take startlingly different forms, of course. An anthropological friend tells me that in some tribes the girl's name is changed from her child's name to that of whatever flower it is that is in bloom at the ritual time – a pleasant variation. My parents, realizing that the change to being 'out' was, as in Jane Austen's time, quite a drastic one, contrived some gradual easing-in for me. I had hardly ever been from home except to Sutton or else to lodgings, or a modest hotel for a continental holiday, but my parents had been in the habit of going off either abroad to stay at some Embassy or Residency, or to one of those famous Edwardian weekend house-parties.

To such parties my mother went with her lady's maid (the beady-eyed Reeves). At home my father did not have an attendant of his own, but was valeted by the butler, Bishop, who didn't go, so I suppose he would be valeted by one of the footmen of his host's house.

As a young teenager, before I was officially 'out', I remember having stayed away with them twice. One such weekend was at the house of the famous millionaire Andrew Carnegie. I remember being startled there: for one thing, in the raftered hall of his house there was what seemed to be a full-scale, church-sized (almost cathedral-sized) organ, and to its rolling sounds we sang hymns – 'Yes, we will gather by the river, the beautiful, beautiful river . . .'

I was also puzzled when, standing before some very large oil paintings (one or two of which seemed oddly familiar), I heard Mr Carnegie explain to my parents that these pictures were all copies, and thus much better than the originals. The reason, he went on to say, was simple: any mistakes that the original artist might have made had all been corrected by highly skilled copyists.

The other visit, a little later, was to Scotland, to the Haldane family. It was my first contact with anyone who had to do with the Sciences.

We had been invited to the house of Lord Haldane, the Law Lord. I, though not 'out', was included in the party. Naomi Haldane, later Mrs Mitchison, tells in her reminiscences of a mountain expedition and of her distress because her brother, Jack (J. B. S.) Haldane, then still at Eton, chose to walk with me. She wrote:

> We used to have expeditions across the Strath to Ben Vorlich. It was here that I was stricken with a fearful jealousy that was like a sudden illness. The Stracheys were staying at Cloan. Amabel had a magnificent, enviable mane of red hair and appeared to me to be superbly confident, almost grown up. And Jack asked her to be his climbing companion! Amabel tells me that actually she was feeling a bit shy and was somewhat surprised by this offer from a young man who rather scared her. Nor, she said, did they have much conversation on Ben Vorlich. I climbed with someone else and raging passion inside me. It was a horrible day. Probably I was thoroughly nasty to everyone. When I calmed down I managed to recognize that this which had come at me was the opposite of delight, was due to asserting ownership over another person.[1]

J.B.S. and I seem really not to have had much contact during the visit, nor did we, I think, ever care for each other in any romantic way, but we did become firm friends. Later he helped me to understand what Biology was about, while Clough and I and Brondanw supplied something that the brilliant, slightly ogreish and restless creature liked and wanted, I fancy.

Policies, biology and poetry – he and I pursued subjects at intervals in Calcutta, in Scotland, in London. The annoying thing about him was that, being a fine researcher and a famous originator in several branches of biology, he yet knew more English literature than I did. Being also all his life a combative fellow, he relished his superiority. Awkward, worthwhile creature! Someone once called him 'the cuddly porcupine'.

As a teenager (flapper was the current word), a good many of the people who frequented my parents' houses still seemed to me to be not quite real and I said as much to my father. 'Transient and embarrassed phantoms?' said he, nodding. 'But not all of them I think.'

There were, however, half a dozen on one occasion, who certainly could be described by both words. They spoke hardly any English and transient they certainly proved to be. They all arrived together at a big party that my parents gave in their honour and at the request of the Foreign Office. They had difficult names that floored even Bishop, our butler, when he tried to announce them. These were members of the Russian Duma. Transient phantoms indeed! What happened to them

when they got back to Czarist Russia after being guests in London I
never heard. But this I know for sure: one, or maybe all of them, invited
the whole family to visit them in Russia and to stay on their estate. One
of them (a small, shy man wearing pince-nez) was incongruously a Don
Cossack. Even at fifteen or sixteen, I knew enough to realize what a
deprivation it was when, at the last minute, we didn't go, because,
forsooth, there was some nonsense about a General Election. My
father, it seemed, 'couldn't leave the Paper.' The final let-down was
that we – without my father – went to Boulogne instead.

And so the seasons went on – spring, summer, autumn, winter – and
then in 1913 came the moment, the ritual moment, of my 'coming out',
the moment when (as I have said) I ceased just to look over the
banisters at the couples going down arm-in-arm to dinner. Had the
date been brought forward, partly because I was tall and fairly
grown-up looking – as Naomi had observed – or partly because my
parents had a feeling that something might be going to happen?

My father, for instance, was busy promoting rifle clubs and having
field days with some Territorial Unit as 'enemy'. He believed in the
possibility of an invasion and had formed a mounted corps of Surrey
Guides. My mother was active in the formation of a Red Cross
Voluntary Aid Detachment – Nursing and Ambulance. I participated
a little in this, of course, even before coming out.

When the ritual moment came, I was rather more awkward and shy
than other girls who had had the experience of going to school, but I
was not entirely unprepared. For the young woman in London and
Paris of 1913 and 1914 the first visible change was that one's hair went
up and one's skirts went down to floor length. Horribly long, narrow
skirts were in fashion when my turn came: 'Directoire' the fashionable
dressmakers called them, those accursed skirts; we called them
'hobble'. They were so awkward that in a really smart version you
could hardly get your foot up on to the kerb from the street. Not only
was such a skirt impeding, but there was yet another horror: perched
on our uncertain hair would be a large hat. My red hair curled and shed
hairpins wildly. These two inconveniences were obligatory. In the
1980s very few girls wear hats, but then it was essential on going out of
the house to perch an enormous hat on your head. Pinned precariously
on to the toppling pile of my red hair, I remember a hat which was
much admired; it was as wide as my shoulders. Not a shady garden hat,
I must point out, but a smart hat in which you might have to go out
when a strong wind blew, and which you kept on as a guest at a
luncheon or tea-party, or when paying calls.

In the evening our clothes were awkward in a different, equally unaccustomed way. Our arms had to be visible and bare except for a pair of long white kid gloves. Also our bodices were very *décolletées*, and our dresses were not only long but often had little trains which, together with a fan, had somehow to be held up when waltzing.

Such evening dress often looked charming, but was not pleasant to wear, and was also very cold. Older ladies might temper the cold of such a costume in houses which seldom had central heating by wearing a fur stole or even a little fur bolero, but young girls might not wear furs – not with evening dress. Nor could a young girl possibly wear any make-up at all, while older women had to be surreptitious and pretend that they didn't.

The hymn about 'little drops of water and little grains of sand' making the mighty ocean 'and the smiling land' had a cosmetic parallel:

> Little grains of powder, little dabs of paint,
> Make your face look nice and smooth, even if it ain't.

Other rules were that you must contrive a chaperone at dances; must not drive about alone in hansom cabs, especially not alone with a young man. You must not walk alone in a street or park. These were some of them, but there were other rules. Why didn't we rebel? Why did we put up with all this sartorial nonsense? The short answer is that I, at any rate, never imagined rebellion possible, and indeed nor did the militant suffragettes (most of them) rebel against the clothes regulations. They defied the police and all the grim and powerful authorities in those dreadful fashionable hats and those long, impeding skirts.

What a girl wore changed not only with her new status, from little girl to young lady, but also changed with the fashions. This means that older women still, in the case of underwear, conformed to yet older ways such as wool next to the skin, long 'combination' garments, and satin bloomers with white washable linings. And then there were the corsets, and the frilly camisoles which hid the corsets, which, by the way, were not washable.

Young men suffered, too, but when I 'came out' the frock coat for London wear was being superseded, though older men such as my father still wore black or grey frock coats in London, and also spats – little white semi-gaiters – and top hats. It was a bold and Bohemian man who wore a felt hat in London, unless he was a painter or a writer. I once saw Henry James in such a hat. In the country, a cap or a tweed hat was permissible for men. A deer-stalker was only permissible for outdoor sporting occasions.

All men wore their hair 'short back and sides', satined down with brilliantine, and nearly always parted on the left. It was not quite the thing – a sign of daring and perhaps decadence – to part it in the middle, as a few bold spirits did, but to do so was to risk being thought a lady-killer or a lounge lizard.

Sir James Laver (very agreeable company he was too) was one of the first men to recognize a now generally accepted fact: anthropology and psychology throw light on the subject of dress. He didn't push his inquiries as far as they have been pushed since, but he did get as far as realizing that dress was not just a covering or an artifact, but essentially a badge and a declaration. The statements were sometimes conscious and sometimes unconscious, and he saw that this fact could be established, and a great deal could be learned from the extraordinary heat of the controversies that arose over dress, and what was good form and what bad. Only if clothes were symbols would all such fuss be possible.

It was absolutely 'not done', for example, for a man to wear a made-up tie, or worse a shirt-front that wasn't part of a shirt, or false cuffs. At least women could practise deceptions like this, but men could not.

In tailors' or dressmakers' shops, the senior men assistants wore frock coats, the lady assistants black satin gowns with long swishing trains and incredible piled up coiffures.

My fellow debs and I had, as was said, been trained to make ourselves agreeable, to conform and to be pleasant in society, and most of us were willing enough. Not so Edith Sitwell, not so young Virginia Stephen and her sister Vanessa, not so Simone de Beauvoir in Paris. As for me, I just played along awkwardly but as well as I could, though I wasn't as happy as I was expensively meant to be. Osbert Sitwell in his Hanoverian style put fair and square what he thought the difficulty was: 'Edith and I and my brother Sacheverall were artists, special beings, often it is true much more difficult and disagreeable than the others, with nerves and brains and a kind of sensitive perception for the gathering of and selection of impressions.'[2]

I knew Edith fairly well over a long time and published her poems in the *Spectator*, while she later dedicated a book of her poems, *Troy Park*, to me. I doubt if she was a great poet, but she was a true one. It was, I suspect, the pain of the grotesque attempt to make her into a deb that later hardened her into an eccentric. This situation is not a matter of sex, as Sean O'Casey and D. H. Lawrence bear witness. Awkwardly, we are not accurately sorted at birth, so year after year both parents and children often get it wrong. For instance, both Edith and I found that our parents' well-meaning efforts were being made to adapt us for an inappropriate group. It was right, mind you, not to let either Edith or me grow up as misfits, freaks or dowdy prigs, or some other sort of deviant. But to make debs of either of us . . . ? The Sitwells are comparable, by the way, in that they were like good raised maps, that is they showed some social points with the raised map's useful exaggeration of the vertical scale.

The clothes we wore and the fact that we had to change every day for dinner, and sometimes at grand house-parties two or three times a day, and that the meals were so elaborate, made it necessary – or at any rate very desirable – to have a great many servants. There were always seven in our house, sometimes ten, and these numbers were kept up I think for the next ten years or more, not of course counting the war years.

My mother had a lady's maid, and so had I; mine was French. There were three servants in the kitchen, three in the pantry – that is a butler and two footmen – and I think three housemaids. There doesn't seem to have been a boot-boy, but my grandmother had one who, incidentally, was very greatly despised by the housekeeper, Mrs Baker, who declared that he was 'a dirty 'abited boy'. I feel that he was probably extremely oppressed.

When I tell my grandchildren about these doings, they are appalled. A French maid? Preposterous! And indeed, there was a great deal that was preposterous about Edwardian glitter. But it is possible to see these tribal rites and taboos in proportion, and also to think of the technical devices that we didn't have then. These are appliances that we use now to keep up the standard of comfort and elegance that our fellow tribe-members had then. This is important for career women who can, if they want to, keep up the 1912 standards with no paid indoor help at all, except of course for much of the important part of child rearing.

Supposing that an intruder (or Father Time himself) comes to my house, Plâs Brondanw as it is now, or to the house of one of my married grandchildren. He has a great sack (no, it has to be a great van) and into it he puts all the diverse things that we have now that we didn't have then.

Consumer durables would take up a lot of the van: the fridge, the television, the radio, the dishwasher, the washing machine, the electric cooker; all the coat-hangers, zip-fasteners and paper handkerchiefs; plastic mackintoshes, drip-dry sheets, nylon shirts and stockings; he rips off nylon lace, takes away the electric blankets. Only cotton, linen, silk and woollen garments would stay in drawers and cupboards. Most picnic, camping, sailing and climbing gear that are now nylon or aluminium or plastic would go. The point is really that after the intruder had driven off in his removal van, everything left would be heavier, more inconvenient and need much more servicing.

But much more important were the differences that would be felt by families in what are now called the 'lower income bracket'. That is to say that the other eighty or ninety percent of families would experience much more loss in a time machine. The difference between then and now is more drastic. Even a clever boy would almost always have to leave school at twelve: some of those who were later my friends went down the pits at that age. It was still common for the bride at her wedding not to be able to write her name in the register; nobody had holidays with pay, and shop assistants worked from eight in the morning and were still at it at six or seven when the shop shut and when they would begin the tidying up. There was no early closing, and builders were not paid for wet time.

And in thinking about the intruder who took all the modern gadgets away from the well-off home, I forgot the medicine cupboard. The aspirin would have to go, and of course all the antibiotics that most of us save from last time they were prescribed.

But to go back to big things again, and to the conditions of the majority of our fellow citizens. When I was a child there was no Old Age Pension, so that to be old was always chancy – positively dreadful for many people. Also, both for reasons of lack of money and for technical reasons, most of them had to do without spectacles or hearing aids, and had to put up with the effects of very poor dentistry.

So much for 'the golden past' and 'the good old days'! But all the same, there was such a thing as 'Edwardian glitter', as Clough called it. There really was. And I am among the few hundreds still alive who participated.

Six

GLITTER

My father promoted causes, not only by writing about them but also by taking practical action. With Lord Roberts and Lord Haldane as colleagues, it was National Defence, which he furthered by organizing a demonstration – a platoon, was it? – of crash-trained *Spectator* infantry, and also by enrolling fifty or so of our neighbours as mounted Surrey Guides. In case anyone got hurt, my mother formed a Red Cross detachment – nurses, stretcher-bearers and so on. I was one of the volunteer Red Cross nurses, a VAD.

All this was dashing, but not eccentric. It was the fashion then for newspapers to go in for practical campaigns. For instance our neighbour and (almost) friend, Alfred Harmsworth, and his *Daily Mail* promoted a rose and some sort of particularly nutritious bread, something without additives perhaps? My father, indifferent to bread and roses, flew at larger game and one of these practical activities of his changed my life, quite fortuitously.

There was in 1913, as ever, a housing shortage so, tangling with a body called The Rural Co-operative Housing and Land Society, he arranged for a piece of land to be bought and a weather-boarded, tile-roofed cottage, costing £150, to be put on it. This, like the houses in Letchworth Garden City, was to serve as a specimen, so an opening ceremony had to be arranged, not just to show the cottage but, as with the china eggs supplied to hens, to inaugurate a competition.

Big-wigs were invited, the day was fine, transport had been laid on, and Lord Middleton, then Lord Lieutenant of the County, was to take the chair. Invitations had also been sent to housing experts, town planners and architects. It is because of this last circumstance that this particular activity of my father's is chronicled here. Activities – parties with a purpose – were the usual thing, but generally of minor interest to me.

So, on that fine afternoon in a marquee in a field in Merrow, where the weather-boarded cottage stood, we sat in dutiful rows listening to speeches from the platform. I lately found a verbatim account of what my father had to say about the affair:

You may write beautiful leading articles about a £150 cottage till you're black in the face! I determined therefore to see if, where paper had failed, a working model might not succeed? You have seen it. Such a cottage would let for three shillings a week, and even if you also had to pay a ground landlord, five shillings would cover it. [After more about finance, and looking about him, he went on] I understand that there are gentlemen here present who believe in the possibility of building a good cottage with three bedrooms, a kitchen-living room and a scullery, for less than £150, indeed for £100.

But at this point, sitting in the front row, I lost the thread. For I had caught sight of something interesting. Among the trestles supporting my father and the rest of the platform there had appeared, quite undisturbed, a fieldmouse. The neat, quick-moving little creature appeared to be (very appropriately) collecting material for a house of its own. I longed to warn this small misguided householder. All these trestles, I wanted to tell it, are not at all a good nesting site, that next day it would be all cleared away and then . . . I watched how, presently, the little creature stopped collecting, sat up, and in the beguiling way of mice began with busy front paws to clean its face and whiskers.

When my father stopped talking, I thought, there might be clapping and, with luck, the clapping might warn the rash little creature into taking cover. Upon this my father's voice came through to me again: 'I make a sporting offer to all devisers, inventors and patentees of cheap cottages, to come and show his mettle by putting up a £100 cottage on my land. If his cottage will stand the test of wind and rain for one year and thus show that it is not merely a butterfly house, I will purchase it from him.'

He seemed to be winding up. I liked his expression 'butterfly house' and decided to attend again. The clapping had the desired effect on the fieldmouse.

It turned out that one of the 'devisers and inventors' present was a young architect, who was there chiefly because it was a fine Saturday afternoon. I learned later that as the meeting progressed he had caught sight of a young woman with red hair who was sitting in the front row and who seemed to be paying deep attention to the speeches. Her looks caught his fancy, and he was intrigued by what seemed an unusual interest in the speeches. Walking about during the tea interval, he decided that I probably belonged to Lord Middleton's party and, Lord Middleton being an acquaintance, the young architect proceeded to make himself as pleasant as possible, 'chatting him up' as this activity would have been described later. Soon it transpired that this red-haired girl was Miss Strachey. The young man didn't know my father; something drastic had to be done. So, on the meeting being resumed and volunteers called for, the young man declared his deep conviction that there was indeed a need for more rural housing and that, in short, he would be a competitor. Fifty years later Clough Williams-Ellis wrote: 'The strategem succeeded and I contrived to see quite a lot, though never enough, of this Miss Strachey.' How I wish I had known about this at the time, though of course I am glad that he didn't know about the mouse.

That notorious 'love at first sight' – to have known she inspired it would have heartened any girl. To this particular, slightly misfit, shy girl it would have made all the difference. Always afraid of not getting dancing partners, knowing that I was too tall for many of them, I was always apprehensive and a little afraid at dances. Was it because I was tall, or because I hadn't the right sort of chit-chat? Anyhow, I felt I knew only too well that I didn't somehow please the dancing young men.

As it was I knew nothing, suspected nothing, was not even aware of setting eyes on this specimen of the 'devising gentlemen here present', as my father had called some of the audience.

One particular 'devising gentleman' diligently drew the plans and presently his cottage began to rise from its foundations. Four rooms it had, and it cost £101. When this unknown competitor reported that it was nearly finished, my parents sent me to ride my mare down from Newlands and show him the way. He had been asked to lunch.

It was wet, raining hard, and when for the first time I saw him, all I thought was that he looked absurd. This was for no better reason than because, over the long, dark, urban overcoat of the day, he had superimposed a much shorter light-coloured waterproof jacket. With his rather rakish good looks, his tall gipsy figure and one of those suspect felt hats, he looked to me peculiar, certainly not much like the usual run of my dancing partners. Having civilly given my message, I turned my horse and cantered off in mildly derisive indifference. At lunch? I don't remember.

Then, and then, at the London balls to which I was taken this Mr Williams-Ellis, now perfectly conventionally dressed, somehow kept turning up. He was, it seemed, a dancing man after all and wore, of course, trousers with braid down the sides, a white waistcoat and white kid gloves, and an elegant, sharply waisted tail coat, all of which admirably suited his long legs, small waist and wide shoulders.

Now, as we danced, I didn't feel at all inclined to be derisive, but soon found myself easy with him, looked out for him, was sorry if he wasn't there, so that next time he had to come down to Surrey 'because the cottage needed a look', I was truly pleased to see him.

All that season we managed to find occasions for dancing together.

'Gold and Silver' the dance bands played, and 'The Merry Widow', 'The Choristers' and 'The Blue Danube'. We danced at many houses where balls were given, and at the Ritz. At Kent House the ballroom walls had been decorated by Paul Sert – on shiny black walls were outlined huge gilt elephants and garlands of swinging apes.

Sometimes the grander London houses would have a small garden lit with fairy lights, a garden in which couples could sit out. This was even better than sitting out on the stairs. He didn't hold my hand, except to help me up, and didn't ever try to kiss me. And yet it did begin gradually to cross my mind that perhaps, like other girls, I had a young man. But I didn't know the form and hadn't even one confidential female friend of my own age. 'Tell me, you who know what love is . . .' '*Voi che sapete* . . .' nobody said a word, so I thought perhaps that it wasn't so.

But it was so, only I didn't know, not for sure. It transpired much later that on one evening – it was at Kent House – sitting out a dance in the garden, he had, as he wrote later: 'almost proposed to my chief partner of the evening. I wish I had! Many months later, and in very different circumstances, I did so propose. . . . But at Kent House terror won.'

I wonder whether it might have been easier if terror had not won at Kent House. Apparently everyone except me seems to have been perfectly aware of the real situation, but I (then, as always, a slow learner) only said to myself with a reasonably cheerful shrug of the shoulders that, if there was nothing more to it, it had been very nice indeed to have him for a friend. For friends we were, not a doubt of that. We amused each other, much as acknowledged lovers do, with light frivolities, for instance with collecting picture-books showing ridiculous buildings 'in the Gothic taste' (on which taste we pretended to dote). I have just found a copy of one of these books again. It is by Mr Papworth, who is endearingly described on the title page as 'Author of the celebrated essay on the Dry-rot'. Was it Papworth or another who delighted us by designing a lodge 'for a nobleman's park entrance' with two rooms down and two up, which was said by its designer to exhibit a 'blending of the Castle and Cathedral styles'? The villas and *cottages ornés* in these books fairly dripped with creepers, many of them had thatched roofs and some of them had bits of sham ruin – disguising a dairy perhaps – tacked on to them: 'the earwig style' we called it. Even then I think I did sometimes pause to pity the lodge-keepers who had to live in such concoctions and who might have preferred Clough's sensible little box, the sort of house that had so fortuitously brought us together.

What was nice for me about this Mr Williams-Ellis (even at this stage I thus thought of him, and thus addressed him), what was so nice, so reassuring was that with him I didn't have to pretend to be either stupid or grand or sophisticated, or anything else that I wasn't. No, not ever. This was so comforting because I often found that, having quite liked some other young man, he would suddenly disappear if he found out what I was really like. I suppose that feeling of assurance – of no disguise – wasn't really important to him, since he was already in love with me.

That we liked as well as loved each other turned out to be absolutely relevant, for such an easy feeling, though much less spectacular than the splendid flame of love, produces a lasting warmth that, for reasons beyond our control, was in our case very much needed. As is only too well known, the devil never loses a trick, and for us there were years of strain to be gone through, of uncertainties and doubts. These, though not of our making, nor made by our respective families, were very real and we suffered long war years and long frustrations.

However, for a short time it was all play. Writing about that London Season and telling of balls and parties, Clough called his chapter 'Edwardian Glitter'. Glitter there really was, that is for the golden boys and girls such as we, so briefly, were. We were happy. Clough's precarious architect's practice was, he realized, budding and looked as if, after the warmth of this summer, it might show leaf and flower. As for the outside world, neither of us took heed of things which other people, my father for example, were obliged to evaluate.

There were as usual strikes and troubles in Ireland, troubles so violent that they rocked a divided House of Commons, and in the London streets girls and women – suffragettes in ornate shoulder-wide hats and feather boas – demanded votes and chained themselves to railings, threw themselves under galloping horses or poured paint into letter-boxes. When they were arrested they resisted vigorously and when in prison immediately went on hunger strike, upon which they were forcibly fed. But in spite of these and other startling and unacceptable happenings, affairs of which week by week my father and his *Spectator* were obliged to take notice, the London Season of 1914 went on brilliantly.

In the politer districts of London, theatre parties were being arranged, there were *thé dansants*, and balls were being given in the bigger houses of Carlton House Terrace and Eaton Square, or else at the Ritz. A small or sometimes a large dinner party was the desirable prelude to a fashionable evening. So on those June nights by seven o'clock in a dozen houses in Westminster, Mayfair and Belgravia, hostesses would be arranging flowers, seeing to the distribution of cigarettes and matches in their drawing-rooms and putting the name-cards around their dinner tables.

Some who were plump and provident would have finished such tasks early and be trying to forestall the effects of good food on a healthy body by soaking themselves in hot baths. Soon they would be contemplating their reflections in gilt-framed mirrors, trying out the effect of this or that set of ruby or sapphire necklaces and bracelets, while their ladies' maids brushed, curled and piled up their hair.

Any efforts to keep down weight did not go uncontested. Downstairs taps poured over the red hands of scullery maids, cooks contemplated the dishing up of sauces or cautiously lifted the steaming lids of saucepans. By seven o'clock butlers would already have padded their last to the wine-bins and were able to stand looking at orderly rows of bottles on sideboards or at the leaning contents of ice-buckets. In a spruce little house in Kensington the cook would be making a clatter, beating up spinach for *épinard à la crème*, and looking out of the corner of her eye at the mousse of sole in aspic with its border of muscatel grapes.

An hour or two later, discreet butlers and footmen or tripping parlourmaids would have begun their intricate motions between kitchens, sideboards and softly lit dinner tables. First the plates and then the dishes, balanced on skilled hands, slid between the diners. Small talk hid shyness or high hopes, or the pressure of a foot. In some houses it was the food that counted. Among the six or seven courses would be perhaps an innovation, a clear iced tomato soup, then perhaps something wrapped in vine leaves served with a sharp sauce, and lastly a sorbet or an ice hidden in a haze of spun sugar and surrounded by the first strawberries.

By ten o'clock, in front of the Ritz, in front of some house in Park Lane, and in front of another in Curzon Street, there would be a queue of cars and a striped awning, while a strip of red carpet had been rolled across the pavement. These were the signs that a dance was being given. A double row of shabby onlookers was nearly always waiting to see the pretty dresses that the light summer cloaks did not entirely hide; they would see the rose or the flower-wreath on the gleaming hair of the girls, while on the heads of the older women were dazzling tiaras.

Soon the hum of voices and the soft waltz notes floated out through open windows.

By August the country was at war.

Seven

COURTSHIP

It is December 1914. In the mud and deafening noise of heavy artillery, the War, which is being fought on the other side of the Channel, has staggered on since August. In Britain, few people – not the generals, not the politicians, and certainly not the public – understand very much about it. True, a great many flags are being waved and there has been massive recruitment for Kitchener's Army, but military preparations have included buying cavalry horses as though for another Charge of the Light Brigade. Economic theory seems stunned into imbecility so that, in the first limp surprise, all the banks suspended dealing and kept this up for days on end, but now that phase is over and the slogan is 'Business as Usual'.

'Gallant little Belgium' has been invaded and overwhelmed, and remnants of her army have reached Britain. They have not only reached Britain in general but our house in particular, for Big Newlands is already a military hospital. Our Belgians are walking wounded and include a very black Congolese corporal of odd and apparently violent habits. He has filed teeth. This is popularly held to be proof that he belongs to a cannibal tribe. It is decided that he has to be returned to a more regular military establishment.

Mr Williams-Ellis is, like me, by now in uniform, in his case that of a second lieutenant in Kitchener's Army. Was it a coincidence that he had joined a battalion stationed somewhere on the Surrey side of London? I think about him from time to time. I am beginning to understand nursing routine, and my feet hurt. And I find the rationale of medical procedures interesting, but I know nothing about the War and very little about my own affairs, and feel fatalistic about both, and my feet hurt.

It is Sunday morning on 6 December and I get up and put on my VAD uniform. Mr Williams-Ellis, who is to lunch with us, is coming down by a morning train to Clandon station and I, not being on duty till later that day, plan to walk halfway down by a field path to meet him. He has come down like this before. Today, although I know nothing, I have a feeling that this is a special occasion and, looking in the glass, I wonder if I look nice in uniform. I could wear my ordinary clothes now and change later, but then I decide not to dress up and that he had better see me as I am. Then, just before I ought to start, the telephone rings. He has missed his train and will have to come on the next. I immediately suppose that this settles it. It can't be a special day after all. Never mind, we can still be friends, and all I can do is just try to make sure that we shall.

It is in this mood that I walk down the field path with half the short December day gone and with it more than half my foreseeing it as a special day. It is just an ordinary day after all, yes, even if he stays on late, for my evening tour of duty will leave very little time.

How green I was! A more experienced girl would also have realized what it meant when we met on the field path and he, in an unusually embarrassed and yet jaunty way, explained what had delayed him. He was not usually a scatter-brain, as I knew, but today he had somehow worn his watch in the bath. Most girls would have realized what all this added up to, and that his drowned watch, missed train, in fact masked a mixture of desperate resolution and a return of the terror that had assailed him months ago at the ball at Kent House.

Why do I now, more than half a century later, feel impelled to recall and formulate what are, after all, only details of an unimportant though unusually long and, in its first years, desperate love story? I suppose it is because I feel, as Prince Genji in Japan said so many centuries earlier, that 'There should never come a time when people do not know that that is how things are.' I think that the Prince meant that people ought to know that the more significant human actions often come from deep sources. Therefore decisions that are momentous for us are only apparently made at haphazard. Thus, events on which our futures depend often seem so dreamlike and chancy; they are not really chance-determined but times when the river of life flows strongly.

Here we both were then, on that December day, feeling other-directed as one often feels in a dream. I was a novice, inexperienced to a degree that was unusual even then, and not knowing what my part in the drama might be. There was he – another novice – who up to now had bolted from other girls in panic. He hardly knew why, having bathed wearing his watch, he had gone on to catch the next train. He didn't quite know why he was here. He didn't want to be tied down. Oh, how he hadn't wanted to be tied down! And up to now he had always bolted. He had bolted because, in those days, young ladies could be compromised and, more important to him, he also supposed that girls might have real feelings and were vulnerable, and had hearts that could be damaged. Thus his conscience had up to now always decreed that he must bolt. Hurting girls wouldn't do, so he had always fled.

But now on that winter's day, how did these two creatures – I, so unversed in the female arts, and he, up to now so liable to panic at the very idea of being tied down – how did we manage to get ourselves engaged?

Above all perhaps comes the question: how was it that such an apparently amateurish business turned out so well? For it did turn out well and was long admitted, even by such of our friends who were most anxious to bolster their cynicism, that here was a love story that – though so shaky, so improvised, so rickety and irrational, and later to be so troubled by Fate – had a happy course. The preliminaries really did turn us almost sick with apprehension, yet the love story survived our generation's protracted separations, and flourished. Year after year, for more than sixty years, our affection not only outlived all the usual physical and emotional vicissitudes of a long life, but also the shocks and carnage of two world wars.

Luck came into it, but it should also be added that neither of us was a complete fool. Though we behaved like dreamers, we were not entirely sleep-walkers. The current that carried us along was indeed that of a strong river. But we did also act rationally.

But to go back to the events of 6 December. Nothing of the slightest moment had been said as we walked together up the field to the house, which was usually full of other people. Clough noticed that they seemed to have evaporated, but I was sadly aware that it was late and it would soon be time for me to go on duty. Clough seemed to have realized that it might be now or never, so that it was in stammering haste as well as panic that we promised to love each other for ever and that we exchanged our first kiss.

He followed me up the stairs to the wards and, as we went, I (always a sucker for the truth) tried to tell him that I believed I should always want to write. It startled me that I should suddenly feel this important, but somehow it seemed essential that he should realize this. His answer was heartfelt: 'I shouldn't know what to do with a whole-time wife!'

Reaching a small pantry, I began with shaking hands my first evening duty, which was filling a great many hot-water bottles, some rubber, some stone. An irate Sister entered (a small starched ramrod little tartar from the London Hospital).

'Nurse! You were late coming on duty. Also Red Cross Probationers are not allowed to bring visitors to the wards.'

To do her justice, though, she did relent, frostily, when I said meekly that this particular visitor had that moment asked me to marry him.

Next day we managed to borrow two of the ponies, pleading that they needed exercise. Later he was given another short leave. Gradually, as we got to know each other better, our love and affection grew, though not without days and especially solitary nights of panic on both sides. Panic happened to me when he wasn't there, and when it seemed quite mad and preposterous to have let myself in for such a thing, and he seemed to recede into being almost a stranger again. Promising to spend my life with a strange man . . . But it was always all right when he was there, so that my need for reassurance was an additional reason for longing to have him there again.

I believe that these symptoms are classic and that true love, first love, which can be one of the great magical experiences of human life, is commonly beset with fear. Maybe the panic, the sense of a receding wave of feeling that Clough experienced earlier and I late, is something that makes the passionate reassurances of lovers' meetings surpass other joys.

> For sweeter far than this, than these, than all,
> Are the first passionate utterances of requited love.

What Byron said is true.

When Clough asked for my father's consent (necessary for I was not yet twenty-one), my father had agreed, only remarking quite amiably that he had rather hoped I might marry a duke, and when my mother showed no particular elation, their reactions scarcely affected me. Indeed, so engrossed was I in my own sensations that I was hardly conscious of this lukewarm, almost sighing atmosphere. I was indeed no more aware of them or of the events in the surrounding world than the rider on a roller-coaster is aware of happenings in the rest of the fair.

It was not till later that it occurred to me to wonder at the dimness of my parents' first reactions or at their apparent lack of sympathy or fellow-feeling. It is not till now, indeed, that with hindsight I have begun to guess at the reason. What they saw was that the inclusion in the family of this young officer was going to mean first to me, and thus to them, that the War was going to cross the Channel. The War was going to come home not just in the perfectly tolerable form of a Congolese cannibal in one of the spare bedrooms, but to our real feelings. In a sense they, and I too, had been immune; now the immunity was broken. If my older brother Tom had lived, he would have been of military age, but he had not lived. My younger brother

John was still a schoolboy; I was a girl. But now my heart, if not my person, must share the common danger and I would suffer as other young women had suffered these two hundred years and more, and as they had endured the consequences of what the ballad called 'The cruel wars in High Germany'. The mounting casualty lists already showed the consequences as a likely matter for heartbreak.

And what about the other family that was involved in what we had just done? The Williams-Ellis situation was quite different. Clough had older and younger brothers and a mother, of whom I was to become very fond. Clough and all the brothers were of military age, and inevitably they were in the War. I did not realize it at the time, but my arrival (he was the first of the brothers to become engaged) in no way added to the family's involvement in the casualty lists, but was regarded instead as something hopeful.

As Clough had already explained to my father, his father had, some years before he died, given Clough (as second surviving son) the second house and the second small family estate that they owned. I had met none of his relations except his mother briefly in London. She hardly ever left Wales but came to visit two of her sons. It was a stiff occasion when our respective mothers, as I now realize, cast appraising eyes at each other and us. The significance of this meeting I, dolt that I was, failed to notice.

So it was not till we were engaged and when I, carefully chaperoned by my prospective mother-in-law, was brought to Wales to meet my new relations, that I first saw Plâs Brondanw. It is of small manor-house size, slightly ivy-grown, and was then also slightly dilapidated, tall, built of native granite, grave, dignified. Inside, it had few modern conveniences; altogether it seemed to be the Welsh equivalent of an English manor, and was clearly loved and cherished both by Clough and by his mother.

His family wondered what the new girl would make of it. Clough's uncles, aunts and cousins, fond as they were of dear Clough, yet saw his romantic notions about the house as definitely odd. He surely didn't expect the new bride, and any staff she might bring, to put up with such things as no servants' hall, with that old kitchen range and its dubious supply of hot water, with that old painted bath, or with that flat scullery sink, or with lamps and candles? A 'strange old place', 'full of draughts', 'such a very bachelor affair', 'awkward for dear May [my mother-in-law] showing her round'. 'Of course, dear Clough didn't have money to do much, but you can see that any money he did have he didn't spend very wisely, just spent it on planting all those yew hedges and making that terrace.' 'Nice old place, but still . . .' 'What's *she* like?' 'I believe they just met at dances, in London, so I wonder if she's any idea about living in the country?'

I think that Clough and Nain – as we prematurely called her, it's the Welsh for Granny – I fancy that these two, or she at any rate, did hold their breath a little. So it was all right for me to say, as I did that very evening, that it was a good thing that I'd promised to marry Clough *before* I saw Brondanw, otherwise I could never have been sure it hadn't been for love of Brondanw, rather than any fancy I had for him, that had made me say yes.

It really was lucky that I came out with this half-joke so quickly and emphatically, for no sooner had I faced all those relations and gone shy than the comic spirit, as is usual in my life, got to work. I felt odd; what was wrong? It turned out I was developing quinsy, which back in Surrey soon made any sort of speaking or swallowing impossible.

Several months passed. My quinsy subsided after an operation. Clough, by now in the Welsh Guards, continued to be an adept at getting leave, and my tours of hospital duty were made to fit.

One day, in a bluebell wood, I am resting half-asleep. Clough beside me has picked some of the sweet-scented, long-stalked flowers.

'Don't beat your wife' I say drowsily.

'I wish she was my wife,' is said in a tone that makes me sit up and take an almost instant resolution. The poor creature is suffering! I am not, indeed I am drowsily happy with things as they are, I am content for a while to go no further with love.

I think young girls often feel like this; I fancy there really always have been such things as maidenly feelings. What I suddenly saw in the bluebell wood was that the situation could not continue: suppose I let things slide and he gets sent abroad, and is wounded or killed?

So, in July 1915, we were married, having romantically decided on eight o'clock in the morning as the time (in order to get a train to Wales), and further that the place is to be St Martha's, a pilgrim church perched on the top of a hill near Guildford above the river Wey. Everyone had to walk the last part.

We caught the train, and settled down – in a first-class carriage for once – and soon realized that, among all our manifold more serious and romantic feelings, hunger was now insistent. But again the absurd had not done with us. There was a luncheon car on the train, but through numerous confusions no one had booked places for us. There were war shortages and it was a full train. So now? In a suitcase of mine that wasn't in the distant guard's van but had mercifully come with us into the carriage, there turned out to be lurking an unlikely thing – a small plum cake in a box, also a small tin of potted meat and, less unlikely, a button-hook.

Somehow Clough opened the tin and, taking turns with the button-hook, we scraped out and ate every scrap of the potted meat and then finished up the cake to the last crumb. Being young and slightly delirious with happiness, we found ourselves delighted with this curious gastronomic combination. I felt that for me, as a young housekeeper, an unbeatable and satisfactory standard of unlikely meals had been promptly set.

Venus, whose slaves we were, is 'the laughter-loving goddess'. I have observed that she laughs at, as well as with, her votaries.

At Brondanw we were greeted with a triumphal arch, a choir and a harp. And for a short time the War let us thrive and rejoice, but this time of being let alone seemed very short to us.

Eight

TRENCH WARFARE

In France, first with the newly-formed Welsh Guards and afterwards
with the new hush-hush Tank Corps, Clough saw a great deal of active
service and indeed had an exceptional amount of what the military
called 'combat experience'. In later life he still remembered details
about the Kaiser's War clearly. The misery was real. For one thing,
tanks, the new arm, though they changed warfare so much, were not
always successful at first. He wrote later:

> It was round about midnight when I got to Agricourt on the eve of the
> battle. It was pitch dark save for the fitful light from the still burning village
> and the flashes of the guns. The attack was to be at dawn and yet there,
> helpless and wallowing in a bog of black mud, were the tanks on which so
> much depended.[1]

But this is not the place to record more than a few tattered scraps of
the bitter chronicle of World War I. We were to relate much of it at
length.

However, the experience of having lived through this time as an
adult is now singular enough to warrant some uneasy glances at what I
felt as the wife of a serving officer, and at his impressions:

> Northern France, indeed Europe from the Swiss border to the sea, was being
> devastated. During the withdrawal the condition of the villagers was pitiful.
> Women and children and old men crazed with fright . . . Tragic indeed is the
> misery of these 'Processions of the Cross'. To members of the Tank Corps who
> witnessed them the impression was unforgettable.[2]

'Unforgettable'? Alas, war misery partakes of oblivion, but to recall
misery briefly is necessary, for it suggests two or three points relevant to
my whole story. If, for example, Clough or the present writer should
later praise the experience of living and remain, on the whole,
'Yes-sayers', our comparative optimism is not a case of our being
simple Drs Pangloss. A young person of the 1980s with today's
problems in mind, might dismissively suppose that very thing. 'You're
lucky', I have been told, 'to have lived then and not now in these
disturbed, dangerous 1980s.' They say to me, 'That was just conventional warfare.'

At about 3.30 am a heavy rain had begun to fall and all day the armies fought amid intermittent storms of sleet and drenching rain . . . Day after day, months, years of trench warfare.[3]

But this book, it must be said again, is not intended as a history of Europe or of the world. So it is enough to say that we speak out of some knowledge of bad, unhappy times, We both experienced, in different ways, the shocking force, the blood-boltered irrationality, and the horrid paradoxes with which from time to time the Dark Powers have infected and convulsed most human societies. Such senseless convulsions have been variously named wars of religion, territorial wars, dynastic wars, racial wars, tribal wars or witch hunts.

My experiences involved no danger, but they were often eye-opening. I had war-work too.

'But, Doctor, he's under the anaesthetic. For an amputation we have got to get the patient's consent.'

I am the young probationer in the operating theatre (I am called 'dirty nurse' because my duty is to deal with anything not sterilized). I look down at the young, unconscious face of the man on the operating table, for the anaesthetist, who is also listening, has withdrawn the mask for a moment. I look at the young face and then at the tattered, shattered flesh and bone of his splintered leg, visible between the turned-back sterile sheets.

To my relief, surgeon and physician decide to go ahead. The sound of the murmuring, consulting voices is replaced by the rasp of the surgeon's saw on bone. Soon someone tells me to carry the severed leg away. It is quite heavy, as I notice with a sigh. He must have been a strong young fellow.

Back at the convalescent hospital (I have been on loan to the hospital with an improvised operating theatre), the amputation patients sit in a long row in their hospital blues for me to dress their stumps. These stumps were all infected at the time of wounding, and are slow to heal.

Clough was present in France at many other tank battles, and I was doing dressings in England, and both of us were unhappy because we so longed to be together, but we were wanted so it seemed irrelevant. We did what we were told was our duty. What seems extraordinary to me now was that we didn't feel more than a twinge of wonder as to why all we young creatures had to be subjected to so much strange, protracted suffering (I, anyhow, did not at the time), or why morality had apparently gone into reverse so that it was now right to engage in certain usually forbidden doings, such as killing and ordering young men to their deaths – things that we had always been told to think of as criminal.

I am nursing convalescents again. I am changing the sergeant's dressing; all wounds received in shell holes are liable to go septic. He is a nice man, this sergeant, and what they call a good influence in the wards, so that in a way the nursing staff are not altogether sorry that his wound is slow to mend. He and I go on chatting as I put on the clean dressing. He has been telling me about an incident in France. He was put in charge of a small detachment detailed to take a batch of about twenty German prisoners back to the base. The way back was, he says, a bog, a maze of half-flooded trenches, and soon heavier shelling started up again.

'So what did you do?' I ask.

'Shot the prisoners, and we all got back to base.'

Naturally I didn't comment and, though the tale stuck with me, for a long time I didn't question anyone – not my father, and certainly not Clough next time he came on leave; it rankled, a wound in my mind that was slow to heal. Long after, I did at last talk about it to an officer who had been fighting in Spain in the International Brigade and who had been invalided back. He said the sergeant had been right.

'How could it be right to shoot prisoners?' I asked.

As this sergeant had described the affair, replied my officer, the whole lot of them would probably have been killed otherwise. 'His duty was to his own men.'

I have already remarked, and shall have occasion to repeat, that I am a slow learner. Wilfred Owen's poems hadn't yet come my way. Owen was of course killed soon after writing this one:

> It seemed that out of battle I escaped
> Down some profound dull tunnel . . .

The tunnel, Owen goes on, is full of sleepers – or are they sleepers? One of them rouses:

> And by his smile, I knew the sullen hall,
> By his dead smile I knew we stood in Hell . . .
> I am the enemy you killed, my friend.
> I knew you in this dark; for so you frowned
> Yesterday through me as you jabbed and killed.
> I parried, but my hands were loath and cold.
> Let us sleep now . . .[4]

I had not yet read the poem, did not ask Clough then or ever what he thought of the sergeant's story. At the time I only asked the Fates to grant me two things. The first was to let Clough survive (which on the face of it was most unlikely).

The second thing was that I should bear his child. This seemed more possible for, though he had so much combat experience, Clough was known as 'the leave king'. He would regularly somehow get back on leave, or on some course or other. After all, courses were inevitable because the tank was a new armament, liable to design-changes and modifications whose precise consequences in battle conditions only a serving soldier could assess. The fact that he often got leave meant something beyond the obvious relief and joy, they meant that perhaps the Fates might grant my second wish. To bear him a child would, I felt, also be my poor counter-move to so much death.

'Tranquillity,' said Dr Henry Huxley with a sigh, when I complained to him that nothing seemed to be happening. He had confirmed the depressing fact. 'With just these hurried leaves and the long trench warfare worry for you in between, it's no wonder really that you don't seem to be getting your baby. I'm so sorry.'

He was right about the long worry in between. Leaves, even for Clough the adept, were short and, as I couldn't help feeling, doom-framed. Oh, slowly, slowly! But clocks and calendars were relentless. The time was doled out, the time when, as a great concession, we had leave to be young and to love one another. Leaves were poignant and brief, and the time between, for me, an anxious nullity. I didn't try to look at casualty lists but just felt long grey gulfs that I tried to bridge by hard work; it is usually the best anodyne. The greyness, the unknowing of these long gaps, was scarcely lightened by delayed and infrequent letters and by printed field postcards that I grew to hate, for they could tell me nothing except that, a fortnight ago, he had still been alive. And what in the meantime? The casualty lists in the papers still filled column after column.

All this went on for a long while and then the Fates, deciding perhaps that they had watched two of their poor puppets dangle for long enough, decided to grant me my second wish, but to grant it in a way that, though logical, was characteristically undignified. The Fates resorted, in fact, to the sort of ridiculous bathos with which my more classically tragic sorrows or dilemmas have often been alleviated or resolved. They contrived that I should suffer an attack of measles.

My brother John, being then at Eton, was said not to be too well. I was delegated to go and see what was up. When I got to his bedside there he was, covered with spots. He had begun to feel better, but it was clear that it had been a mild attack of measles.

Back on duty at the hospital, in due time (the incubation is a long one) my throat began to feel sore. Home, still a military convalescent hospital, was no place for such a patient. So, before the first spot could declare to our military overlords the ridiculous truth, I found myself in bed with a high temperature at the top of our London house with, of all things, a Zeppelin raid going on, amid furies of flak from our anti-aircraft guns. The raid was little more surprising than it was short.

But for a grown-up young woman, measles can be long and thorough. However, it was over at last and I was out of quarantine. How Nanny Holland had managed I can't imagine. I was incurious as well as grateful. So then my hospital routine was resumed and, after a while, Clough again got leave.

I am in Dr Huxley's London consulting room again. The examination is over. I just manage not to burst into tears for joy when he confirms that it really is so.

'But why', I ask, 'this time?'

'Because you had the measles.' He goes on to explain all: mucus membrane surfaces had been inflamed . . .

From the nearest post office I send a brief and cryptic telegram – telegrams often get through fairly quickly, at any rate to staff officers, which is what Clough is now. I must share the news as fast as I can. Then I write and write to him.

In due time the profound, everyday miracle of a human birth was accomplished. My baby was born in a house in Guildford let by Roger Fry, which had wall decorations by Duncan Grant. Once more a telegram was sent off: 'Susan! Both well.'

Much as I had wanted that baby, I found the experience of bearing it moving to a degree that I hadn't guessed. Not till I had managed to repeat it twice more, with Charlotte and with Christopher, did I also manage to formulate what I had felt and then try to set down something of the common yet extraordinary experience. This first time, with Clough not there (however much I longed for him), only two thoughts surfaced into consciousness. One was a frivolous thought: it was to wonder how, after such a very undignified and basic experience, Queen Victoria had managed to stay so pompous and still to be so very much the Queen? The other was to remember and repeat to myself over and over again that ancient, that anonymous, that compassionate summary that the Orthodox Version of the Bible has immortalized:

A woman when she is in labour cryeth out because her hour is come. But when she is delivered of the child she remembereth no more the anguish, for joy that a man is born into the world.

Born into such a war-torn world? Yes.

Nine

THE BELLS RANG OUT

On 11 November 1918 the bells rang out – the War was over. Already for weeks we had expected, as well as fervently hoped for, the release of our combatants. But like thousands of other women, I did not hear for days (or was it longer?) that he was alive, nor if and when he would be coming back.

Tales flew round among the men and the nurses of our convalescent hospital, dismal tales about garrison duty in defeated Germany, worse tales about death and maiming in the last of the heavy shelling that was said to have gone on after the cease-fire in some forgotten island in the sea of mud; sometimes this was said to be from our own guns.

Like other women, I had to wait. The tension built up. Couldn't my father find out? Surely an Editor could get access to news? Couldn't my mother find out? As Commandant of a hospital that would soon be evacuated, she would surely get early news? Yes, they did both get early news, but alas it was quite general, nothing about individuals. I heard nothing from him. In the confusion of that huge demobilization, letters, telephones, telegrams from the front were piling up, jammed inextricably.

The news, however came at last: he was alive, unwounded, though he had indeed been in the final battles.

With the War thus over, 'normality' was as much one of the official words as 'reconstruction'. It might be supposed that once the church bells had stopped ringing we must all have begun trying to take stock, to define the word 'normality', and to ask ourselves what the dickens the War had all been about. Not a bit of it! Certainly I can remember no such immediate and appropriate stock-taking even in our news-conscious family. There were those – often ex-conscientious objectors – who could, and later did, stand back the better to look forward, but as a whole, as I remember, the nation seemed to react much as individuals react when they are said to be in shock. Sometimes a shocked patient – obsessed and in a daze – will go after some trifle as if their life depended on it. Perhaps they will insist on rescuing a doll from a shipwreck. Another will react with diffused anger and paranoid suspicion after an accident, blaming some irrelevant individual: 'It was all his fault,' they reiterate. Another, when in shock, won't react at all but will stay for long in a paralysis, completely stunned, almost in a coma of pain, fatigue or grief.

In that last month of 1918 it was common for soldiers, especially those who had seen a lot of action and who had perhaps won awards for exceptional courage and fortitude, to suffer a frenetic, an almost hysterical need to get away, to put the whole thing behind them. Thus some of these men who were at the end of their strength had for months been preparing an early escape, much as a prisoner prepares to escape. Though he was in command of his feelings, among these was Clough. He had never shirked, he had never given way, he had medals and mentions, but now he could take no more.

He had planned that, the moment honour allowed, his professional services as architect and planner should be officially requested by the ministry whose reconstruction job was to provide 'Homes for Heroes' or, more exactly, modest houses and smallholdings for returning servicemen. There, in France at HQ, he showed the official application to his General.

'Not at all!' said his Commanding Officer, handing back the letter, 'I shall want to keep you for some time.'

It was, as his Commanding Officer pointed out, equally urgent, indeed far more urgent than 'Homes for Heroes', that a book telling the history of the Tank Corps should be prepared at once. The General's tone implied that this was an order. I think this interview must have been one of the worst moments in Clough's whole life.

Seen from the Corps Commander's angle, the order and the choice of poor Clough to write this infernal book was rational enough. As Second-in-Command of Tank Corps reconnaissance, Clough had seen more of the fighting than anyone except his immediate superior, Colonel Hotblack. The last the Corps Commander had seen of that exceptionally gallant officer was lying on a stretcher being carried to the rear, unconscious with his fifth or sixth serious wound. It was undoubtedly important for the future of the Army that the achievements of the new arm should be realized. Therefore it was clear that Clough could not be released, but would remain on garrison duty in Germany, and that there he would write the necessary book. He would of course have access to all the official records. The General asked if he thought he would need a year for the work?

I have never ceased to wonder how Clough managed to escape. I fancy that, for one thing, General Elles – a true leader of men – realized that it was ludicrous to suppose that he would get the book he wanted by means of the only final disciplinary resource at his disposal – a Court Martial under the Defence of the Realm Act. Such a book should be full of immediacy, balanced, accurate and also 'a good read'. A piece of work of that sort could hardly be conjured out of a totally miserable, disillusioned, dejected and impatient author.

Clough made the next move: he put before the General an inspired scheme that was half-rationalization, half-humbug. How much better, said Clough, it would be for such a long piece of work if all the necessary official material could be handed over to him at home. There he could study it properly. Moreover, at home he would have the help of a professional author. After a while the General gave way.

And who, it may be asked, was this professional author? Readers of *The Tank Corps* have sometimes asked this very question, wondering about this 'A. Williams-Ellis' on the title page. The benevolent General Elles either knew the answer at the time, or found it out soon after. But, after approving the typescript of the chapters as they came along, he was merely amused by the answer.

What he fortunately did not know—I had only just realized it myself—was that I was with child again. I had supposed, when I so heartily agreed with Clough that he must somehow get out of the Army as soon as possible, that as I was still suckling our first child we need take no family planning precautions.

A year had been spoken of, but now the law of nature declared that it would have to be nine months. With Clough doubling as a town planner and designer of the Ministry's 'Homes For Heroes', it was clear that the solid work of writing the book would have to be done by me.

Writing about all this in his autobiography, Clough boasted that he was 'out of the Army, out of uniform and home for good' within a fortnight of the Armistice. I think it was in fact rather longer—it certainly felt longer. The point is that we kept our bond. He wrote:

> Amabel in fact did almost all the writing while I fed her with memoranda, eye-witness accounts and official documents, and raw material generally. . . We delivered book and baby by the dates agreed, the book being duly published by *Country Life*, half the proceeds going to the Tank Corps Benevolent Fund. . . Surprisingly our book became a recognized official military work of reference.[1]

The production of the book was, he goes on to admit, more 'domestically dramatic' than the military authorities or its readers ever knew: 'for my co-author was expecting our second child and it was a race between the baby and the book. Fortunately she found the race exhilarating . . . the text was even serialized at length in the *Daily Telegraph* as newsworthy . . .'[2]

Neither the writing (with those masses of official papers needed) nor the architecture (with the need for site-visiting) could well be done from Brondanw. Brondanw really was then rather remote and of course without a telephone; nor could such work be done from Clough's family home, Glasfryn, still more remote. Money would be scarce. With one child already and nothing but Clough's exiguous Ministry pay until the book was written, and even then half of that money was promised to the Tank Corps Benevolent Fund, we had no money to take a house. My ever supportive parents solved the problem of where we were to live while we worked. Clough and I, our baby, our nanny and our piles of official records, went to their house in London, where I had had the measles. All this was contrived while my mother superintended the demobilization of her Newlands Corner Hospital and the dismantling of all the apparatus there. How she managed in the confusion of the time to organize all this is still a mystery and it is only now, looking back, that I see how much she accomplished, and how she let me off to get on with my urgent writing job.

My father's task on the *Spectator* was equally demanding. John's task at Eton was to get on with the history studies that were to give him a scholarship to Magdalen.

So, committed to hard work as we all were, it isn't perhaps so strange that we didn't ask a number of relevant questions. Like the nation, our small family was also in shock, trying to make up for lost time.

During all those post-war months, the day-to-day news was explosive and much of it ridiculous. 'Hang the Kaiser' shouted the *Daily Mail*. However, that prudent Emperor had already taken refuge at Doorn in neutral Holland, from where not even the *Daily Mail* could winkle him out – as Lord Northcliffe no doubt very well knew; this was perhaps why he allowed his editors to shout so loud.

Much worse were constant shouts for reparations: 'Germany started the War! She must pay to the last farthing', 'We owe it to our war dead to bleed them white!' There were deeds as well. The Allies instituted a blockade which half-starved a whole generation of German children. Shouting nonsense (and wicked nonsense) proved to be as catching as influenza, of which we in Britain had an immediate and killing epidemic. Old clichés flew about like bats: 'We must beat our swords into ploughshares', 'Nothing too good for our gallant lads', 'They are all smiles as they walk Civvy Street again'. The vast task of demobilization seemed to get more and more snarled up as the months went by.

I didn't at the time stop to wonder how much my father knew about what was really going on. For example, did he know that in Britain the demobilization muddle was so grave, so much resented, that in the middle of London three thousand British soldiers had mutinied? This happened, it seems, on Horse Guards Parade in sight of our house. Three thousand men – still with their side-arms with live ammunition and frantic for liberty (as Clough had been) – refused to entrain for garrison duty in Germany. More important, did he know what was going so wrong at Versailles? The statesmen there never questioned 'German war guilt', being so busy exacting huge reparations. Their conduct caused such misery, starvation and humiliation as, quite predictably, to prepare a second world war. It came, as a war against the Nazis, a war which Versailles made inevitable, a war for which we, the Allies, did not, alas, even prepare militarily. We did not even build enough tanks, for example. Did father and his readers know about all this? Did he know what the Allies were up to in Russia? There we were, only weeks after we had stopped fighting Germans, now fighting alongside them against the new government that the Russians, our allies of two months ago, were struggling to form.

But like many others, we as a family were ludicrously hard at work – irrelevant, well meant. There were deadlines: the delivery date that Clough had promised for the tanks book; there was my own biological delivery date; my parents had urgent tasks.

Forming, contemplating and then sifting that great pile of official documents was a little daunting. For instance technical design changes – Mark II and Mark V and so on – how did they differ? Then there were the complexities of often strangling orders that came to the firing line from London or army headquarters. Every so often I would turn to Clough both for explanation and for a bit of 'immediacy' and, resourceful as always, he would give it to me. A personal memory was very often what he gave, or he would help by pointing out to me the relevant combat report. When I had managed to piece a couple of chapters together, we would go through them adding or subtracting, correcting muddles, preventing libels or (more often) giving honour where it was due. Then the draft would go off for verification. Speed had been demanded and, because of that other private delivery date, speed was essential. Clough was, of course, also struggling with his and Sir Lawrence Weaver's 'Homes for Heroes' job. Alas, like so many of the bright promises of the Lloyd George administration, this reconstruction scheme seemed to be getting nowhere.

After a while we wondered why post-war reform didn't go better. Clough was reading Bernard Shaw and H. G. Wells, as well as what his fellow-architects and town planners had to say about the hold-ups. What his professional colleagues wanted was a better environment, a better planned rural and urban Britain. These people were becoming

incensed by some lesser but symptomatic private sector manifest-
ations.

These pioneer environmentalists formed lobbies. Outdoor advertising was one of Clough's special hatreds. This, of all things, was then a
growth industry and not even the sky was the limit. The *Daily Mail* was
sending up clever little biplanes to do sky writing. 'Buy the *Daily Mail*'
now said the clouds. At night, in London, advertisements for blacking,
soap and pills were projected on the facade of the National Gallery and
on to Nelson's Column, and even on to the White Cliffs of Dover. There
was building activity, but what went up were buildings such as Gordon
Selfridge's large, ornate retail shop. This was by no means a shopping
place for demobbed servicemen.

In the Press, advertising became a major power. I confess that in a
dark comedy mood I enjoyed some of the advertising copy. Selfridge's
shop went in for a new sort of press advertising in a big way, and I still
cherish copy put out a year or so later for Messrs Jaeger which skilfully
anticipated Bauhaus architecture and décor in the language of the
bright young people:

My lovelies! With Paris and Berlin doing the most ANGULAR things with
concrete, glass and metal – so stimulating – one does heave the old bosom just
once to find mahoganized, diluvian London shedding the mildew at last. I
mean, on the new floor of Jaeger's, positively ALL the fungus has died in the
night.

My dears, they've gone COMPLETELY chromium! Tubey chairs, vulcanite
tables, glass walls, plus-ultra pictures and WHOLLY immediate carpets . . .

It has been calculated that a hundred million pounds (pre-war
pounds, and valuable) went on advertising in the early 1920s.

This is a close-up view. This is how it felt to one of the fortunate.
Thus do I remember effervescent post-First-World-War Britain, the
Britain we had allegedly been fighting to preserve. Do I remember the
whole muddle, all the evil as a total disappointment? No, I don't.

Ten

THE PLEASURES OF ARCHITECTURE

So there we were in 1921, precariously solvent with my parents as a safety-net, and feeling that we were unusually lucky, with the years of fear, suffering, uncertainty, boredom and frustration behind us. Alas for contemporaries who were either almost extinguished by grief and doubts; also for those who seemed slightly manic. Fortunately there were also lively, optimistic and productive people.

Believing, in our innocence, that human beings can be independent, Clough and I sought and achieved enough apparent financial self-sufficiency to persuade banks to bet on us with overdrafts. Thus we gradually hived off to live on our own. Clough, as he began to rebuild his private practice, again had to have an office. To live over the shop was, we thought, quite the thing. Freed by the presence of a nanny and a succession of very odd and experimental home-helps, I was also free to try to earn, and started work on the literary side of the *Spectator*. It was obvious that on a weekly paper, much of the sort of work I did could be done at home by a nursing mother.

Out of my *Spectator* work came a book called *An Anatomy of Poetry*. Re-reading it now, I dislike it intensely, though I still have an affection for some of the Georgian Poets, but I have no intention of now publicly repenting the book's shortcomings. Clough in his *Architect Errant* recalls that some satirist or caricaturist depicted me as the conductor of 'the Georgian Omnibus' with the famous Eddie Marsh as the driver.

The Pleasures of Architecture, the next book, published in 1923, was a different matter. Its genesis was something like this.

After the day's work, Clough would be standing at his drawing-board; I would be sitting on the floor knitting, doing proofs or playing with one of the babies, according to circumstances.

'Are you talkable?' I would ask.

A desultory conversation followed if he was. I would probably ask what he was at; the answer might be a cornice or an entablature. I would perhaps ask what sort of cornice – for outside or inside? And what was an outdoor cornice supposed to be for? The answer might be, to throw a shadow. Sometimes he would drift on as he drew, talking about the proper arraying of windows – 'the art of fenestration' – about the voids in the facade of a building and how they were as important as the enrichments; or he might report a discussion on town planning or conservation at what I called one of his 'indignation meetings', at which they had been protesting about some nasty bit of ribbon development.

After a while I began to realize that he had been teaching me to enjoy and notice things about buildings that, in all my sightseeing with my parents, had never struck me. ' "Firmness, Commodity, Delight",' he would quote. 'That is, the thing must do its job, not fall down, and give me pleasure. I don't care a bit about all that puritanical "truth to construction".'

I soon began saying that I thought his 'indignation meetings', his denunciations of bad building and town planning, ought to be balanced by an explanation or a celebration of the odd, out-of-the-way, often unobvious pleasure that could be got from good buildings or a nice bit of lay-out, even if it was all on an unimportant scale. He ought, I said, to write a book.

All I got for some time from the drawing-board was 'Humph' and a sidelong, slightly suspicious look. I didn't twig at the time why this was, or why he seemed dim about my propaganda, even when I became quite eloquent about the extra pleasure he had taught me to get from buildings. What I didn't twig was that to write was my natural way of forwarding some notion or of expressing my feelings, while his was to do. His impulse all his life was to make something tangible. He agreed with me – of course, he agreed with me – but his way of proving that sort of point wasn't by writing about it. Well, in the end it dawned on me (it took a long time) that what he wanted was to build, to build a village, or better still to persuade someone to let him build a whole town, a little port perhaps. He didn't say much about why he hung back about this book, because the feeling belonged to a private, imaginary world, too impalpable to be put into words.

Then I suppose it occurred to him that a book needn't be an alternative to building – perhaps the contrary. After a little more cajolery on my part I think he saw that it might be fun to collaborate again on a book. So, Jonathan Cape, the publishers, concurring, we set to work on a really pleasant comradely job. The result was *The Pleasures of Architecture*.

Letting ourselves go on jokes and enjoyment, on inventing ridiculous names for the styles we disliked, soon proved agreeable. Among much else Clough produced a splendid drawing of a modest house with all the architectural faults that he could cram into it. 'Nasty little bits of bad detail add up,' the drawing implied. He went for bigger monsters, too, making fun for instance of the plans of some badly designed stately homes. Still more congenial was pointing out the virtues of good buildings, both old and new.

Clough, by the way, gives quite a different account of the book's genesis in his autobiography. Whatever started us off, the book was, as he says, 'most cordially received'. Indeed it went into five fairly large editions. For many years we were greeted by people who said that their first inkling that architecture wasn't all country churches, Norman fonts, solemnity and early Gothic, had been *The Pleasures* that we had enjoyed pointing out.

Anyhow, the book was somehow lucky. It was an extra bond that added to our obvious partnership over children, a house and everyday life. Later the products of our respective professional skills became diverse so that it was, I fancy, good to have this added bond. What I mean about our work becoming diverse is, for instance, that I often did not go to see his building sites, his jobs in the making, while he scarcely more than glanced at my books once they were done, and only shared to a limited extent in the vicissitudes attendant upon rearing three children. We told each other about the more dramatic happenings with great relish, but as we settled down and as our activities absorbed more and more time and energy, they might have tended to be divisive. But I'm not sure that this is not a fanciful notion. We were unlike in a dozen ways, but the stern lesson of the long war years had made us deeply aware of our interdependence and of the seriousness of the partnership of love, so that time and again we winced away from any real threat to the life and vigour of our marriage.

I have never become indifferent to architecture, and when we travelled either abroad or at home, architecture and town planning could always give me pleasure or pain, and to this day I refer what I see in this context to Clough's imagined or remembered opinion. True, there really is pain in such enhanced awareness. There is obviously pain in the more horrid, intrusive and inescapable results of Brutalism and of the fashion for imitations of Art Deco, the Bauhaus and Corbusier styles. But in a way, I rather wish I had been allowed to like the Taj Mahal and not, as I must now, see it as 'That exile from the mantelpiece'. However, the pleasures still greatly outweigh the pain. What, after all, are eyelids for if not to exclude the unwelcome?

If there is rather less in this book than might be expected about Clough's works and about Portmeirion, this is not accidental but stems from something much more practical. Clough himself wrote three autobiographies, two of them still in print, while two biographies are, even as I write, in active preparation. It's good that he should be so amply documented. For example, it is largely due to his skill and exertions that many of our motorways are so carefully landscaped.

My interests were changing fast. I recall clearly all the steps that at this stage made me cease to be indifferent to politics. But science? It is an odd fact that, with no scientific training beyond that little bit of classificatory botany already chronicled, plus four years of surgical nursing, something set me off trying to understand a little about the natural sciences and especially about scientific attitudes and methods.

When Miss Green, my governess, had made me every summer write out those printed schedules the better to identify wild flowers, a vasculum and a pocket lens had been our only scientific equipment. But I had been taught nothing about ecology, and she didn't tell me anything general. I was never taught that collecting and observing, counting and recording were part of the essence of scientific procedures. I didn't know for a long time that not only botanists but also other kinds of biologists and scientists in general tend to have to carry out such down-to-earth work. I found this out for myself, and that there was such a thing as a history of science, Charles Singer's classic, for instance. And why had they bothered so much about wild plants? It had been because of the confusion over medical herbs before the Swede Linnaeus thought up the distinctly Freudian idea of sorting living organisms according to how they reproduce. Not a word of all that had she taught me.

There was another source of my curiosity. Even the most junior VADs had to know something about anatomy and we had a few elementary lectures on it. I was, as usual, inquisitive, but while the War was on I hadn't time or energy for much more than an occasional quick look at a medical dictionary or for being shown do's and don'ts about the handling of an injured limb or a haemorrhage.

All this, even if you throw in child rearing, doesn't seem very much of a foundation for a lifelong and, as it turned out, not unproductive interest in what was going on in scientific research.

Looking back, I seem to see as well a specific, professional motivation. This had to do with my apprenticeship to weekly journalism. When I was put on the editorial board of the *Spectator*, you would have looked in vain for articles about any of the sciences in any general weekly or daily, though all editors repeat vehemently that they are looking for new topics and fresh ideas. I began asking at editorial meetings what the *Spectator* had to say about, for instance, Einstein's Theory of Relativity, or about Rutherford's atom-splitting, or what

Niels Bohr was doing, or the rediscovery of Mendel's work on genetics. I kept on about it.

Again I am boring an editorial meeting:

'But surely anyone can see it,' I say. 'Scientific research will soon be changing the world. We could make a feature of science, reviewing it would be a real breakthrough. You just get bare mentions in most papers. Current scientific events often aren't comprehensible unless readers are given at least some idea of what's going on.'

Sceptical looks all round.

Another time I go back to it in a medical context. X-rays? Asepsis? No response. No-one quite knows how aspirin works. Or a nice chat about telephones, which are beginning to supersede telegrams? Or yet again, how about what Rutherford is up to at the Cavendish?

'The Cavendish Hotel?' asked a shocked voice.

'No, the Cavendish Laboratory.'

'There isn't anyone on the staff who could handle that sort of thing. And anyhow, does all this really affect people in general? It's not current affairs.'

'Astronomy, for instance, that doesn't seem practical!'

Next time I go at it again.

'How could we find the right contributor? It's surely very difficult to explain even the least thing about the sciences . . .'

'Difficult? Easy!' I say. (This wasn't true, of course, but no matter.)

'How would one set about it?'

'Easy!' I say again. 'You take in *Nature* and the *Lancet* and perhaps some of the specialist scientific journals – take them in regularly every week. There are generally at least a couple of articles in *Nature* that anyone could understand. The letters too – some of them. And then there'd be their reviews of books. And in most fields there are research people who would be perfectly willing to give relevant advice on their own subject.' (This wasn't quite true either.) 'And then what about reporting the big British Association meetings, and occasionally doing an interview? It wouldn't really be any more difficult than getting the review books out, or the concerts and pictures and theatres each week. We wouldn't claim too much for it – "Layman's Sciences" it would be, "Voters' Science".'

They wouldn't have it. 'Our readers wouldn't want it.' The final verdict was clear. 'Nobody', they said, shaking wise heads, 'ever has to vote on a scientific issue.'

I gave up in the end – I gave up at editorial meetings, that is. But I wasn't finally beaten.

Eleven

AVIGNON EPISODE

For all of us the early 1920s were effervescent, cheerful and confused, a time of recovery. Our family had been fortunate and the outlook was hopeful. There was for us this feeling that 'the time of the singing of birds' had come.

My brother John was now an Oxford undergraduate at Magdalen and, as was proper at his age, he was trying out life-styles. Clough and I, going to Oxford mainly to visit him, found him one Sunday morning at about eleven o'clock sitting comfortably at his fireside, dressed in a brocade dressing-gown and red morocco slippers, and breakfasting placidly on crème-de-menthe and chocolate cake.

Like the more recent Flower People, Teddy Boys or Skinheads the more spirited of the young were busy creating various life-styles. 'The Bright Young People' were not exactly like their later counterparts, nor were they like the much earlier 'intense' sets of whom Gilbert and Sullivan made fun. They were upper class, unlike the Teddy Boys, and neither as amiable as the Flower People, nor as vindictive as the Skinheads, nor as fanatical and surrealist as the Punk Rockers of the 1980s.

For some of them, being a 'bright young person' might mean something similar to John's Lorenzo di Medici phase. For others it was practical jokes and treasure-hunts, often carried out without much regard to other people's feelings or property. Sometimes there was wild behaviour which led to conduct of a highly inconsiderate and inconvenient nature. This irked many a respectable family. One young man complained of a girl I knew: 'I shouldn't mind her being drunk so often, but it's her monkey always being so drunk!'

With John the phase of elegant *magnifico* didn't last. Some of the wild girls with whom he was involved were fascinating in their imaginative and inconvenient way. They made me feel very 'square'. Indeed, John would have been hard-hearted if he had not sometimes sighed after one or other of them even when, as he soon did, he turned to more permanent concerns and a far more serious kind of love. How the change happened in John I don't know, for I was busy with my own demanding affairs. Anyhow change was then the natural state of things and I, being seven years older than John, was often just round the next corner, always at a different stage.

I was concerned with our marriage, about which I cared a lot, with solvency, with promoting Clough's practice, and with wondering how children ought to be brought up. About that I foresaw problems. What, for instance, were they to be encouraged to believe in? Then there was how the *Spectator* ought to be run, and which of all those Georgian Poets were viable! All these activities, all these calls for decisions, presented themselves to me then against the background of 'these unprecedented times'. What I did not know then is that all the times in which we happen to be living, including the 1980s are always 'unprecedented'.

Thus preoccupied, I had only sketchy notions of where John and his ideas had got to, though I did know, for instance, that he had been travelling in the Danube region with various friends but had dutifully returned to drive our parents on a motor tour of the south of France. Then to us in London came a series of telegrams from Avignon. John had gone down with acute appendicitis, had had an operation that sounded as if it had been in some way unsuccessful, and was now in a clinic in Avignon being looked after by nuns in a manner that our poor mother (no nurse herself, but so lately the competent and observant commandant of a hospital) could see was inadequate. My own five-year surgical nursing experience wasn't altogether relevant, it had been of a different sort.

However, after hastily seeing to the welfare of Clough and the children, I sought advice on nursing techniques for what sounded to me only too like a burst appendix accompanied by a high fever. There were, as yet, no antibiotics, also apparently no international telephone available, not to Avignon. I don't remember how we communicated, only that since telegrams from France were garbled, I did not really know the situation till I got there.

'We have all of us prayed so much for your brother,' said the gentle little nun.

'*Nous avons beaucoup prié pour Monsieur*,' echoed another.

They were, I suppose, of the Franciscan order called, I think, Poor Clares; anyhow their habits were brown and black, their wide coifs white and, as they spoke, they inclined their innocent heads and, as the religious do, hid their diligent little hands in their wide sleeves.

They had watched and prayed, they had been endlessly kind, but I saw at once with alarm that John, half-delirious, lay tossing flat on his bed – not propped up. This propping up, as I had been warned in London, was essential; lying flat meant that the infection was free to spread upward to his diaphragm and lungs. Less important was that (as a hand under the bedclothes proved) they had done nothing to relieve the misery of soaking wet pyjamas as the poor thing tossed and turned in fever.

What followed were days of surreptitious nursing. I had contrived a little spirit-lamp, a bowl and two water-jugs. These I hid in a drawer by his bed. Clean pyjamas also somehow appeared and were put on. The usual ways of propping a very weak patient into a sitting position, also the ways of keeping him propped, succeeded fairly well.

The little nuns' prayers and the kindly 'blind eyes' they turned on my unheard-of nursing techniques, or the help of a young surgeon whom our parents sent for from London, or else the patient's vigorous will to live, gradually brought results – at least his temperature went down. But the London surgeon had a piece of bad news. He told us that his French colleague had, alas, failed to remove the offending appendix; in fact the French surgeon's help turned out to have been only an affair of rubber drainage tubes.

Too occupied and anxious to think, I can only now imagine how much, before he took the turn for the better, my poor parents must have endured. The danger had been protracted and the sinister fact was that it had been just about at the same age that Tom, their elder son, had sickened and died. They had been stoical. I had been concerned only with my patient and no help to them.

Clough's arrival in Avignon lessened the tension. The most resolute of sightseers, he was able to tell me about the venerable beauties of Orange and of Aigues-Mortes and other notable local sights. These I have never seen and at the time Clough's animated descriptions made me feel a little wistful once John seemed to improve. When journey preparations began, it was found that, characteristically, Clough had collected a very large, tall, mysterious package which, incidentally, proved no help at all on the journey home. Well packed in straw, what Clough had got were half a dozen sapling cypress trees, each then about the height of a tallish umbrella. Now in Wales, in the garden at Brondanw, each cypress waves its green-clad trunk and pencil-pointed head some twenty to thirty feet above the grass.

This was not all. At that time travellers returning to England from the South of France by *wagons-lit*, had the option, instead of changing trains in Paris, of staying in their compartments and being trundled for an hour or more round the railway that then surrounded the city, the famous *ceinture*. I shall never forget that particular circuit, which turned out to be not so much a medical as a social and psychological challenge.

I think our parents knew, I certainly did, that John was in love again, and that this time it was serious. To me he had let fall a few facts: she was French, came of a military family, had been married to a general and was now a much-travelled political journalist; she was older than John. From Avignon he had contrived to send her a telegram: could she possibly manage to join our train and sit with us as it clanked and rattled round the successive stations of the *ceinture?*

She came, and the catalogue of Yvette's particulars, as I had understood it, proved a less than adequate preparation. There came through the station murk a creature who was lovely in the most surprising and incongruous way. All cream and roses, Yvette looked twenty. With a flawless complexion, enormous blue eyes, and in her light, floating summer dress her milk-maid freshness seemed to light up in turn all the weary stations through which our train successively bumped.

Then at the Gare du Nord she vanished. She was often thus to vanish. For years I was to wonder why couldn't, or wouldn't, Yvette marry John. The mystery remains. At different periods there seemed to be different answers. Sometimes Yvette was said still to be unable to get legal proof of what had really happened to her husband when he had disappeared on a night patrol in a desert incident in Senegal. Sometimes it was supposed to be because Yvette, taking the risk, was now married to someone else. Later it was because John was married to his first wife, Esther. But quite often it seemed to me that it might be because of some sharp political difference between them; for Yvette was as much of a political animal as John.

At some stage it seemed that Yvette gave John an early nineteenth-century copy of Benjamin Constant's celebrated tale *Adolphe*. He once showed me where in her pointed writing she had written three words on the flyleaf– *Ce triste Adolphe!* What Constant tells, as the reader may remember, in this small masterpiece is the tale of a man who falls desperately in love with a woman older than himself. In the story, she warns him, he over-persuades her, and disaster follows. But John's and Yvette's affection and respect survived all vicissitudes till her death from cancer a generation later.

Twelve

NOAH'S ARK

Our son Christopher was born in 1921. Once more my mother let me use her largest spare room for the birth and another spare room for my monthly nurse and the baby. Everything else was laid on as needed. All this was very good of her, for she had an orderly and anxious temperament, and babies are not usually punctual or particularly orderly. However, what she did for us, and did so well, was at least the expected and proper thing.

At that time very few young women for whom good home care could be contrived, either from the family or professionally, chose to have their babies in a hospital or nursing home. A baby's birth and early care was an intimate, hopeful and protracted family affair. It was protracted since the new mother was not supposed to put a foot to the ground for a fortnight, and for another fortnight to be a fragile, much congratulated convalescent. After this second fortnight, she was supposed to return to normal life. The monthly nurse left and the responsibility for the baby fell on the mother or nanny. If everything went well, this was, even in a less *de luxe* version than I had, a very agreeable arrangement and had many advantages, for instance that of involving a lot of co-operation from grandmothers and aunts, and even to some extent the males of the family.

In my three birth dramas, all went well and nearly everything was done in the traditional way. The only modern touches were that in the case of Charlotte and Christopher, the professionals allowed Clough to be with me till the last moment, and that this ultimate anguish was softened for me by a light anaesthetic. So, after the pain and stress, there was immediate comfort and a general sense of shared communal achievement. For me there were large meals ('Remember you're eating for two, dear').

In a dreamy, milky fashion my leisurely thoughts wandered forward and back, rather as a traveller reviews the way already traversed and considers in this light a proposed itinerary for the way ahead. Such recollections and imaginings will usually comprise a series of disconnected pictures. For me one definite picture was of my sense of loneliness when Susan was born. I had had every care, especially from Clough's much-loved mother, but Clough, my partner, wasn't there, and with the two others he was. I pondered why it should have made such a difference; it had not been necessary for him actually to do anything.

It was when my thoughts reached such a point, as they often did, that something sharp and professional awoke in me and caused me to wonder in a more lively way why the dickens it was that no one seemed to be writing about the oddities of marriage. In a fairy tale it was 'So they were married and lived happily ever after'; in real life it was often, 'So they were married and were perfectly wretched and hated each other ever after'. Neither conclusion seemed very profound. I began to wonder what happened in marriages and what couples tried for or expected. Also why, over that quite usual consequence of marriage – the birth of a child – there was hardly a word. The door of that room seemed always to be shut in the reader's face.

Such musings were the foundation of my first novel, which I called *Noah's Ark*. I still like it. Since it was published in 1926, I feel now (as I believed at the time) that it was in its way exploratory and pioneering as well as being what might be called 'a good read'. I wanted to say rather a lot about marriage. True, I was young in experience, but in spite of that I had quite an urgent message to put over. Looking back, it seems that *Noah's Ark* had, for me, a real function. The novel is what might be termed 'a scenario', setting out in some detail what may be the consequences of a particular decision: what might be expected if one or both partners try to eliminate differences of taste or contrasting priorities, and what might be the consequences of considering the marriage as a goal in itself, regardless of its effect on the individuals. There is the danger of the partners ending up in a state of stupefaction.

In the book I came down sharply against too much adaptation, feeling that a spirited man didn't want a faint carbon copy of himself, and that a girl might well marry a man just because he wasn't a bit like her or her family. Obviously it would also not do to develop out of shouting distance of each other. Watching middle-aged couples in trains or restaurants, I wondered why some of them seemed no longer to have anything whatever to say to one another. 'Utterance', as one of Shakespeare's contemporaries called it, might be lacking so that if she talked to him about her feelings she sounded glib, and when he didn't even try to communicate, she felt him to be a dull blockhead. 'Utterance' really is difficult. Plain statements belong to science, but seldom convey much truth about feelings. Suppose somebody needs to know how a young man feels when head-over-heels in love. Robert Burns answers, 'Oh my love is like a red, red rose that's newly blown in June/Oh my love is like a melody that's sweetly played in tune.' But the scientist answers 'sexual over-estimation'. The trouble is, of course, that the first answer when given by a less gifted fellow than Robert Burns can, and often does, sound glib and silly.

I suppose that all through such musings I was really thinking of our own marriage and felt pretty sure that it would not do for either of us to try to change ourselves too much. I made a character in the novel say tartly to the young heroine: 'If you go on adapting yourself to Edward, you'll end up not giving yourselves room to live.' There was another abrasive admonishment: 'Edward loves you, but you know there's a degree of direct female kindness which no man can stand. And the man will be right! If you're so kind to him now, if you cut off bits of yourself, you'll send him the bill later on. You'll have every scrap of it out of him some time later.' I imagine that novels are often heartfelt clarifications of this sort, a thinking forward.

Almost more than all this precautionary stuff about marriage, I felt that I wanted to celebrate something; I wanted to open the door that hides our old friends Pity and Terror as they show themselves in the business of giving birth. This may be, after all, the most urgent and compelling adventure and experience for women – the neglected half of humanity.

I hadn't then read Lawrence's *The Rainbow* so that, as I began to think how scurvily and inadequately this everyday miracle had been treated by imaginative writers, my thoughts went to older books such as *Tristram Shandy*. There was a notable case of the shut door. Mr Shandy and Uncle Toby sit in the parlour philosophizing, while Mrs Shandy gets on with it upstairs. And then there is the tragic scene in *War and Peace*. True, the door was opened a crack but, because it is a tragedy, Tolstoy leaves out the second half of the tale, the reconciliation.

I'm not sure at what point it was that I remembered an abominable sentence which had long annoyed me, because the birth of a child was something I thought should be celebrated. That engaging Elizabethan, Francis Beaumont, in his *Triumph of Love*, had made an affectionate attempt to convey the domestic loving and kindly aspect of a birth, and this had been Charles Lamb's comment: 'It required at least as much address to ennoble a lying-in as Pope's much praised giving of dignity to a game of cards.'

How, I fumed, had the fellow dared to make such a comparison? A game of cards indeed! The drama of giving birth, after I had been through it three times, seemed to me like most major experiences: dramatic, magnificent, tedious, agonizing, trivial and absurd. Great journeys, sea adventures, great explorations, all have these characteristics; Stendhal makes his hero discover this when he finds he has been at the Battle of Waterloo.

So I made an attempt to record and to generalize a little. Not every woman feels the experience as I made my heroine feel it, I knew that. Sometimes the whole thing comes a little more easily, sometimes with far more difficulty, but there is always drama for the young mother, and often a preliminary fear, like stage-fright or that of an athlete attempting some difficult feat.

The warning to the chief protagonist in a sleeping house can often be subtle and lonely: 'There hadn't been any sound, but there had been a summons all right – something purposeful had moved in her loins. This was like a hand slowly, gently gripping and then as slowly loosening its hold. She lay limp. It's now, it's today, it's come at last! She was pervaded by a growing excitement, but tried to hoard her strength.'

Tedium then prevails for a long time; there is ignominy too, before the real drama begins:

She began to drift away into a phantasmagorical world where it seemed she had to use her wits to get over each of the pains – it was like an obstacle to be surmounted. She would feel one coming, and it was as if she had to be cunning with it, she felt as if she were fighting with it, for now it seemed as if any one of them might tear her. And then when it grew intolerable, it would ease off again and she would have a breathing space that seemed like heaven – that made it impossible to believe that the pain had really been there . . . Later, the waves broke in a spray of pain and receded, and broke . . . This one was unbearable. The sweat broke out on her. It was like a demon now, tying you into knots . . . you felt like a bit of wrung-out cotton . . . Quick, quick, she would get away – it was coming on again . . . the smell was sweet. She took a long, frantic breath, as if she was running – running away from the pain, away, away . . . she felt a sense of exultation as she raced down the long road and heard – far away – a long bellow of a scream and saw that poor thing writhe again. She didn't care, it was funny . . . She began to listen. It was something she had heard, something very exciting . . . There was something in the room, something odd, not just people moving about, something exciting . . . She heard the magic wonderful sound again, the new sound – new in the world. Someone was towering over her. The sound was close, and then of themselves her arms unglued themselves . . . sprouted as if they'd been angels' wings and clasped themselves round an old shawl, and there was a red, soft, downy head, and breath that she could feel on her face, on her face down which the tears were flowing like a warm fountain. So near it was – her and not her – she was too near to see – she could feel it though. It moved – it had a soft mouth, its breath came and went softly, hurriedly. It seemed as if it was giving her back her life . . .

So, over half a century ago, I was trying to say something of which experience had made me sharply aware. I knew the imperious, implacable way in which our bodies can use us, I had been carried on one of the strong tides that carry us all at some time past what we had thought of as the goals of reason.

There are other ideas that arose then that have stayed with me ever since. One such idea is how strange it is that so many intelligent people have written and thought as if adult Western men were the archetype of humanity. In fact, even in the West, adult men are one third of the population, adult women another third, and the rest are infants and juveniles. Being a slow learner, I did not at that time take in the further fact that all these Westerners are far from being in a majority. Homo sapiens is mainly brown, black or golden.

So it was that the early 1920s turned out, for me, to be the time of my first stocktaking as an adult. All sorts of other things rattled about in my head. Insistently I kept wondering how we were going to answer the difficult questions that our three little creatures were sure to ask. I fancy that Clough would have thought it silly if I had said much of all this to him. About the children's questions I think he would have said amiably, 'Why not wait till they ask them?'

Thirteen

THE POLITICS I WAS
TRYING TO AVOID

There was hardly anything political in *Noah's Ark* nor in *The Pleasures of Architecture*, but my brother and I belonged to a political family, so that it was natural in the early twenties for me to wonder about father's political circle. I wondered, mothering my small children, about the causes of the war that had left such a deep mark, about why conscription had shown that our young men were in such poor shape and that, physically, we were what was currently called 'a C3 nation'. I wondered why there should be so much unemployment, not only here but on the Continent, and in general why our town planners were so discontented, so that what Clough called 'a Britain worth fighting for' didn't really seem to be materializing.

Neither the big-wigs of the Conservative and Liberal parties who continued to frequent my parents' houses in Surrey and London, nor the equally distinguished foreign statesmen ever seemed to me to shed much light on such fundamentals, a singular fact which did not seem to surprise or perturb my father.

It is obviously natural for grown-up children to disagree with their parents' tacit assumptions about the world, but in our case there was one point about which I and my brother did not disagree with them. We believed, as our parents did, that public affairs mattered, and that it was a constant duty of good citizens – and particularly the privileged citizens – to try to understand the issues of the day. But, as it seemed to me, in contemporary politics there wasn't much to be hoped for. Politicians were a write-off. Politics ought to be more fundamental; as it was, it seemed to me somehow a mediocre activity.

By the time John came down from Oxford, I had become very lukewarm and was surprised to find how seriously he took his duty of understanding public affairs.

Clough's conscience was mainly visual and I was in a mood of having all-round doubts, so that I found myself sometimes saying to John that it seemed to me odd that a civilized and honest man like Father could keep up such a keen interest in politics. Neither the Conservative nor the Liberal politicians, so I grumbled, seemed to interest themselves in 'real life', and still less with producing a 'land fit for heroes', either in the town planners' terms or in mine, that we had so lately been promised. What had either party really said, far less done, about unemployment, housing or education, or the regional planning that Clough cared so much about? They played politics much as they played bridge, only – I said nastily – more frivolously. So how could Father, who didn't play bridge, who was an honest man, humane and patriotic, attend seriously to all those callous calculations and manoeuvrings?

Then, one day, John began answering, as it seemed to me, like a young St Paul. He said I must know that there was a political party that was neither callous nor frivolous, and that there were men active in politics, members of the House of Commons even, who knew that the condition of the people question and fair dealing between classes were what mattered.

He may have quoted the old Chartist hymn to me – 'Not crowns and thrones but men'. Certainly, as we talked and later when he made me read Tawney and Engels, I began to believe that some form of socialism was the faith that he had found and that I was looking for:

> He found in socialism something for which he must have been looking for a long time . . . Man must have something in which to believe. He must rest his ignorance of whither, which and why, upon some rocks in which he can have faith . . . it offered, as it seemed, Reason, or the chance of its introduction into human affairs. For Reason indeed Strachey had a paradoxical but passionate enthusiasm . . . [1]

It was a while before I began to realize that to the accepted premise that politics matter something else had to be added. For us the honest thing to do was to join the Labour Party, specifically, as we felt, the Independent Labour Party (its left-wing ginger group). To do so was likely to have most unpleasant consequences; I did not see this at once, though I fancy John saw it clearly. I recall that I felt a tremendous sense of relief: I no longer had to condone injustices that had long irked me. I was optimistic and felt sure that socialists had the knowledge and determination to find cures.

Apart from the Sutton Court situation, of which John knew nothing, our dilemma as 'class traitors' was peculiar, even unique. Consider its ingredients.

Father – St Loe Strachey – had, as I've said before, an unusual political position, which was still as it had been when Tom died. The party manipulators knew that father was honest and believed him to be talented. The *Spectator* was still exceedingly influential in a way that has no parallel in the 1980s. He still called himself a Whig, a cross-bencher, a broad churchman, an independent, and Oliver Cromwell was one of his heroes. For many years, week by week, on one question or another, Government and Opposition statesmen had courted him when they needed support. It was known by a generation of wheeler-dealers that the offer of almost any sort of inducement to speak or not to speak – inducement such as money, or honours – however delicately insinuated, was likely to prove violently counter-productive in the case of the Editor of the *Spectator*. He had not steeped himself in the Elizabethan dramatists, Dryden and Pope for nothing: his invective was often brilliant and never lacked polish; you did not need a rest-camp in the middle, as some wag said of Garvin's articles.

So there was often flattery and unexpected political support for one of father's causes such as rural housing, access to mountains, the National Trust, or his odder-seeming para-military activities. But there was surely one benefit that he could hardly throw back at them: benefits accruing to St Loe Strachey's politically minded son, John, could hardly count as bribery. In short, John could have found an early and happy career in either of the dominant political parties. But there was more than a parliamentary career at stake. It had been assumed (by me at any rate) that when father retired, John and I would inherit the *Spectator*.

Nor would such an event have been a scandalous piece of nepotism, as the censorious and puritanical young of today may probably hastily assume. I, for example, had been carefully familiarized with most aspects of running the literary and business sides of the paper and, by apprenticeship, had had what amounted to a sound professional training. Even with my now heretical opinions, I could probably still have functioned on the literary side, as indeed I did for quite a while, when father's health at last gave out.

But with my brother, the case was different. The tacit assumption had been that John would succeed to the more important political control and that in the meantime, till father retired, John would go into politics. He was a great deal better fitted for political promotion than most of the new crop from the universities. He had been a history specialist at Eton, and at Oxford had clearly shown himself to be a highly political animal. So, taking this into account, I don't think that as I mused in the nursery or over review books I was being too cynical or too affectionately partial in thinking that John could have a political career which, for speed and brilliance, might be second only to that of the younger Pitt.

It was plain that the *Spectator* could not become socialist and live, though John did contribute a few Leftist articles. John knew that, however sympathetic and kind father might be, he had ultimately to be disinherited because of his new left-wing convictions. I didn't realize at the time that there was so much about John that would be a drawback in the Labour Party. Many of his traits which would once have made for success were now far from being assets: he belonged to the old school network; he had an upper-class accent; liked good food; knew something about wine; and had friends who would be assets among Liberals or Conservatives, but would be liabilities among trades unionists.

As for a safe seat and easy promotion, even when Labour was able to form a government, membership of the Independent Labour Party was no ticket to the front bench or any kind of seat. The path to these things was thick with stalwarts from both the TUC and the constituency parties, men whom it would be impossible to pass over for a safe seat in favour of a young 'parlour pink', a Johnny-come-lately.

There was obviously also a painful personal side. How John and our parents sorted it out, I don't know, and here my almost total lack of knowledge seems an excellent example of the classical Freudian theory of forgetting a wounding, and especially an ambivalent, situation. I only know that John was steadfast and that there was no quarrel, and that the *Spectator* published some of John's articles on economics.

One of the many gibes that he met with still annoyed John years later. It came from our fashionably Freudian friends and was to the effect that John's conversion to socialism was merely the result of a desire to disoblige his father. Anyone, John would answer, might have motives of which he was unaware, but he denied in principle that a right argument or an honest line of action becomes paltry or downright dishonest if it should happen to coincide with some emotional drive. Stupid objections from the Right of being a class traitor and from the Left of being merely a fellow traveller seemed not to ruffle him. Also there were those in the Independent Labour Party who were both congenial and welcoming: Clifford Allen, then its chairman, and his wife, for example. Professor Hugh Thomas, in his biography of my brother, sums up like this:

Clifford Allen himself believed that it was he, always on the look-out for intelligent young men, who introduced Strachey to the ILP. But the Webbs probably played a part, while it was certainly Arthur Ponsonby, himself a convert to Labour from Liberalism, in 1918, who introduced 'an ungainly young man' to the ILP's new Organizing Secretary, Fenner Brockway . . . 'It turned out', Brockway said, 'that he was good at writing. We found his spelling very bad, we couldn't understand why someone who had been through Eton and Oxford could spell which "wich". But still, he could write all right.'[2]

Remarks about spelling raise a slightly sheepish smile amongst all members of our family, and did so when this Hugh Thomas biography first appeared. The fact is that an inability to spell, indeed an almost infinite capacity to spell wrongly, is a family characteristic.

'Never mind, my dear!' my father (sharing this inconvenient trait) would say to me, 'the printer can spell!'

Bertrand Russell was, as far as I can recall, almost the only one of our eminent friends who could manipulate the extraordinary intricacies and obscure vagaries of standard English spelling. They are standard, by the way, for a mere two hundred years. Sir Walter Rawley (Raleigh, Ralegh, etc.) spelt his name in a dozen different ways. As for Hakluyt, John Donne or Chaucer, I find their infinite variety most consoling.

Fourteen

MERIONETH

Even with the fraught situation of being a disappointment to our parents and of becoming class traitors, despised parlour pinks or fellow travellers according to whether Right or Left was criticizing us, cheerfulness kept breaking in, as it is so apt to do when you are young. Anyhow, unlike my brother, I had a bolt-hole. All this happened in London and, as I soon realized, Westminster politics did not signify at all in north Wales, between the mountains and the sea.

At last it looked as if we should have a chance to spend enough time there, on and off, to make the foundations of a home at Plâs Brondanw, the tall, old granite house that Clough had loved for so long and in which his mother had so kindly and nervously received us as an engaged couple.

Clough's practice was coming along nicely, the children throve, in fact we were full of life, set to make up for the wasted war years. Clough, like my favourite saint and my favourite Anglican divine (who were and still are Sir Thomas More and Sydney Smith), seemed to feel that it should be one of his aims (whenever present) to keep his wife laughing for at least a couple of hours every day.

Domestically, the Griffith family had for some time been Brondanw's caretakers. Now they looked after us, not, it is true, in a style of which a majority of Clough's aunts could approve, but in a way that taught me a good deal about that elusive concept, 'the Welsh way of life'.

The mountains were a delight even in the rain, and so was the coast. As for the sea, the children and I took to bathing, and Clough bought a small cabin cruiser which was moored at Portmadoc. Her purchase proved the foundation of one of our lifelong shared pleasures, whenever work or wars allowed.

Clough described *Twinkler* as 'a small Hillyard sloop'. She slept at least two and had a centre-board in the middle of the cabin. He had messed about with dubious, often home-made boats, often keel-less, with only an oar for a rudder, vessels that were not much improvement on the boats of the Stone Age. Thus, the prospect of sailing a nicely balanced, seaworthy little cabin-cruiser was for him intoxicating.

Any sort of seafaring was entirely new to me, but I took to it almost as immediately as I had taken to the mountains and the tall old house. I soon became a tolerable deck-hand but never, oh not ever, a galley slave specializing in saucepans and primus stoves. Clough, not very domesticated ashore, was decent about sea chores.

A friendship that proved lasting began during one of our escapes from London to Merioneth. When the children and I (Clough was elsewhere) got out of a train at Penrhyndeudraeth station, an unknown young man, who was also getting out, lent us a hand. He had observed that I was travelling with three small children, a pram, two cats in baskets and a typewriter – it was the typewriter that made him curious.

A couple of days later, having worked out that this oddly en-cumbered young woman would very likely be the Amabel Williams-Ellis with whom he had already corresponded over a poem that he had offered to the *Spectator*, and Brondanw having no telephone, Richard Hughes suddenly fell at my feet, literally but never metaphorically.

He fell at my feet, literally, off a motorbike whose always unpredict-able steering was this time, I fancy, made still more odd by its rider suffering from a sudden attack of shyness. Anyhow, the fall broke the skin on Diccon's shins and also the social ice, which further receded as I dealt with what seemed like half a pint of blood. Weeks later, but unknown to me for forty years, he wrote me an immensely long letter. The letter itself and the fact that he never sent it or told me about it convey a good deal of information about him as the author later of that excellent book *The Fox in the Attic*, and also about the 1920s Oxford approach to literature. I still feel impressed by many of his insights.

Dear Mrs Williams-Ellis,

I have been meaning for a long while to fulfil my threat of sending you some sort of a poetic Athanasian Creed in a letter, but haven't been able (owing to plastering chiefly); however, I have now reached a stage when I have time to sit down and start picking the quick-lime from between my eyelids . . .

Art is not imitative: it is creative: creative of beauty. Music creates beautiful sound: plastic art beautiful form: poetry – literature – beautiful *Idea*-images, if you like: mental processes. Art does not extract beauty from nature, imitate nature, in any sense: all beauty in Art gets these by parthenogenesis. In fact, beauty in nature lags behind, imitates, beauty in Art . . .

He goes on to say he is not advocating Clive Bell's abstract form. On the whole he uses the visual arts to illustrate his points in general, because he thinks them 'the most concrete form of Art', simplest and plainest. Also he feels that they have been, to a great extent, cleared up 'by the Bloomsbury school'. I think Diccon wouldn't have held to the next part of this credo about the Arts and Beauty when he was a bit older, though he kept to his 'Beauty is a kind of rhythm'.

Later on there is what still seems to me a useful and excellent distinction between the sentimentalist and the genuine artist: 'The artist teaches, the sentimentalist reminds.' Several pages later he remarks that he 'expects that RG [Robert Graves] will have shown you his essay'; then he adds that he very much wants me to criticize all this, 'as I don't yield an inch to Robert in my admiration of your critical abilities'.

Reading this forty years on, I applaud Diccon's dicta about symbols: 'The use of symbols is part of man's pattern-making propensity.' The use of the word 'propensity', being made in 1921, was surely ahead of current poetic opinion and is now endorsed by modern explorers of human drive.

I should so much have enjoyed reading that letter at the time. I should not then have minded the bit about 'picking the quick-lime from between my eyelids'. Such a phrase was perfectly all right in that kind of letter, and I shouldn't have felt it as ominous or a foretaste of a stylistic trick that often irritated me later.

Shakespeare was said to 'invigorate his readers with a giant or a dwarf', but Diccon got into the habit in writing and conversation of, so to say, jumping out at you from behind a door armed with a fire-cracker. All very well in that letter, but when he did it later in speech or in the course of careful narrative prose, I had wrathful thoughts which I sometimes even put into words. I didn't think, and I still don't, that such a good and careful writer, a writer who could and did wreathe the bright coils of his words so skilfully round his subject, ought to resort to schoolboy tricks of style. It is all very well in a first draft, in a letter written in 1921, but not in a tenth draft written in middle age in mid-century. The dead child draped round the shoulders of his hero with which he begins *The Fox in the Attic* still seems to me an example of this fire-cracker trick, though I know that many people tolerate and even admire its boldness. There is another instance I recall where he uses a face-to-face encounter with an enormous octopus as an analogy.

Writers' tricks and their ways of working are diverse and often come from deep down. Could this trick of Diccon's and his agonisingly slow way of working, of writing one meticulous version after another, have the same source as the reflex shyness that caused him to initiate our long friendship by falling off his motor bicycle?

There are as many ways of writing (or being unable to write) as there are authors. Joseph Conrad is said to have sat for an agonizing year in front of a blank sheet of paper before a novel that he had planned would come. How Pasternak wrote his splendid, chaotic *Dr Zhivago* we have not, I believe, been told.

I remember asking Lytton Strachey one day when he seemed fairly communicative if he re-wrote much. In that high precise voice came the answer with his usual little pause: 'It comes out – in faultless sentences!' Yet, in the end, his years of writing produced no greater abundance than Diccon's. With Diccon the intense labour of recasting whole chapters and minutely reshaping every sentence time after time were clearly connected with the way he lived his life. Often he turned, as it seemed to onlookers, in a sort of desperation to less demanding things – digging, plastering, clearing out gutters, repainting or re-rigging a boat, or dreaming about sailing her. His whole way of working was completely different to Margaret Storm Jameson's or Rose Macaulay's, for instance.

When Diccon came to live nearer to Brondanw or Portmeirion, nearer than Ann Jones's cottage (where the unsent letter was written), he used in the sailing season to frequent Elias Pierce in his boat-building shed on the beach of Portmadoc harbour. Mr Pierce, elderly in the 1920s, had been ship's carpenter on more than one of the voyages of the small Portmadoc schooners that coasted or 'went foreign' as they carried slates from the quarries of Blaenau Ffestiniog. By the time we knew Mr Pierce, he had come ashore for good and was building admirable dinghies, better and cheaper than those to be had from yacht yards.

Elias Pierce, like John Griffith and his family, taught me a great deal about the Welsh way of life, for he was elegantly articulate in English as well as in Welsh. When Clough and I came down to the harbour after an interval, his greeting to me would be: 'And what have you been composing?' A poet rather than a prose writer, he meant, of course, like any other author, that I should wave away his question and ask him what *he* had been composing.

Diccon Hughes, on much the same 'fellow-writer' footing as I was, reported what might be called one of Mr Pierce's 'storm pieces'. The heavily laden little schooners were often not coasters but blue-water craft. The description of this particular Atlantic storm ended: 'You know, Mr Hughes, after so much peril a man is apt to give way to his natural impulses! I went below and I wrote an ode.' This was the sort of remark to make any writer feel 'natural' in Wales, and not a freak.

Mr Pierce could listen as well as tell. Once, after we had had an alarming time in *Twinkler* rounding Anglesey's North and South Stacks (tall inshore rocks they are, the water shoaling here and there with cross-currents and a tendency to kick up a nasty sea in certain conditions of wind and tide), I told him about our uncomfortable time, wondering whether he would think that we had done the right thing, had judged the wind and tide right. We followed the Cruising Association handbook's recommendations, the august Admiralty Pilot being silent on small-scale technique.

Mr Pierce: Ay, that's a terrible place. What do you say in English? A raaace we call it.

Me: Yes, it's the same in English; a race, a rip.

Mr Pierce: And, do you know, there was a schooner once, she was taking the inshore way and getting in that raaace and there'd been a lot of wind . . . they had a following wind, ay! She was tossing about something terrible.

Me: There are cross seas off there.

Mr Pierce: Ay! And the crew, they were very downhearted and thought she would never live through it. The captain, he sent them down below and locked them all in under hatches, and him the only one on deck. Then he lashed the helm and then, do you know what he did? He took his concertina, ay! his concertina, and there he sat himself down on the skylight, and he played it. There was the crew down below and crying because they were downhearted, and there was the captain sitting on the skylight of the cabin, and playing that thing. And she came through it all nicely too. Ay, she did.

My parents often came to spend a week or a fortnight with us, which was brave, as my father was by then often ill and we had as yet none too many conventional comforts at Brondanw.

However, luckily, our Mrs Griffith, who cooked and cleaned, was very much impressed by these London visitors. For instance, she made special rice puddings for my mother 'like the gentry have' (Clough and I were only given ordinary puddings). Another of her tributes to anyone she considered very special ('a very eminent man' or 'lady' was her phrase) was to pile on extra blankets and a second eiderdown on the bed, even in the hottest summer weather.

There was, though, one item of domestic comfort over which Mrs Griffith had no control: this was the bath water. The intricacies of our plumbing were too difficult to be explained here. It is enough to say that if Clough turned on the fountain in the garden (and he loved to do so as he passed or whenever he had an audience for it) then there was no cold water for baths. I have a vision of my father in a bath towel, steam rising behind him from the open bathroom door, and calling down with only slightly plaintive patience, 'Could someone, please, turn the fountain off?'

My parents' pleasure in the Welsh mountains, and their patience
with our odd domesticity, made me almost oblivious all this time to the
way John's political defection must have hurt them. My father often
looked pale and tired, and his frustration over John reinforced my
efforts to please him by writing better. What he demanded in a writer
was 'the extreme characteristic impression of the thing written about'.
A surviving notebook shows the way I tried to exercise myself
technically, the equivalent, I suppose, of a painter going back to attend
life classes. This is a nearby estuary:

High water, neap tide. Channel, pale pewter colour. Across the other side,
grass fields quilted by their grey walls. Rectangular houses, barns, also
grey-roofed, dotted haphazard. Light on hills and woods beyond makes the
trees look lettuce-green, but a distant mountain crest is ink-blue. Blue sky. Soft
clouds in six or seven shades of grey. Very quiet. A pair of shelduck flies over.
Sounds, later, a tinny chapel bell, far away, sheep, rooks, oyster catchers, just
audible, hardly heard. Cuckoo only just guessed at. Whole effect, unemphatic
Sunday peace.

I don't know how many other prose writers try this way of making
more or less abstract studies 'from the model'. I often did.

There is no really dependable way of writing well. One day,
depressed by a chapter in one of my books, I turned to Diccon: 'What's
wrong with me?'

'Too busy living,' was his answer.

Living in Wales, I have always thought, was better than living in
most places. Elias Pierce and the annual Eisteddfodau are the proof. A
writer needs peace but does not like to be a freak.

Fifteen

CLOUGH AND PORTMEIRION

In his memoirs, *Architect Errant*, Clough has something characteristically elusive to say about the purchase of *Twinkler* and how he got her round to Wales. The fact is that there was more to it than just his natural pleasure in at last possessing a trim little craft after the water-logged old boat of his boyhood that had so often run aground among the water-weeds of the lake at his old home Glasfryn. This is his account of how on this occasion he thought in two layers:

> I did not explain everything about my buying of *Twinkler* to my wife . . . I was perhaps not quite aware of my own motives. I had begun to feel that I should try in actual building to show an example of what I meant, and that I must find a site, preferably on the coast, perhaps an island, which would provide the sort of remote and unspoilable setting that I demanded for my cherished though still fluid ideas. I was like a sea-bird seeking a nesting place.[1]

Building development was going on all around in the 1920s. He was active in writing and speaking as a town planner and a conservationist. What he was saying was that change was often needed and was all right as long as it was heedful, the right sort of change. He did not merely want to be against growth. He believed that even a very beautiful site could be developed without harming it. He said again and again that beautiful places might even be enhanced, as they so often are in coastal and mountain districts all over Europe. But for him words, though he used them well, were not enough. He was a builder; building was his natural language.

So we sailed and I as his crew soon learned the rudiments. A sheet was not, as might innocently be supposed, a sail but a particular kind of rope. An anchor was an anchor, but it was also a kedge, and in inexpert hands the deck-mop in some circumstances was a less damaging tool than a boat-hook.

Thus we sailed Cardigan Bay, poking into little ports as tides and wind favoured. In the end, however, it was not *Twinkler* who found the 'nesting place' for Clough; the clue came in a letter to us in London from an uncle in Wales. The uncle asked Clough if he knew of a suitable tenant for a biggish house, Aber Ia, with stables and two cottages, about four miles from Brondanw on the Dwyryd estuary. Clough was startled. How odd! He had heard of but never seen the place. Further correspondence followed.

Old Mrs Haig, an eccentric recluse, had just died. She had long held the lease. 'The grounds', the uncle intimated, 'are rather overgrown and the house possibly in need of a little repair.' This remark turned out to be the understatement of a lifetime.

Clough has told the story of what happened next, of how the half-derelict Aber Ia and its jungle setting was explored, rescued, and by the summer of 1926 was on the way to becoming the prestigious beginnings of Portmeirion.

We were in the habit of giving parties in London, so Clough decided to give a party at Portmeirion and to my alarm invited a collection of friends, clients and Press people, most of whom were rather grand connoisseurs of the comfortable. He invited them for an Easter weekend, having decided that an hotel was what Portmeirion was to become. Everything went wrong: the water supply and electricity were not as intended, the food was atrocious. Did a wail go up from all those prestigious guests? No. The weather was radiant and Clough carried it off so that, when explained away by him, horrors became hilarious. Though all this was fun for an invited party, there soon came a time when amateur slapdash didn't seem quite enough and a certain discontent among a paying public began to manifest itself.

A. P. Herbert happened to be staying once when pouring rain, managerial ineptitude and plumbing infelicities combined. Always looking for a subject for banter, he lampooned Portmeirion in *Punch* at some length and with wit. Clough was hurt by the article and did what he rarely did when his friends got in home thrusts; he wrote protesting that though funny, such an attack on his infant venture was unkind. Herbert agreed that perhaps he had been a little barbed, but Clough must realize that after all, as a journalist, he did unfortunately have to find something to be funny about every week. He was not really letting down the propaganda for town planning and any publicity was always better than none. Reconciliation followed. Clough took the point that good regional development might be helped by good digestion, and he soon managed to persuade James Wyllie to become manager. True, Jim Wyllie was a painter first, but he had also run an exotic but excellent and prestigious restaurant in Oxford, and by the end of that summer Portmeirion began to flourish.

This is not the place in which to trace out a Portmeirion chronicle. For one thing its story has been written and re-written (as I've already said), in books and in hundreds of articles here and in America, and in French, Italian and German, while two more biographies of Clough seem to be in preparation. There is another reason: there is a good deal that to this day I don't really know.

Notice Clough's phrase: 'I was perhaps not quite aware of my own motives.' One motive was of course to declare once more that architecture could be a pleasure. Not knowing his own motives was a frequent state of affairs for Clough. When he was building, either for himself or for a client, he reacted after he had had his usual precise look at something – a site, an existing building or the curves of a river. He had immediately taken in a dozen things about what was before him, but he often did not formulate, still less announce, the conclusions he had come to or whether he meant to act and if so in what way. So it was with Portmeirion.

This apparently almost dreamy way of working is, I think, common in the Arts, even including planning. Now in the nineteen-eighties it has become, surprisingly enough, once again a recognized procedure in Science. I noticed, for instance, at a meeting of the British Association in 1980 how a speaker urged his fellow-scientists: 'Let your unconscious do your research for you.' That usually precise, even demure, body took the advice as natural and proper.

Such a way of composing was certainly natural and proper to Clough. Could it be because he always had such an instinctive way of designing that his buildings continue to give so much pleasure? For pleasure is what they do give, both to those who are unused to expecting any emotion whatever from a building, and also to those in the profession who fear that they ought to write Clough off as a perverse fellow and no scholar. What I am trying to suggest is that Clough didn't quite know why he bought *Twinkler* or sought a use for Portmeirion, and that I certainly couldn't follow all the ebbs and flows of this long development of his piece of practical propaganda.

But such points need not be laboured. That great biologist Thomas Henry Huxley wrote about 'the vulgarity' of supposing that there was such a thing as 'a single cause' for anything. What is sure is that his building of Portmeirion to prove his propaganda points had many side benefits, but which of them he foresaw who can say? I fancy he just had glimpses. There was certainly not just a single cause for his 'I did not tell my wife', and also no single cause for my not being intrusive and thus never knowing everything about Portmeirion during its long and unexpectedly successful history.

At the beginning I certainly felt ambivalent about the whole enterprise. For one thing, for Clough to build on this scale was of course financially madly imprudent. He had no partners or backers; he had only his professional earnings. Though banks were friendly (at five to seven percent), the whole thing put us deep into debt. Such conduct in a husband even for a likely project is apt to scare a wife, especially if she is, as I was, also the mother of his young family.

However, from my point of view, there were two very favourable aspects of Clough's truly roller-coaster guesswork exercise, his demonstration that might well have become a financial horror. The first good side-effect was a minor one: this new bout of building meant that Clough might now let Plâs Brondanw's exterior remain un-adorned and unimproved, as I fervently hoped. But the second reason was far the more important. Over the next fifty years, I found it most delightful and satisfying to watch Clough's continued pleasure in the enterprise. He was embodying and summarizing his convictions and feelings about the environment; he was turning thankfully from little black words on paper and from spoken words to expressing himself in structures:

An architect has strange pleasures. He will lie awake listening to the storm in the night and think how the rain is beating on his roofs, he will see the sun return and will think that it was for just such sunshine that his shadow-throwing mouldings were made. The wind will circle cunningly round his house trying to lift the tile, or level the chimney, but they are firm. It is the rain's part to descend, it is his roof's part to keep it out. The waters will swirl round his bridge or, in calm, exquisitely double the colonnade on its banks. The clouds will help his picture, or a fall of snow give its surprising underlighting. In architecture the work of art becomes a part of the earth in a peculiar degree. His building will form an integral part of a sunset, a moon-rise, or it will blot out a patch of stars.[2]

He so seldom spoke or wrote like this about his feelings, directly in so many words, that I am obliged to rely on that passage and on one other written at much the same time. The second one is about marriage and parenthood. His comments are in thirteen lines, whereas I had felt impelled to use a whole novel, *Noah's Ark*, in which to be objective on this. Notice how he sticks to analogies of building:

What is a happy marriage? It has something to do with the deep satisfaction to be found for both concerned in the planning, building, extending and maintaining of an ambitious structure of tensions, thrusts and reactions in a balanced equipoise that can yet be carefully though confidently pulled about and altered whenever that seems wise or necessary, because its foundations are secure. One might assert the belief that the greatest happiness in marriage is to be found in an intellectual growth and adaptation, in quickened sympathies and perceptions; or again, and with equal truth, in my case, in the conviction that a family of adventurous children is both educative and pleasant, even if slightly alarming. To give them their due importance and proportion as the real stuff of which one's life is made. I'll just leave it at that: one way and another I do find myself happy.[3]

These were our feelings in the 1920s and in a world that was, as usual, changing fast. How fast it was changing we did not quite grasp.

Most people in Britain think of 1926 as the year of the General Strike, a recession that was far worse in human terms than that of the 1980s. Our marriage was to us a chief concern. There was Clough, eleven years older, thriving professionally and much more sure and single-minded that I was, aware of change, if not of wider public happenings, and happy at the need to adapt and grow. In domestic affairs each of us led in one field and followed in another.

Clough liked his surroundings to be much grander that I did, and I accepted that in such things as house furnishings it was his pre-delictions that ought to prevail. To myself I called them 'his chandelier complex'. I taught myself to be amused by his tendency to treasure a good many impractical things. For instance, when I first tried to keep house at Brondanw, I counted fifty or more charming-looking china teapots that adorned shelves or half-filled cupboards; I found that one was cracked, another lidless and that a third had no spout. They had been so tastefully disposed that the poor things' tea-making impotence wasn't apparent. Such was often the case when he was called upon to provide an occasional table or an electric lamp.

As for the children, note his 'slightly alarming' phrase. The decisions as to what in the way of morals and manners we were to teach the children were (legitimately, I felt) left to me. Years later, writing as a grandfather, he wrote: 'I am not completely at ease with the young of my own species', and went on to hint that it may be that he felt them too much of a responsibility simply to be able to enjoy their vitality and refreshing irresponsibility. He was, in fact, the sort of father who used to be known to mothers as 'a good provider', a man who is willing to spend hard-earned money and to adapt himself generously to their needs and interests, but who alas gets far too little of the fun that is his due. A man who misses this in the early years, risks feeling strange to it later. Clough's case was not as bad as that.

Although I breast-fed each child for four months or more (not always easy for a theatre critic, as I was for some of this time), I delegated a good deal of their day-to-day care. Most young mothers delegated more in our circle. I'm not sure now, but then I didn't question whether this was right or not. Apart from meals, walks and bedtimes, there were larger matters to be decided, for instance, what was the best standard of civilized manners, and where should the line be drawn in the context of freedom and obedience?

In the early 1920s the children were still small, but I had already begun to consider their education. Dora and Bertrand Russell's views, on the one hand, were very different from the standards represented by Eton for the boy and governesses and a finishing school for the girls on the other. It soon seemed to me that in such things it was important to observe the children themselves. They were likely to be different so that, even granted that as their parent you were sure about what you wanted each of them to learn, you had better be as flexible as you could. The same codes of behaviour and the same sort of skills might need to be presented in almost opposite ways. Anyhow, who could be sure what skills and behaviour were going to be appropriate in a changing world? And then what about emotional ties?

As the three began to develop I could see that this latter might be the most tricky problem of all. This was in fact the area in which I seem to have made an outstanding mistake. When, a year or two later, his two sisters ganged up against Christopher, I tried to protect him. It wasn't till much later that I was shown how stupid this had been.

I also made lesser mistakes with both the girls, mostly in judging what they really wanted in small things. Charlotte, at least, from the age of seven left me in no doubt of her main interests. But though I sometimes blundered, I loved them and they flourished.

Sixteen

MICROSCOPE AND TELESCOPE

At about this time, while Clough was so closely involved in thinking out his concerns and I was busy with political dilemmas, mostly in the context of the children, the subject of religion made one of its recurrent incursions into the upper layers of my mind. In my teens I had taken seriously the Church of England's injunction to love the Lord your God with all your heart and with all your strength and with all your mind, and your neighbour as yourself. With my mind? Brought up in what were then called broad church principles, taught especially by my mother to know whole passages of the Old and the New Testaments by heart, I had not noticed what at last seemed to me a strange fact: it apparently never occurred to either of my parents to go to church. They were buttresses of the church, supporting it from outside. So, I pondered this 'with all thy mind' and when we were in the country, I used to walk two miles on my own to the village church.

It seems that my mind, which I supposed ought to be involved in a straightforward rational way, began to boggle. But I did not ask my apparently placidly believing parents which of the two accounts of the Creation was to be believed and thought of as holy writ. Neither did I question them about the doctrine of atonement, sin or eternal punishment. I suppose I felt there was something about their way of thinking that satisfied them and that this ought not to be disturbed. I may well have felt that the rational approach wouldn't make much of straightforward questions and answers. Indeed I felt obscurely that to ask them might make something go very wrong in some way – in a way that at fifteen I couldn't at all think out.

As for the principal rites of the church, I knew that I had been christened and I knew that until I had sorted things out myself I didn't in the least want to raise the question of whether I ought also to be confirmed.

Later on puzzles recurred. Clough and I were married in church and our children were christened, but it was always clear that Clough considered it my affair what to tell the children about the sensitive subjects of religion and sex.

I tried my best, but I squirmed one day in company with my in-laws when I heard a pleasant six-year-old voice asserting, 'Mummy says she isn't sure about God but she thinks Jesus was rather sweet!' Or when another child asked suddenly in a full bus which had stopped at traffic lights, 'Babies are like their mummies, but why are they like their daddies?' The silence in that bus, the waiting to hear what I would say, was electric! At some point later I tried to indicate that, while I might be asked anything and would do my best, yet there were a few things that I didn't want to tell about when there were other people listening. With a note of perfect comprehension came the reply, 'Yes, don't tell ladies!'

I now console myself when thinking back at what were then no doubt my clumsy answers on sensitive topics, by remembering the curious ways in which children interpret our answers. A paediatrician friend of mine, for instance, remarked the other day that his little boy having learned the Lord's Prayer, was heard repeating: 'Thine be the Kingdom, the Car and the Lorry, for ever and ever, Amen.'

Somehow or other we all saw a good deal of Bertrand Russell about this time, and naturally I was influenced by his ideas about manners and morals. We often found ourselves side by side pushing prams along the Embankment in London. We didn't just talk about children. For one thing he was always a splendid gossip. He was one of those who used to tell me particularly eloquently how dreary the food was at the Sidney Webbs: 'They are far too high minded,' he would say. I recall other pieces of gossip from those term-time pram walks (I should explain that we were depositing descendants at schools). One tale was about Sir James Frazer of *The Golden Bough*. At that time younger anthropologists had begun to shake their heads about him, for he declared emphatically that he never had visited a primitive community and never intended to do so. Field work could be done by other people. Not that Bertrand Russell blamed him for this; after all, he would say, Frazer was usually dealing with history and myth – the folklore of the Old Testament say, or the tale of 'the priest who slew the slayer and shall himself be slain'. Bertie would laugh, throwing his head back: 'All those people in togas and those Babylonians couldn't be visited, not even by Malinovsky.' (Malinovsky was not only the fashionable anthropologist of the moment but had spent years with pre-literates.)

Anyhow his gossip about this founding father of anthropology was not just about his methods but also about his extreme honesty. In the summer vacations Frazer, he said, would usually go back to Scotland. Obviously for writing such a work as *The Golden Bough* a great chestful of books was needed. This was supplied, as was so proper, by the

London Library, and sent by train. It appeared, after a lapse of some years of these regular book consignments, that Sir James had been underpaying the railway. Frazer insisted that he must have a bill and must make good the deficit. The railway complained that it was a small matter and to put it right would mean re-opening accounts running over many years. They suggested it would be much better to think no more about it. 'Not so,' said Frazer and insisted to the discomfiture of the accounts department on having a proper invoice and on paying up. How honest are we to teach them to be, we asked ourselves, looking at the denizens of the prams.

This was at a time when Russell was thinking about plans for Telegraph Hill, the progressive school that he and Dora established. Telegraph Hill was to express his already passionate feeling about the importance of education. He was too language-conscious to call what he had in mind an experimental school. Progressive, yes, but the word 'experimental' was inappropriate. However Dartington and Summerhill and other progressive schools did sometimes use the word experimental. Once or twice I remonstrated with Bill Curry, the talented head of Dartington, over this. If they used it, couldn't they make good the word? Couldn't they follow up and see what happened to children brought up in their new method? Couldn't they at least attempt some evaluation, try to find out the results of their new approach? To which I always seemed to get the answer, 'But how are you proposing to evaluate the results? To evaluate success is, of course, impossible.' I went on wanting some sort of evaluation.

Much later, when Bertrand Russell was again available (not having disappeared to China or the United States or wherever), I several times suggested to him that UNESCO might be invoked in trying to evaluate educational results. But Russell did not see how they could help. I fancy he had no very great hopes in that direction. Well, I would say, galloping along with enthusiasm, each member nation could take a microscope and a telescope into the past to help it decide on, say three of its most eminent and excellent citizens. It would have to be people of the present or recent past, I thought. Their own academics would then try to find out how each of these 'exemplary' people had been educated. It wouldn't do to go right back in history, I said, you would have to limit it to the time when education in developed countries had been regularized and when there had been such a thing as a 'thorough grounding'. Then when reports came in, we might have some idea whether learning the *Koran* by heart, or the names of the minor prophets, or the analects of Confucius, or composing Latin verse resulted in excellence. Or, in contrast, study whether the principle of the kindergarten or Madame Montessori's ideas were the better bet. And which had been the most fruitful.

'Or at any rate the least harmful?' interposed Bertrand Russell.

I went on regardless. 'They might set up the research if you told them to, and anyhow it would be fascinating to see which citizens various countries would choose. I wonder would the Poles put in Madame Curie or would it be Chopin? And who would the Italians choose?' He was amused at this notion and we extrapolated.

Nothing whatever seems to have come of all this, but I still have hankerings. We saw a good deal of Bertrand Russell on and off, for he was for years a near neighbour in Wales, but by then he had gone off education and all his energies were for his Peace Foundation.

Though it was never easy to deflect him, he was always admirable company. Our children were friends with his grandchildren. At some period (it must have been some long time after the pram-pushing period) one of our daughters said, 'I know Bertie's very famous, but why? What does he *do*?' I tried to explain that he kept trying to find out what numbers were. 'But everyone knows what numbers are!' I referred this comment to Bertie. He had a splendid laugh, not like that of a hyena which is unkind, but more like that of the genial kookaburra, that admirable Australian bird. 'You tell her to try adding up the Seven Deadly Sins and the Seven Sleepers of Ephesus.' This I did, but all I got from my daughter was a snort which I took to mean, 'But I shan't ever want to do sums like that.'

What to say about philosophy, sex and religion? Could this lead to using the telescope on anthropology? Evaluating the formal ways in which other tribes of homo sapiens educate their young? Play it by ear was the conclusion I came to at the time.

Communicating about science seemed a great deal less full of uncertainty than the things philosophers and mathematicians got up to. I had so much pleasure out of my contacts with science that, like all converts, I wanted to pass on my own new-found satisfactions. Baulked in my efforts to pass them on to the readers of the *Spectator*, I gradually realized that half or more of our children's very proper and insistent questions were really questions about science.

One of the pleasures I felt was that, under the sands of conjecture in politics and value judgements, I had here come upon a causeway of fact, and this causeway seemed to lead the way that I felt I wanted to go. What also pleased me so much and was such a relief from conjecture was the way in which scientists set about solving a problem. It seemed to me incomparably better than the way in which the rest of us argued from a single instance and muddled along. Even the ways of law courts,

though not too bad, were superseded in my esteem by science. The tag
was that in law 'you set two skilled liars to lie against each other and
hoped that the truth would emerge'. So that for me to learn the
procedure which would be used for some bit of scientific research was
delightful. In the experimental sciences you started off with a
hypothesis, used a controlled experiment to test it, then you went on by
describing this procedure so exactly that someone in a different lab, in
Tokyo or New York, would see if they could repeat it. This seemed then
to me to give results that must be utterly definitive.

Such was the way, I believed, in which to establish a whole series of
truths, and I thought that our three children should not grow up like
those whom the board of the *Spectator* supposed to be so darkly ignorant
of scientific procedures. I must repeat that I had begun to perceive that
the children's insistent questions so often needed scientific answers.
Why does milk turn sour? Why don't fish drown?

I looked things up and tried to get ready for what now seems to me
very like the BBC's *Mastermind* machine-gunning of questions from the
children. I would get them books, I thought, with the right sort of text
and pictures. (Meantime I was encouraged when a daughter with a
seventh birthday coming said she wanted a microscope.)

It turned out, however, that at that time, in the early Twenties, there
seemed to be no such books. So I tried by trial and error, and using a bit
of cunning, to see if I could make shift with do-it-yourself techniques to
pass on some of my own pleasure.

The first result was the manuscript for a little book called *How You
Began*. The opening sentence was 'Once you were a little lump of jelly
no bigger than the full-stop on this page,' and the text was embryology
plus evolution. A draft was tried out in a school for seven- to
ten-year-olds by a kindly headmistress; the children liked it even
without pictures. I sent it to a publisher, the publisher sent it to their
scientific reader, the scientific reader said I had got it all wrong.

By then I had a number of scientific friends. I complained to the most
relevant of them, J. B. S. Haldane, whose sister Naomi had once been
so jealous of me. I wrote to him to say that I had read it all up very
carefully and that though I knew that the 'recapitulation theory' of
which I had made use wasn't quite approved, it made sense for a child
and I hoped that I had safeguarded myself by saying that before they
were born they had 'played at' evolution. Why had the little book been
thrown back at me?

'No, you haven't got it wrong,' wrote back J.B.S. 'What you've done
is to state a lot of things in simple language, consequently the
publisher's scientific reader can't understand you! That's all.'

It ended in J.B.S. writing two prefaces: one for children, one for adults. He was of course already famous, a trump-card, and was to become not only one of the top research geneticists but also one of the best simplifiers. His preface for children went like this:

I think this a good book. I know of no book like it. All girls and boys should know how they grow. I did not know this when I was quite young. Now I wish I had. But there was no book like this then . . . I have to teach people who are going to be doctors. I should find it much easier if they had read a book like this when they were children. Besides it is such fun to know that you once played at being a fish, and later had fur. How I wish I had kept my gills and my fur coat . . . and I am sad that I have lost my nice tail.

For grown-ups he wrote:

It is the only book of its kind, so far as I know, which is a scandal . . . The account of evolution strikes me as being more nearly correct than either of those two recently published by well-known scientific men.

How You Began did break new ground. Since then there have been many good children's books on most of the sciences, while the very best communication about science for the citizen is through television. Here the BBC is outstanding.

As the years went by I wrote more of such books, privately laying down rules for myself: children's questions should be answered briefly, truthfully and, if possible, in a lively way (very much what Marshak had said at a conference in Russia). But trust children for smashing up all nice snug generalizations! Strolling innocently in the garden at Plâs Brondanw years later with one of my sons-in-law, Euan, one of his daughters aged about twelve called out as she flew past us, 'What's electricity? Animal, vegetable or mineral, or is it a gas?' I took to the coward's device and I left it to him to answer.

One of the things I enjoyed about biographizing scientists for children was keeping such agreeable company. There was innocent, brilliant Michael Faraday, the book-binder's apprentice; then, in contrast, moody, disgruntled Newton being persuaded by Edmund Halley to write down what he had discovered about the stars in their courses, and about his liberating concept of the Calculus. Then there was Quaker-faced, poker-faced Benjamin Franklin, who enjoyed scientific jokes. Of him a French contemporary said, 'Yes, he is famous, but he really only invented three things: lightning rods, political hoaxes and the American nation.' Franklin said of himself that science had taught him to look facts in the face, while he had taught himself never to say that a thing was so, but only to say that it seemed to him so, and he added, 'I often regret that I was born so soon; it is impossible to imagine the heights to which science may yet be carried.'

Was it this sort of attitude in Mary Kingsley, an anthropologist before anthropology, which had dazzled me as a six-year-old? I suppose she was the first of the research scientists that I have known. They have been very various: Patrick Blackett, enterprising and disciplined; Dame Janet Vaughan, warm and decisive; Dick Synge, who thought I might enjoy *Peer Gynt* read to me in Norwegian; Norman Heatley, gentle and heroic; Norman Pirie, hoping to feed the world on dark-green leaf protein; David Lack with his robins and swallows; J. D. Bernal, that Renaissance polymath whose brilliant conversation seemed to make him irresistible to women; Solly Zuckerman, who could insinuate statistics into the heads of generals and whose baboon, Betsy, was for long a member of our household because he thought she needed a peer group (i.e. our children).

All these 'Inquirers after Nature', as Franklin called scientists, opened doors for me and made me free in a world that I found new and fascinating. Thank goodness now a younger generation still helps me to see something of strange worlds.

I often wondered why novelists had so largely neglected all this. There was, of course, C. P. Snow with his *Corridors of Power*, but the emphasis was more on the dominance game than on the actual feelings and motivations of a research scientist. However, what Julian Huxley knew about the biological sciences shone out briefly in at least two of his brother Aldous Huxley's novels: in *Antic Hay*, for instance. There were those who thought that in this tale his character Shearwater was drawn from J. B. S. Haldane. This I don't altogether believe, except that his Shearwater, like J.B.S., is shown briefly as often his own experimental animal: '"When he's with hens," Lancing explained to the visitors, "he thinks he's a cock. When he's with a cock, he's convinced he's a pullet." '[1] Over the years we all saw a good deal of J.B.S. and he seemed to me an outstanding creature, so that I was glad when later such a good judge as Sir Peter Medawar in his preface to Ronald Clark's *Life of JBS*, said of him:

> He could have made a success of any one of half a dozen careers – as mathematician, classical scholar, philosopher, scientist, journalist or imaginative writer . . . He could not have been a politician, administrator (heavens, no!), jurist or, I think, a critic of any kind . . . He became one of the three or four most influential biologists of his generation. In some respects – quickness of grasp, and the power to connect things in his mind in completely unexpected ways – he was the cleverest man I ever knew.[2]

During several summers J.B.S. took to driving himself to Brondanw from London, starting quite late from his lab and often arriving really late at night. He would say to Clough and me, 'Don't go to bed yet, the benzedrine hasn't worked off.' Benzedrine was the pep-pill of the day. Clough would creep off after a while, but I would loyally sit up with J.B.S., getting sleepier and sleepier while the benzedrine in him talked delightfully. He had a habit of contradicting his interlocutor and indeed you had to look sharp with him, and though I couldn't meet him on his ground, the irritating fact was that, as Medawar suggests, he could meet me on mine and would quote, for example, line after line of Shelley's *Prometheus* or of *Paradise Lost*.

In *Antic Hay* Aldous Huxley wrote of a visit to Shearwater's laboratory:

The rats who were being fed on milk from a London dairy came tumbling from their nest with an anxious hungry squeaking. They were getting thinner and thinner . . . But the old rat, whose diet was Grade A milk from the country . . . was as fat and sleek as a brown furry fruit, ripe to bursting. No skim and chalky water, no dried dung and tubercule bacilli for him . . . In their glass pagoda the little black axolotls crawled . . . A fifteen-year-old monkey, rejuvenated by the Steinach process, was shaking the bars that separated him from the green-furred, bald-rumped, bearded young beauty in the next cage. He was gnashing his teeth with thwarted passion.

A vast, unbelievable, fantastic world opened out as Lancing, their guide, spoke. There were tropics, there were cold seas busy with living beings, there were forests full of horrible trees, silence and darkness. There were ferments and infinitesimal poisons floating in the air. There were leviathans suckling their young, there were flies and worms . . . all were changing continuously, moment by moment, and each remained all the time itself by virtue of some unimaginable enchantment. For they were all alive.[3]

Seventeen

VENICE AND RUSKIN

In going on to tell the tale of the later 1920s, I try as ever to choose or allow to come to the surface whatever seems now to have had the most lasting or significant effect. In the three years 1926–8 I find myself besieged by the recollection of a crowd of events. It would be wrong, or at any rate against my principles, to make even a very ordinary slice of human life sound more orderly and coherent than it is, to try to arrange events as neatly as they affected my opinions at that time and as they now come to the surface.

Unconnected events, if they crowd one another, seem to me to have the same sort of effect as musical notes played as a chord, that is to say as in harmonics secondary sounds are produced and what arises is a sort of natural counterpoint. The result is not at all the same thing as notes played leisurely one after the other. The notes, as far as I was concerned, may not all sound very loud but they do definitely sound out one on top of the other, producing these secondary sounds or 'beats'.

The General Strike of 1926 was the result of an unemployment situation comparable to that of the 1980s. As far as I was concerned it was the year when I found myself addressing envelopes in Transport House in the company of Ishbel MacDonald, helping those organizing the strike, but also helping Clough to entertain those who were soon to help break it: the young who joyfully drove London buses, for example.

During the following year we travelled a little, but for the most part I was trying to fill the anxious hours of my father's terminal illness by working on a biography of John Ruskin, a part of whose history and influence had intrigued me. We were able to travel partly because, with Jim Wyllie in charge of the guests and the kitchen and with Clough's talent for getting the news disseminated, Portmeirion was beginning to prosper.

Two journeys stick in my mind. Not surprisingly and perhaps reprehensibly, our socialist principles did not cut us off too much, especially if holidays and enjoyment could be shared by those with the same ideas. Oswald Mosley (of whom more later) was already dissatisfied with the Conservative Party, already on the brink of crossing the floor of the House, though I fancy that nothing had yet been said publicly. We were asked to join a party with the Mosleys, Nancy Cunard and, I think, Bob Boothby and others in Venice. Perhaps Tom Mosley fancied himself as the new Byron; Professor Galbraith was to remark later that, if he did, this was better than for him to see himself as the British Mussolini, as so tragically he did eventually.

It was a glittering week: apartments in a palazzo (I forget which), gondolas, swimming on the Lido:

What, they lived once thus in Venice where the merchants were the kings . . .[1]

In the incomparable city there lived and live on incomparable presences, from Boswell to Ruskin, on again to the author of *The Aspern Papers*, and from Canaletto to Mozart, and Thomas Mann.

Did young people take their pleasure when the sea was warm in May?
Balls and masks begun at midnight, burning ever to mid-day.[2]

Generation after generation, 'delight of the eye', has lived there. They took their pleasure in that beautiful faded city where sea winds have dimmed an oriental magnificence, an over-plus. They lived, they kissed, or they plotted:

Till in due time, one by one,
Some with lives that came to nothing, some with deeds as well undone,
Death stepped tacitly and took them where they never see the sun . . .[3]

Clough and I also went to America in 1927, probably on some sort of architectural visit. Anyhow, we stayed with Joe Brewer, an old friend of my brother's, and we met a lot of people, as is so agreeably usual in that hospitable country. I talked to a doctor friend who was the brother to the celebrated *diseuse*, Ruth Draper, about my father's illness. He seemed to have no strength or vitality in him, and a letter had come from England saying that they had diagnosed pernicious anaemia. It seems that in America they had begun to treat this with liver, but it had to be raw liver and you had to eat a great deal – a pound I think it was – every day. They were trying to synthesise it, but that hadn't been managed yet.

We tried to get through to father's doctor to tell him about this in case there was anything in it (it came from very reputable sources), but it sounded like moonshine I think to the medical faculties in Britain. Indeed it was an almost intolerable thing to have to prescribe; you couldn't force a patient to eat a mass of raw liver every day.

The next development was, looking back, something that seems rather strange. Father didn't like hospitals or nursing homes, so we arranged that we should make the drawing-room of our house into a sick-room for him till he was better, as we hoped.

Why he didn't go to a nursing home or to a big house they had in Chester Square, I don't remember. Anyhow, there he was with a day nurse and a night nurse. My mother, I think, remained in Chester Square. I did a certain amount of nursing myself. The children were at boarding school; Clough, always amiable and knowing what a debt we owed to them, put up with the whole situation. Since I was doing some of the nursing, I was very glad indeed to have something quite different that I could do in the intervals.

I had been startled into taking an interest in John Ruskin. Always in the habit of asking questions, I had already asked several Labour Party people if they could remember what had first made them take up left-wing politics. At that time A. J. Cook was one of the miners' leaders and, as editor-in-chief of *The Miner*, was my brother's boss. I felt pretty sure that Cook's answer would be *Capital* or Marx in general.

'Arthur,' I said, 'what made you a socialist?'

'Reading Ruskin,' was the answer.

Probing further I found to my surprise that there was a lot of evidence of Ruskin's influence on the British Left, and I began to wonder if these (to me) unexpected answers had something to do with the differences in the feel of the talk and writing of what I knew of the Continental Left, and what I heard and read here. Obviously there would be many other sources of difference, but this unexpected referring back to Ruskin made me inquisitive. I knew very little about him and associated him vaguely with the mild opinions of the 'Arts and Crafts' movement of the Twenties, that is with nice, slightly wistful, old gentlemen who wore tweeds and William Morris ties, not knotted but pulled through seal rings.

It seemed that Carlyle, who had known him well, had called him 'ethereal Ruskin' and, when at best, 'an insubstantial creature' and, when at worst, 'silly'. I supposed him to have been rated as a man brilliant and fashionable in his day but who ultimately thinned into a beautiful voice.

Surely, I thought, an influence of that kind, so unscientific and whimsical, must have been regressive. After all, it had been Marx and Engels, not the wistful romantics, who had carried so much of the endlessly fruitful scientific method into political economy; it was they who had observed, thought quantitatively, framed hypotheses, and who had most influentially formulated the aspirations of the workers. (Yes, and unfortunately written lamentable sentences like that one!)

So why had Ruskin's earlier biographers been all admiration, had a great deal to say about his classification of a huge collection of Turner watercolours, and about his relations both with the pre-Raphaelite Brotherhood and with two or three romantic young ladies? Then there were also those who were interested in what the Evangelical and the High Church party had to say about him, and with what psychiatrists might tell. But no one at that time had apparently thought to follow up the results of what Ruskin had to say about politics and economics. Since I wrote my *Tragedy of John Ruskin*, a great many private papers have been released, so what has been on offer since has primarily been the tale of how his pretty wife Effie got away by means of a nullity suit and married that robust character Millais, and how other girls (luckily for them) evaded his wistful and oppressive adoration.

Reading what accounts there were of his politics, I came to the conclusion that his strong influence on the Labour Party had been very largely technical or literary. It had been largely the beauty of his prose that had so unexpectedly taken his message clear and whole to the hearts of those who read it. His prose still worked, as I found by experiment, for I tried it out on meetings, speaking his luminous cadences as best I could; I could feel how an audience responded:

> A great cry rises from all our manufacturing cities, louder than their furnace blasts . . . We manufacture everything there except men. We blanch cotton, and strengthen steel, and refine sugar, and shape pottery; but to brighten, to strengthen, to refine, or to form a single living spirit, never enters into our estimate of advantages.

This particular scrap comes, by the way, from *Stones of Venice*, one of his most popular books on aesthetics. Nobody took any particular notice when he wrote it. It seemed, perhaps, just an odd little interjection and was perhaps no more than a plea for better town planning. I thought perhaps that it was his tremendous reputation as an art critic that had for long lulled his European public so that even other sayings of his, sayings which didn't at all fit into an 'Art for Art's sake' message, could be overlooked. Anyhow, it came about that his advice could still be asked for by the Establishment – by 'the proper' as Ruskin called them. But gradually 'the proper' began to feel perplexed.

In 1860 he was asked to give evidence before a Committee of the House of Commons whose leading member was Sir Robert Peel. This committee had been set up to see whether the usefulness of picture galleries and museums could be improved. They wondered, for example, whether those whom the members of the committee spoke of as 'the lower orders' or 'the workmen' might want to take a look at the nation's possessions.

Ruskin said that he wasn't sure that they would, because he noticed that in Britain, more than on the Continent, there was a sort of awkwardness between the classes: 'The workman is often so ashamed of his bad clothes as possibly to be unwilling to go to such places.'

Further on in the proceedings, when asked if 'they' didn't want to better themselves, Ruskin used a phrase that has since become a Labour Party slogan: the aim of the individual workman should be, Ruskin answered, 'to rise with his class not out of it'. Again the perplexed committee wanted to know if, in Mr Ruskin's opinion, the masses were anxious for self-improvement. 'Yes,' said Ruskin, '. . . but I find that with an ordinary constitution the labour of a day in England oppresses a man, and breaks him down, and it is not refreshment to him to use his mind after that . . . his mind is languid with labour.'[4]

Ruskin, asked his opinion about the attitude of the classes to one another, said that he noted 'an increased kindness of the upper towards the lower'.

And did not Mr Ruskin think, asked a committee man with the correct Victorian belief in progress, that the lower orders had improved in the last twelve years?

Ruskin would not have it: 'No, while greater efforts are made to help the workman, the principles on which our commerce is conducted are every day oppressing him and sinking him deeper.'

Here the chairman interposed with the remark that he was sure that Ruskin did not intend to cast a slur upon competition.

'Yes, very distinctly,' Ruskin answered. 'I intended not only to cast a slur, but to express my excessive horror of the principle of competition in every way.'

Ruskin finished his evidence with a touching phrase. The committee, completely baffled by his attitude, finally asked him what he wanted done, in a cultural way, for these lower orders. Ruskin said that they would soon understand if they would suppose that 'the workman' was a son to one of them, that he had no means of rising into another class. They were then to imagine that the life of a manual worker was to be made such as should be lived by one of their own children.

In *Unto This Last* and soon in articles that began to appear in Mr Thackeray's *Cornhill* magazine, Ruskin began in so many words to attack the main presumptions of the Establishment and the basis of Victorian economics. He declared that he didn't believe that 'progress' was in fact happening, he didn't believe in competition, he thought that even feudalism (unjust as it was) produced less deplorable results than 'the play of the market'. The articles caused a major scandal. Thackeray discontinued the series. Such indignation about doubts expressed of the workings of the laws of supply and demand seems almost incomprehensible, unless we are ready to agree with Marx that nothing matters to a class except its means of subsistence and domination.

The contemporary Press outdid itself in abuse of this aesthete who formerly could do no wrong. These economic essays were called 'intolerable twaddle' and the author 'a perfect paragon of blubbering'. This critic went on, with exquisite lack of humour, to call his own willingness to argue with a man like Mr Ruskin, 'who can only write in a scream', as 'condescension'. 'The world', said another, 'is not going to be preached to death by a mad governess.'

I find it touching that in the 1980s up and down our industrial towns there should still be Ruskin Halls where beer is drunk and snooker played, and that one of the principal centres for adult education, a centre for 'the second chance', should be Ruskin College. I wonder if a good many of the saints and martyrs to whom churches are dedicated in much this way, may have been rather like Ruskin? Men and women, that is, who inconveniently came to unpopular conclusions and felt it their duty to keep on saying what they thought in spite of 'the proper'?

Ruskin wasn't tortured or burnt at the stake. Looking at what the media and Amnesty International have lately found out and proceeded to tell us about 1982 world-wide, I am inclined to think it a good point for Victorian Britain that Ruskin was allowed to go quietly mad in a comfortable house in the Lake District. Nor do I suppose that it was just the plight of the 'labouring poor' that drove him mad. Life is not so simple.

A collection of his drawings can still be seen in Coniston, and Sir Hugh Casson tells me that he finds them as exquisite as I find the prose cadences of our poor 'mad governess'.

Eighteen

RUSSIAN JOURNEY

After he had had appendicitis, my brother John edited *The Miner*, the organ of the National Union of Mineworkers. The Independent Labour Party had undertaken the issuing of a series of short studies, each one describing the structure of a specific Russian industry.

In 1927 John was invited by the Russian miners' trade union to go to the Don area to study the working of what was left of Soviet coal-mining. About this assignment John wrote:

> In 1920 the Russian coal-mining industry had almost ceased to exist. The Great Don Basin coalfield (out of which comes some 80 per cent of all Russian coal) had been pillaged and laid waste by three years of civil war, of famine and disease. The pits themselves were, it seemed, irretrievably destroyed. All that had water were flooded; the winding engines were smashed, the shafts had closed in; the roofs fallen . . .[1]

The invading armies had been, of course, those of the British and the other Allies of the 1914–18 War who, in a trice, had begun co-operating with their late mortal enemies the Germans to smash Lenin's attempt to reconstruct Russia. As soon as these White armies withdrew, though still with bandits roaming the country and famine pressing, the Russian miners' union began the heroic job of reconstruction. Production had been a matter of counting bucketsful, but by 1928 some upper levels of the mines had been resuscitated and it again became possible to speak of 'coal output'.

But it seemed also that the Soviet miners' union was putting up the price of coal; after all the historic role of a trade union has always been to make hard bargains on behalf of its members. It was also necessary that miners should have enough to eat. But now it was the coal-users who were protesting, especially the railways. This hard bargaining, they said, was out of place. The miners' union should remember that they were bargaining with their fellow-workers – the railwaymen, who couldn't get the food to famine areas, and the factory workers, who were trying to produce essential goods. Hard bargaining by any one union might lead to impeding all those who were trying to get industry going again. Some sort of national plan must be organized. Yet the miners had a good case, for workers' control was obviously an important part of 'the dictatorship of the proletariat'.

The details of how the new People's Republic was succeeding in getting round this sort of problem and somehow organizing production, were of the greatest theoretical interest to politically minded people and to economists, whatever their sympathies. To many of us the Russian effort seemed important. Might it not truly be 'the Fatherland of the Workers'? But with the means of production devastated by intervention, could the regime survive? If it could, might some version of its experiment be the best hope of a world where peace, with famine over half Europe, and our own 'Land Fit for Heroes' had proved so disappointing? All kinds of economic fact-finding were of the greatest interest.

I managed to get myself included in this, John's first Russian visit, and we set off for the Donbas in the January of 1928.

John was soon deep in detailed studies, both of the main organizational structure and also of the situation of the individual miner. These had to be as far as possible contrasted with our own, though conditions were so different. We wanted to find out what existed and what was being aimed at in the way of hours, time-rates, piece-rates, differentials, work at the face, work above ground, number of shifts worked per week, housing, protective clothing, fuel allowances, and so on.

The answers, of course, were given in Russian through a Canadian interpreter who understood coal-mining. But who could translate from the Poods Rouble to the Pound or the Dollar per shift in those desperate, hopeful, forward-looking circumstances? Pasternak, that splendid poet, had not yet written his *Dr Zhivago* but in talk – often through interpreters – I began to piece together the story of what I myself saw and heard then, and also later.

What was in front of my eyes were the mining villages. The one of which I saw most I called 'Yelenskaya' in writing about it in a story entitled 'Comrade Spetz':

It was intensely cold, long icicles hung from the eaves of the station buildings; the breasts and nostrils of the horses were soon fringed with ice; snowcrumbs spurted up off the sledge runners, and the wind cut their faces and crept round their legs. Yelenskaya was bigger than the first mining village, but a part of it had been shattered. The fronts of some of the houses were gone, the snow had crept in and lay on the stoves, and beams showed pitted and black against the white ground and pale sky. Again the streets looked draughtily wide, again the one-storied houses were dominated by the slag heaps, chimneys and winding gear, which had been visible for several miles

across the steppe. There were differences however. At Yelenskaya there was a
river. It ran at the bottom of a ravine whose banks were brown with the bare
twigs of willow, rowan and birch . . .[2]

The big shed that was the headquarters of the miners' union was
where I picked up most of my stories about Yelenskaya and other
mining villages. In one of them, it seemed, there had last year been a
mammoth row.

'Production!' the chairman, an old leading Party member had
shouted, '*Ugol. Ugol.* Coal. Coal.' But the rest of the workers would not
listen; to get the flooded mine going again was impossible – the old man
was living in a dream.

'Comrade Chairman, you must just open up that store of spares.
Wire. Nails. Tools. We can make pots and pans and little things out of
the wire, metal and stuff that's in there. The women can trade such
things for bread, trade with that Cossack village over there.'

But at last the old trade unionist had said no; all things in the store
would all be necessary. It was madness to dissipate them! 'Ugol,
comrades.' They'd nearly lynched the old man, for already the children
were half-starved.

It had taken time but that mine really had somehow got into
production again, and there had been bread – yes, even though it had
been a bit worse than Yelenskaya; all the machinery had had to be
patched and the winding gear had been so dangerous that it made your
hair stand on end with only home-made brakes.

One day it thawed while we were at Yelenskaya and then froze again
in the night, and a crust formed on the smoke-blackened snow, and in
the railway sidings there was trouble with the points. In the main yard
the crust on the snow was hard so that neither foot nor sledge-runner
went through. Peasants kept going and coming as usual and their
sledges skidded over it, sideways, and the one much-prized pair of
Cossack trotters had to creep. Out beyond, the whole surface of the
steppe gleamed like marble and near at hand the big black smuts from
the powerhouse chimneys skated along when the wind blew.

At night the small electric light bulbs on corner buildings were
Yelenskaya's pride. But it was mostly by the light of the stars, after a
session over tea or (if possible) vodka in the miners' union headquarters, that we picked our way over intricate railway lines back to the
guesthouse. Luckily John had a good head, for now that there was coal
again, now that the rest of the winter wouldn't mean starvation, it was
the amusement on special occasions to try to make him drunk. To
refuse to drink any toast was not possible. I, as a female, was spared.

We left the Donbas after bursts of statistics, after descents under-ground, after feasting and drinking with these formidable trade union comrades. They could make heroic speeches, brandish statistics even when they had fortified their neat vodka with cayenne pepper – just to make it a bit stronger!

Our Canadian trade unionist and another guide-interpreter – a Russian this time – were to go across country to see the oil installations at Baku, travelling on newly repaired but still untimetabled railways. In the course of many changes John and I got lost. We knew that this would greatly worry our interpreter, who indeed later declared, almost in tears, that he had 'never before lost a delegation!'

However, though we hadn't got lost on purpose, we also saw this as a good chance to answer the doubters' chorus of 'They only show you what they want you to see.' So we managed to find ourselves in an unexpected town and to see an unexpected light engineering factory. The workforce there was mainly female, but the two chief managers were male; both of them tall, dark, slim and handsome. Both wore the traditional dress of that part of Russia – high-collared, belted, blue frock coats, Cossack boots and Astrakhan hats – very unlike the miners' usual work-worn gear and quick bow-legged way of getting about. These two had been elected to their positions.

I forget the statistics, but we felt that in this mainly feminine factory the election of these gorgeous beings made workers' control seem a reality.

Both in the Donbas and later, I had needed to work less system-atically than my brother, and was therefore freer to try to find out what was going on. It was known, of course, that property and criminal law were being changed, also the marriage laws. A progressive – the famous Lunacharsky – was Minister of Education, and Lenin had laid down that 'every cook must learn to rule the state'.

Whenever we felt critical of the actual execution of plans that sounded admirable, I reminded myself of how things had been in the Donbas, and how we had not even seen famine areas, though I had heard plenty. Above all, how huge was the scale of the Russian task, the new experiment, so huge as to silence criticism, so huge, tragic and daunting as to induce humility in the well-fed Westerner.

It was a little later, at a time when the most primitive problems of the survivors showed signs of being solved, and after other visits, that I began to write stories about people in Russia: 'The volcano of war and revolution has thrown up a new formation with a stratification of its own. What now lies on the top in Russia already has a history.'[3] There was as yet no epic from a great poet to clarify and clothe this history and make us shake at the tale.

Meantime I had had a cold and got bronchitis. It does sometimes thaw in Moscow in January, but not this time. The temperatures were very low, and in a real Russian low it isn't advisable for anybody with bronchitis to go outside at all. My brother needed to get back; what was I to do?

Somehow he fixed me up superbly. Ivy Litvinov, the English wife of Maxim Litvinov, the Commissar for Western Foreign Affairs, took me in in the kindest way. She and Maxim were both Jewish, she typical of the most lively Hampstead intellectual, of the Bohemian, outspoken, large-hearted sort. As the wife of a Commissar, she was much occupied with official entertaining. Being who she was, she was inclined to find official protocol-ridden parties a chore, and to agree with a saying of Talleyrand's: 'Human life would be perfectly tolerable if it weren't for its amusements.'

It was with the Western ambassadors and their staffs that she was mostly concerned. She found them full of 'official stiff upper-lips', old-fashioned protocol, the whole diplomatic works. I hope what she did for me may have been a nice change for her. For me it was more admirable than can well be imagined. She couldn't give me a great deal of time, but there were plenty of servants in the 'Sugar King's Palace', which was what people called the ex-tycoon's magnificent house that had been taken over for the Commissar. I wasn't confined to bed, only to the warm house. She gave me a room or two and excellent meals came up at unpredictable intervals, usually accompanied by a samovar. She topped this hospitality with an enormous tin of caviare with instructions to keep it on one of the window-sills between the inner and outer panes of the double glazing, the usual deep-freeze in Russian winters.

For reading matter she gave me *Ulysses*, then a banned book in England but she had it from Paris. She would manage to escape from protocol and from looking after Misha and Tanya, their two children, for gossip and my highly unofficial news of London and Hampstead. This was the beginning of lasting kindness on Ivy's part when Clough or I, or both of us, visited Moscow, as we did on two other occasions.

Ivy sometimes suffered from nettlerash and, on a summer visit under literary auspices, I had been put up at a 'Home of Rest for Writers' in the country. Coming back to the ever-hospitable Ivy, I gave her a dramatic account of how the bed-bugs had bitten me there. A real tribute to my powers of description ensued. Ivy, as I told her, came out in nettlerash in exactly the places – neck, chin and wrist – where I had been most savagely bitten.

Nineteen

SAILING

'But why do you do it? Explain.' 'But surely you must know where you mean to go, and when you mean to get back?' Thus spoke our older non-sea-going relations and friends when we began to make more than a day sail of it in little *Twinkler*. 'Just up the coast or down the coast, I expect,' we would answer truthfully. But to them it seemed that we were just being evasive.

'But it's dangerous and so uncomfortable.' 'And you know you're often sea-sick.' 'Only at first,' I would answer.

When we ventured further and stayed at sea for longer, and didn't come back, 'they' were apt embarrassingly to alert the coastguards. They never thought it might be that we had had to wait for enough tide to cross the bar, and that was why we were late. This is the one real disadvantage of sailing in Cardigan Bay. It is as beautiful, with its background of mountains, as any sailing coast in Europe; its little ports are snug, but to get into any of them you will have to submit to the inexorable fact that you will have to negotiate a bar, and that in many of them the harbour dries out at low tide.

Thus it was that when Clough substituted *Scott* for *Twinkler* (with her retractable centre-board and comfortably to 'take the ground') we often sailed from other ports, Scotland or the Channel, and over to France, or later chartered foreign. *Scott* was described by Clough as 'a most comely old 15-ton Loch Fyne ketch' and he added, 'I bought her rather cheaply because of her age and some dubious timbers.' He went on to describe her as 'a picture of sea-kindly grace' and her auxiliary engine as 'elderly if honourable'. We never raced or went to regattas, and thoroughly despised all yachts of the ignoble tycoon-owned class such as those of St Tropez. We were neither posh nor tycoons, nor did we think kindly of motor-boats.

As an old sailing mate of ours, Arthur Ransome, in his preface to Captain Joshua Slocum's two great books, so truly says: 'A close intimacy with winds and seas depends on small crafts and is less or absent in great ships especially those "machine propelled".'

Ransome's own craft, *Rann*, had extremely heavy gear but was splendidly sea-worthy. He had always been a great traveller and in the course of travel a great collector of Russian traditional stories. That came about because, intending to learn Russian, he travelled in some conventional way or other to the frontier, where he bought a donkey and cart, and thus equipped, ambled slowly to Moscow, always playing with the children in the villages and learning Russian in that way. It may well have been because he learned the language so well – real colloquial Russian – that he became the only English newspaper correspondent with whom Lenin thought it worthwhile to talk. Anyhow, I believe it is now generally acknowledged that that is the right way to learn a language, the donkey and cart not being absolutely obligatory however.

Erskine Childers, in his equally famous *Riddle of the Sands*, gives an account of our sort of sailing that is only slightly and agreeably exaggerated. The tale begins with the setting out of such a small yacht as *Twinkler.* The narrator, a grand regatta-yachtsman, has crossed to a small port in Schleswig-Holstein and in all innocence has joined the owner, Davies, for a fortnight on *Dulcibella*. Davies is a much more adventurous yachtsman than we ever were, but the embarkation described by Erskine Childers is comparable except that we forewarned guests. The dude yachtsman has brought a suitcase – far too much luggage. They walk down to the dinghy in the gathering dusk:

> Heavily loaded, we stumbled over railway lines and rubble heaps, and came to the harbour. Davies led the way to a stairway whose weedy steps disappeared below in gloom.
>
> 'If you'll get into the dinghy,' he said, 'I'll pass the things down.' I descended gingerly, holding as a guide a sodden painter which ended in a small boat, and conscious that I was collecting slime on cuffs and trousers.[1]

He slips and ends with one foot in the water:

> I climbed wretchedly into the dinghy and awaited events. 'Now float her up close under the quay wall, and make fast to the ring down there,' came down from above ... I took hold of the slack of the sodden painter and grappled with this loathsome task ... A big dark object loomed overhead and was lowered into the dinghy. It was my portmanteau and, placed athwart, exactly filled all the space amidships.[2]

By the time everything was on, including the portmanteau, Davies, sculling out into the harbour in the fading light, remarks: 'I'm lying a little way down the fiord, you see, I hate to be too near a town ... There she is! I wonder how you'll like her?' She carries a riding light and becomes gradually visible. Then they begin the laborious task of handing up the contents of the loaded dinghy.

1 Holding my new brother, John, in 1901

2 My beautiful cousin Mim, after she was presented at Court; she became Lady O'Hagan

3 Riding at Newlands Corner, Surrey, when I was about fifteen

4 John before he went up to Oxford

5 The Great Parlour at Newlands, when it was a hotel

6 Clough and me leaving the church after our wedding in 1915

Sailing with Clough and some friends in the Mediterranean on *Oronsay*

8 Me in the mid-1930s

9 My daughter, Susan, and her husband, Euan Cooper-Willis, surrounded by family and friends at Brondanw, April 1945

10 My mother, Amy, holding her great-grand-daughter, Menna, in 1

11 Clough and me, looking untypically pensive, at about the time of our Diamond Wedding Anniversary

12 With my favourite cat

13 Feeding the ducks in the garden of my home, Plâs Brondanw

Hazily there floated through my mind my last embarkation on a yacht: my faultless attire, the trim gig and obsequious sailors, the accommodation ladder flashing with varnish and brass in the August sun, the orderly snowy decks and basket chairs under the awning aft. What a contrast with this sordid midnight scramble . . . Down below a complex odour of paraffin, past cookery, tobacco and tar saluted my nostrils . . . 'Mind your head,' said Davies, striking a match and lighting a candle . . .[3]

Like *Twinkler*, *Dulcibella* had a centre-board. 'You see she's a flat-bottomed boat, drawing very little water without the plate; that's why there's so little head-room. For deep water you lower the plate; so, in one way or another, you can go practically anywhere.'

It isn't till the poor young man is on deck that it suddenly strikes him that if it had been raining it might have been much worse, and he observes that the little cove is still as glass, stars above and stars below reflected in the water, and the peace of a quiet evening anchorage steals over and dissipates his feeling that the whole affair is sordid and that he himself has been mortified by bringing all this wretched luggage so unsuitable for *Dulcibella*. His mood changes there and then, sitting on his ridiculous portmanteau and savouring the peace of his surroundings. At the cry of 'Grog's ready!' he goes down below and finds that all traces of litter have miraculously vanished and a cosy neatness reigns, glasses and lemons and the fragrant smell of punch deadening all the previous smells.

In the novel *Dulcibella*'s owner has a secret and laudable purpose for his voyage. At first Clough, in our exploration of North Wales anchorages, also had a purpose which he did not divulge. I had no purpose and soon, with the founding of Portmeirion, Clough's purpose had been accomplished. As he said himself, 'The wandering sea-bird had found a nesting place.' But for sailing a purpose is by no means necessary. I had none, ever, nor had our sailing companions, except the purpose that the dandified narrator discovered that evening on the deck of the *Dulcibella*.

David Lack, the expert on bird migration, Lord and Lady Esher, architect and painter, Lord and Lady Brownlow, Norman Heatley of penicillin fame, and Adrian and Karen Stephen, psychoanalysts, were all notable as sailing mates. Some of the more professional with whom we sailed thought that Clough, when skipper, courted danger more than was right, the secretary of the Cruising Association saying to him severely when he asked advice on what should be done in some hypothetical difficulty: 'Difficulties ought never to arise.' Nor was Patrick Blackett convinced that there wasn't a touch of small boy's daring in Clough's attitude to wind and tide and what the sea can do. Patrick, an ex-Naval Officer, was reported to me as remarking, 'Clough doesn't seem to think he's had a proper holiday unless he's hazarded his ship.' However, when Patrick again went to sea, now commanding his *Red Witch* (another Loch Fyne ketch), he became once more the Royal Navy Officer he had been before his famous researches into physics and his notable organizational power brought him so much renown. I crewed for him several times, and his style was very different to Clough's. I never aspired to a higher rank than deck-hand but, as I remarked in the context of our little *Twinkler*, I always refused, no matter for whom I might be crewing, to become a slave to the galley with its saucepans and frying pans, even if, as sometimes happened, I was the only woman on board. With many a sailing companion and commander have I thus bargained, but not with Patrick, he being entirely sound on this as on larger aspects of human rights. But there are dark stories afloat. Only this summer (1982) I again heard from a capable young woman who had just been 'foreign' for the first time: 'The rest were all men and they just assumed that I'd as soon be down below in the galley as up on deck seeing the first sight of a new port and helping to find an anchorage or pick up a mooring.'

Helping to victual a small cruising yacht, especially in a foreign port, can be fun and many women are better at judging how much to get for how long a passage, and what will keep and what won't, and how not to buy things that need slow cooking (often impossible at sea). Of shopping and victualling, I think females should be willing to do rather more than their share, but they should not be prevented from taking the dawn trick at the wheel, they must not be prevented from watching the moon rise or catching the first sight of a little fluttering land-bird after days and nights at sea, or savouring the scent, sound or the outline of land from the cabin-top when the sun has come out warm at last after heavy weather. Not to get a fair share of these intense pleasures has turned many a girl away from the water. Let me state here, once and for all, that we females need such pleasures, need sports and especially those where competition or slaughter doesn't play too much of a part. I am thinking of such things as surfing, or under-water adventure, rock-climbing, ballooning, certain kinds of camping and explor- ation, walking and trekking. We should not be shouldered out of what need not be after all exclusively manly pleasures, for these occupations make against over-softness, inability to cope, and make for those states of muscle and physical fatigue that so strangely enhance that state of being which in another context is called 'enlightenment'.

We never did anything spectacular when we managed to get away to sea, but we did see and feel and experience enough of the wonders, formidable beauties and dangers of seas and oceans to enrich our lives and give us a sense too of the home comforts that it is so easy to take for granted: hot baths, a warm bed with clean sheets, and something to sit on that doesn't take a sudden slant. Also the social side of the sort of cruising we did was both amusing and invigorating.

Karen and Adrian Stephen were frequent sailing companions. It must be remembered, in order to relish the tale, that they were both psychoanalysts. We had jointly chartered the usual kind of modest cabin-cruiser, this one called *Plover*. My memory is vivid of an occasion when we were tacking as we made passage out of the Medway, the channel here being marked by very large (to us towering) black buoys, numbered in white. The picture comes back.

Clough and I are in the cabin making breakfast. We can hear the two Stephens in the cockpit:

'I think with the tide as it is we should leave No. 4 to starboard.'

'Plenty of room with *Plover*'s draught either way.'

'But what about the wind on this tack?'

'Yes, she does make a good deal of leeway.'

This placid debate goes on for several minutes when we hear a loud bang and feel a shiver run through the boat, almost sending the full boiling coffee-pot out of Clough's hands and the bacon out of the pan that I'm holding on the stove. The bang and shiver are followed by a scraping sound. We put our heads out and see, as expected, *Plover* scraping along the black side of the towering No. 4 buoy as the tide races past. No remarks are made and since our fenders are still out (though they shouldn't be) a few scratches to *Plover*'s not originally immaculate paint is all the damage. All the damage except to my own simple-hearted belief that a civilized discussion is always the way to find an answer to any problem. Either side of that buoy would have been all right.

Plover provided us with a more mysterious psychological event. She wasn't an immaculately maintained little craft and I recall how, tacking in her this time also in a narrow seaway, a good and freshening wind caused her to lay over a good deal on each tack. We soon perceive that the helmsman of another boat, also tacking up, is clearly anxious to speak to us urgently. What could this urgent message be? At last after several tries on his part, our respective short quick tacks bring us near enough to make out his shout. This is what he at last manages to make us hear: 'Your bottom is white with barnacles!' After he was sure that we had heard, he was off and away. I have since often pondered and wondered about why it was so necessary and urgent to reproach us.

Placidly at anchor in some intended port, or storm-bound unexpectedly, there is no better place for social contacts than round a
cabin-table. Sheltering in storm-bound Canna in the Inner Hebrides,
the whole island having run out of bread, they taught us to make a new
kind of scone; in Sicily we were three days in Marsala with such a gale
outside that we put out six warps to secure our stately chartered *Oronsay*
to the quay, and learned that there are more than six varieties of
excellent local wine.

Once, sailing *Scott* this time, we managed to transfer a particularly
unwelcome sailing companion on to another yacht which was short-
handed for a passage to Ireland. Did Clough warn the second yacht
about what he was so obligingly relinquishing? I hope so. Did he warn
our own crew member that the second yacht's skipper was both daring
and a disciplinarian? Again I hope so, but I know that we on *Scott* found
it best to make a particularly early start next morning. It was of this
crew member that we heard something afterwards that sticks in my
mind as an example of saintlike charity: 'Poor gentleman,' his cleaning
lady had said of him, 'poor gentleman. Suffers dreadfully from his
temper!'

It may seem strange that we should often have chartered, but a look
at the map of Europe will justify chartering by people with professions
and limited time. One of our holidays, the land part of which turned out
far too dramatic, began with a rendezvous with a Dutch craft of a kind
called a Botter Ark, an auxiliary sailing barge, flat-bottomed, with
exceedingly heavy lee-boards that had to be raised or lowered if we
wanted to tack. This was at a time when the children were, we thought,
too young for real seafaring. She was essentially a canal boat. We took
the car to Holland and Karen Stephen and later Diccon Hughes joined
or left us as their jobs allowed. Clough, being Clough, was not content
with just canal cruising but insisted that we put to sea, though only in
the inland Zuider Zee. A pleasant craft enough in a canal, we found our
Botter Ark with her broad beam and bluff bows an utter pig at beating
to windward – butting and crashing into the waves. A speechless little
old Dutchman who was the paid hand who came with her had only a
chart of quite a different canal complex. He also had a habit, which
delighted the children, of wearing a complete set of oilskins when it was
fine and taking them off if it rained. They also liked the melancholy
little horn on which he tooted when we were either in fog in the Zuider
Zee or when approaching lifting bridges.

Clough, the children, Diccon and I planned to return the Botter Ark,
collect our car and go on to stay in Austria for a week. We got back to
the mooring and Clough, Diccon and our eldest, Susan, decided to

have a last bathe, since the weather was fine.

We were to stay for a week with Aemethe, one of my mother's VAD detachment who had subsequently been a star mathematics student of Bertrand Russell and was now married to Count Leo Zeppelin. They lived in what sounded like the very best sort of castle, Schloss Wernberg. For me the next two months were a nightmare and that in spite of the fact that both our host and hostess were kind and long-suffering beyond measure, and their castle everything that the most romantic heart could desire. Clough, much later, wrote of it and our host:

> . . . the castle was very large and built around a courtyard on a rocky bluff above the rushing river Drau with cone-topped towers, winding stone stairs, a vast empty and echoing 'Prälaten-saal' with frescoed walls, surviving from its religious past, and great wolf-hounds prowling around . . . Count Leo, a lively muscular little man usually in national green hunting-dress, leather shorts, feathered hat and so on – extrovert and pleasantly eccentric. For example, attending an auction while we were there to buy a bull for his farm, he came back with a lion cub he had taken to instead.[4]

So what went wrong? To realize how wrong it went, it has to be remembered that this was a time before antibiotics.

First, our poor Susan had to be carried off to a hospital twenty miles away with a high temperature and dangerously ill with mastoid caused by the last swim. While I was with her and the surgeon was telling me when he proposed to operate, Clough arrived on a stretcher, delirious and in equal danger from double pneumonia. There followed the most ghastly version of the old puzzle of the goats and the cabbages, for in our party at Schloss Wernberg there were Diccon, ill with an infected tooth, and our two younger children. Aemethe had also on her hands a couple of English friends who were strangers to us. The surgeon and physician at the hospital were obviously young and competent but the nursing was, by English standards, exceedingly sketchy. My German was not very good, but I could understand it only too well when I was told not to fuss about getting some sleep myself in a cot in the passage since it seemed unlikely that Clough would live for more than a couple of days. But knowing that he might and thinking of the children, I insisted that occasional sleep was essential, and even an occasional breath of fresh air in the hospital garden. I think they thought me heartless.

But he didn't die, and they didn't muff the asepsis in Susan's mastoid operation, which had been one of my various dreads. Anyhow it was autumn before we all got home after protracted kindness from the von

Zeppelins. I drove my two convalescents by slow stages, all three of us
in overcoats that a local tailor had made for us, for by now it was frosty
among the mountains. I remember one strange thing about the drive
and this was that at that time in Austria the rule of the road was that
you had to drive on the left in built-up areas and on the right in the
country. This called for a town planner's delicate sense of definition. So
that, lovely drive as it was, I wasn't sorry when I got my passengers
safely across the Austrian border into countries with less whimsical
ministers of transport.

But let no-one suppose that the so nearly fatal consequences of our
voyage in that Botter Ark in any way stopped our family tendency to
escape to water. This has continued to the third generation, but
sometimes shows itself in a rather different way: one daughter, our
eldest grand-daughter and a great-nephew declare that what is under
the sea is far more entrancing than what is on top. When it comes to
watching life around a coral reef, I agree wholeheartedly. There is
hardly anything on land so strange, jewel-like and beautiful as the
intricate living labyrinth of those reefs. The glorious fact is, of course,
that in six or seven favoured regions, both delights – sailing and
diving – are available to adaptable addicts. Alas for us northerners, all
of them are a long way off and mostly in places where it is hard to make
a living and bring up a family. However, this has been and is being
done by some of the adventurous young of my acquaintance.

In my mind I often go over the question of our non-sailing friends:
'But why do you do it when it is so dangerous and uncomfortable?'
There is quite obviously no rational answer to such a question, but
certain elements definitely come in. There are many other activities of
which the same question could well be asked but is never answered by
those who participate in them. Why do people go down the Cresta
Run? Why do so many people take to rock-climbing and caving, to
down-hill skiing, gliding and hang-gliding, surfing and wind-surfing?
I feel pretty sure that one of the answers is that without this love of
adventure, this *Take It To The Limit*, as Lucy Rees called her alarming
book on rock-climbing, such a creature as homo sapiens would not
have survived the dangers of the natural world. In many of us the
strongest possible feelings urge us to match ourselves against danger.

Apropos of courting danger, I remember discussing with an ex-Navy
man the disasters of the Fastnet Race in 1980. A general feeling among
yachtsmen is of reprobation of those who don't stick to their boats.
Slocum, the great circumnavigator, writes that he had taken care that
both his vessel *Spray* and the smaller *Liberdade* should be completely
watertight if they should be overwhelmed or laid on their beam ends.

All openings – hatches, portholes and the entrance to the cabin – should be completely watertight.

Twenty

THE THIRTIES BEGIN

It is said by people who didn't live through the 1930s that political loyalties and moral judgements must have been simple. The sinister rise first of Mussolini and then of Hitler must obviously have made them so. 'These wicked men', as Churchill was to call them, must have made loyalties clear and moral judgements easy; you knew where you stood.

Don't you believe it.

If the issues now seem clear, it is with hindsight and also because it is easy, looking back, to make important omissions. By the late 1920s there were in Britain and America millions of unemployed, and neither sticking to market economics nor the Labour Party disastrously led by Ramsay MacDonald seemed able to prevent starvation in the midst of plenty. We of the various progressive parties found this intolerable. In America, in 1929, there came the spectacular Wall Street Crash, when the comfortable supporters of capitalism, unshaken by the General Strike, began to share our discomfort and uncertainty.

There were three nations, with apparently contrasting ways of conducting their affairs, who seemed to be growing rather than wilting: Russia and the two Fascist powers, Italy and Germany. The politics of the decade come back to me as presenting a constant series of value judgements (i.e. moral problems) about foreign and home affairs that became successively more urgent and more difficult.

Consider the situation of a few of my own friends and fellow-writers, say Rose Macaulay, Storm Jameson, E. M. Forster, H. G. Wells and Bertrand Russell. As time went on we found ourselves deciding and, being writers, having to declare, in favour of providing arms for the legitimate Spanish government. This was when Franco rose against it. France and Britain, we had to protest, ought not to stay neutral but ought on the contrary to re-arm themselves. It was urgent to respond fully to the young legitimate Spanish republic's plea for help. It was not only the crisis in Spain that brought up the moral questions; they happened again and again in the context of Hitler's various invasions – the Rhineland, Austria, Czechoslovakia. It wasn't easy for the likes of us to say successively that Hitler ought to be stopped at this point or that by force. Even many successful writers, like Charles

Morgan, who were either Conservative or politically numb, suffered bewildering and unexpected doubts.

There were questions in home politics also, like those of the Sphinx, to which wrong answers might be politically fatal. Was it 'loyal' to go on supporting such a Labour Government as the one led by Ramsay MacDonald, or patriotically to tolerate that lamentable coalition, or a government led by Stanley Baldwin or Neville Chamberlain? In this context there were urgent economic questions. There were two million unemployed, which seemed intolerable for Fabians such as Leonard Woolf and for the Independent Labour Party, and for parliament-arians such as Aneurin Bevan and for my brother John. For them one Sphinx question succeeded another. For anyone in Parliament, it must be repeated, it would have proved to be political death to give certain answers.

Such was the background, as we saw it, to the creeping, malignant Fascist growth, for abroad as well as here there was economic recession, but magnified. The unemployment crisis was made humanly far more poignant by a means test that further constricted life on the inadequate dole, social services were few, in fact there was nothing that could be called 'Welfare' about the State.

The famous march from Jarrow with little Ellen Wilkinson heading it really was a 'Hunger March'. The Liverpool march of early summer 1981 was – thank goodness – about jobs and about the right to work – and not about enough food for the marchers' children.

The 1980s, so far, have been a time of miserable frustrations, but nothing like the winters of the 1930s, winters of dole queues in the streets in cold and wind. Young people today have never seen the ill-shod, overcoatless, winding queues that I watched then, winter after winter, watched in my brother's constituency in those Birmingham winds, and in the rain of the South Wales valleys.

We asked ourselves what ought to be done and wondered whether it would help for those who could to give up all their normal work and pursuits in view of the economic crisis. Few of us did that.

Historians tidy up periods of doubt, unrest, and alternate hopes and fears so that a reader may get the impression that, in time of crisis, everyone relegated their ordinary lives to second place and gave their whole attention to public affairs, but I'll wager they never did, not even in the run-up to the Civil War between Charles I and the Parliament men.

For hours and days and weeks in the 1930s I was busy writing a school history of England with a historian colleague (F. J. Fisher) and I know, and knew then, that I and my collaborator somehow made events seem unnaturally rational. So I can give no true impression of what the 1930s felt like if I tidy things up and say nothing about cross-cutting, contrary currents, ambitions, desires, impulses, the ambiguities and irrelevancies that constantly intruded. They must not be forgotten in the interests of producing a couple of tidy chapters.

I cannot pretend that we never forgot, never enjoyed life. It was, however, in the second half of the Thirties that one definite shadow now and then crept up on me, as it must have done on many other mothers. Our son Christopher would soon no longer be just a boy. Girls had not been conscripted 'last time', so that our Susan and Charlotte seemed unlikely to be at risk.

Anyhow, as yet they were all three children and developing normally, so they were asking questions. This was why I was writing a history, for now these questions were not quite the questions of their earlier years such as 'What are birds for?' but questions that were still stimulating. I asked various friends if they thought writing a school history a useful thing to do. Storm Jameson, a political mentor of mine, thought yes; my brother John thought no.

Clough's practice was flourishing. Among usual jobs for clients, he was working at something that he found fascinating. This was the rehabilitation of Stowe, perhaps the most famous of the eighteenth-century country houses in England. Alexander Pope, who knew them all, had seen Stowe as exemplary: 'Nature shall join you/Time shall make it grow/A place to wonder at/Perhaps a Stowe.' Clough was happy. There was a great avenue, temples and terraces, and it was one of those half dozen houses which, legend asserts, had a window for every day of the year. Clough's task was to make the great neglected structure viable (others were to make it financially possible) as a new public school. When, for the first time, he walked up the great steps leading to the grand porticoed entrance, he found a handbell on a little bamboo table with which to announce his arrival. The plumbing was on the same scale, for it consisted of one water closet and one cold tap in the basement!

It would need, they said, to Clough's great satisfaction, subsidiary buildings. Stowe had long been famous for its temples and pavilions, and for new structures a very respectful hand was needed, for the great house, vistas, temples and trees had been a splendid and integrated work of art.

Would it have been right to try to pass on worry to Clough, so happy and well engaged? His Portmeirion was flourishing too. Clough was having the greatest pleasure with that on a scale that seemed charmingly miniature compared to Stowe – urns, vistas, a waterfall, as well as elegantly rural little buildings and now a clientèle that sparkled. Not the least of his delights at Portmeirion was not having a client. Clough could be the sole arbiter, for there were also, then, no Building Regulations, no Town and Country Planning Act, no regulations about Historic Buildings and, though he thought there ought to be all these things (and he said so repeatedly), privately, secretly, he relished their absence.

I was busy writing the history book, being a wife and mother, and, as usual, I was trying to learn to write better; and, oh yes, also trying to enjoy myself, and succeeding. Clough was teaching me to sail and I was improving, and there was the more obvious kind of pleasure, of going to parties and giving them. Clough's *Architect Errant* is full of accounts of parties that we gave at our Romney House in Hampstead, for there was, as there had been in 1913, plenty of glitter.

Bob Boothby, for long a friend of my brother, an MP and a great party-goer and country-house visitor, was one who called the years between 1925 and 1935 'the happiest and most amusing' of his life. Those, as he wrote in his *Recollections of a Rebel*[1], were, once more, the days of the big country houses that Henry James had described so well. They were again the days of butlers and footmen, of gleaming silver, log fires and private golf courses. 'Fortunately', as he wrote, 'the unemployed were out of sight; and I'm afraid, out of mind.'

There were said to be five great hostesses. Of these Lady Colefax was the one that we knew. The Sitwells made a speciality of mocking her as a climber, and indeed I remember thinking to myself that at one time we all stood together on one level, and then with much amusement we watched her ankles disappearing up the ladder of social success. The Sitwells put it about that she insured her visiting list and address book for thousands of pounds. I know what the Sitwells meant when they sent her a postcard from the Alps: 'Wish you were here, the climbing is splendid!' But all the same I found that what she did was often enjoyable. In her house in Chelsea she specialized in luncheon parties for writers. These became famous. Arnold Bennett, H. G. Wells, and Max Beerbohm were often there, and it was at her lunch table that there took place one of my favourite conversations. Mrs Patrick Campbell, the eminent actress – Eliza Doolittle in Shaw's *Pygmalion* – had a most beautiful voice, soft, deep like black velvet. Sitting next to my cousin Lytton Strachey, she said:

'Oh, Mr Strachey, you will write a play for me, won't you? The sort of part I want . . .' and, going on in considerable detail, she ended up, 'You will write it, Mr Strachey, won't you?'

His high falsetto came back with one word: 'No.'

Was such social life and conspicuous consumption shocking? I think not. Bob Boothby, for instance, though apt to trip from time to time over the rich folds of the red carpet of his life, played a valiant part in trying to convince the Establishment of the dangers of Fascism. Often unselfishly and even diligently he used his position in the Conservative Party, in smart society and in the House of Commons to help in what we also were doing in our more nitty-gritty way.

The workers seemed generally more concerned with the recession, and didn't look abroad so much. This was no wonder, considering how sharply the economic situation affected their lives. As for my own associates, we felt that we had remedies for the recession but not for the foreign situation. It was a little alarming to us that the workers should not be more aware, but in all the propaganda I have ever done, it has always seemed more difficult to get an audience to look abroad. This was for long not, I think, indifference but diffidence. There was a feeling that people abroad should be left to settle their own affairs; a feeling opposite to the 'white man's burden' of the Establishment.

So we felt our job was to warn our apparently supine leaders that Germany was re-arming, and under the guidance of the most cunning, ruthless and efficient gang ever assembled since the days of Genghis Khan. But like the rest of us, Bob gradually found that there are indeed none so deaf as those who won't hear.

Tom (Oswald) Mosley had crossed the floor of the House from the Conservatives to become a member of the Labour Party, chiefly on economic theory. He and my brother were, like Bob Boothby, apt (as on our Venetian excursion) to enjoy themselves, but they were less thorough about it than Bob Boothby. Pleasure was only pursued between anxious moments and was often quite different to the pleasures promoted by, say, Lady Cunard. She, by the way, at about this time changed her Christian name from Maud to Emerald. This is what Clough wrote of one of our politically more relevant pleasures:

It was at Amabel's instigation that I joined the ILP and lectured on town and country planning at one of their summer schools at Lady Warwick's Easton Lodge. All the left-wing top brass of the time were there – Ramsay Macdonald, James Maxton, Aneurin Bevan, Jennie Lee, Clifford Allen, Oswald and Cynthia Mosley, H. G. Wells and my brother-in-law, John Strachey. Of our almost incredible hostess, Daisy Warwick, we got a more intimate close-up later on when we spent a quiet weekend with her. We both fully appreciated the fascination for which she had so long been famed. Certainly she charmed me into planning her a model village which she proposed to establish in her park. [It never got off the drawing-board.][2]

I don't think Clough's list of notables is right, but no matter. In a novel that I wrote, *The Wall of Glass*, I put in portraits of some of the people who came to these summer schools. Aneurin Bevan for instance, with his sense of fun and the stammer that he used so well; James Maxton, the only orator who ever really moved me; and of course Oswald (Tom) Mosley.

Many people in the Labour Party had already begun to admire Tom Mosley, and yet felt doubtful; after all, before he crossed the floor of the House, he had had minor office under the Conservatives. Mrs Sidney Webb wrote of him in her diary, after first meeting him as a potential Front Bench Labour man: 'The perfect politician who is also a gentleman. Tall and slim, his features not too handsome to be strikingly peculiar to himself . . . a pleasant voice . . . an accomplished orator in the grand style . . .' Then, old political hand that she was, she added: 'Is there in him some weak spot which will be revealed in time of stress by letting your cause down, or sweeping it out of the way?' Aneurin Bevan, like Mrs Webb, felt the attraction but, like her, had doubts.

Writing in my *Wall of Glass* (the title, by the way, signifying the way in which in the class struggle the two sides saw each other but often communicated so imperfectly), I tried to show by fiction rather than by fact something of Tom Mosley's effect on the ordinary ILP member, and chose as a symbol his arriving at an ILP summer school with much too grand luggage. I seem to remember a pigskin suitcase and he may have taken golf clubs as well as a tennis racquet. Comrades pausing before the literature stall to flutter the leaves of *News From Nowhere* or a pamphlet on the Capital Levy might have eyed him and his belongings with more than mild surprise. In Labour gatherings such as a summer school he was apt to walk through the life of the place, but this was seldom if ever resented. After all, he genuinely wanted to know other people's views on currency or Communism, and what votes could be expected in this or that constituency. The impression was of a keen-eyed champion.

Maxton and Jennie Lee were among those who particularly stick in my mind. Jennie, whenever she appeared, was the cynosure of every eye, and it turned out that she was one of those beauties whom, like Virginia Woolf, the passing years make more beautiful. It is impossible in print to reproduce the lovely cadences of Maxton's voice. He had a Clydeside accent, rolled his Rs, had slightly modified grammar, and had deep-set meditative eyes; he gesticulated constantly with a cigarette-stained hand. There are those who considered Aneurin Bevan the better speaker, but though he was so invigorating, he never moved me as Maxton did.

The Labour Government, in spite of ginger from us of the Independent Labour Party, seemed to be failing, and the other parties seemed to have nothing to give. Lady Violet Bonham-Carter (Mr Asquith's daughter), a leader in her half of the Liberal Party, suggested that neither Conservative nor Labour nor the Liberals had anything to offer. As in the 1980s, no constructive policies seemed to have a chance of being accepted or put into operation; certainly they were not being put forward by any of the three traditional parties. (The recession, as I write this, is the same; the danger is different.)

In the 1930s the home question was could the Left unite? But it must be repeated that many of us looked more uneasily abroad. For pacifists, many of them in the Independent Labour Party, moral choices felt particularly difficult. Many members of the ILP held typical, Christian, non-conformist views. Many of them were indeed active members of the Society of Friends. How were they to answer the successive Sphinx questions about the rise of Fascism? And what about the differently orientated 'one world' advocates, non-Christians like Bertrand Russell and H. G. Wells?

There wasn't too much common ground. The Fabians, some specializing in foreign relations and the Empire–Leonard Woolf for example, who couldn't stand the Communists–and others who were in Economics–notably Maynard Keynes, the Webbs, and writers such as Bernard Shaw–had at least got in common such things as that they were people for whom reparations had been all along an increasingly dirty word. They had seen the Versailles Treaty as poison. All these found themselves involved, as the situation developed, in continually making new and crucial value judgements. One of these was whether, or how far, it would be possible to make a united front with the Communists. The Webbs and Shaw said 'Yes'. In general, the question arose of whether or not it would be possible for all the varieties of left-wing opinion to combine. Could they stick together? They had before them the fatal example of the German Left, which in 1933 was being far too easily overrun by the Nazis because the various opponents of Hitler and all he stood for failed to unite.

I was one of those who found it possible and necessary to work with the Communists. Leonard Woolf, more diligent, single-minded and particular than I, found it impossible. He was later to be revolted by what he called the 'savage stupidity' of the Russian Communist Party under Stalin. 'Russian Communists were', he wrote in 1964, 'continually torturing and murdering their fellow Communists on such grounds as that they were either Right deviationists or Left deviationists.' The Fascists were, however, worse:

In Italy there was established a dictator who, with a political doctrine purporting to be the exact opposite of Russian communism, produced much less efficiently the same results.

In Germany the same phenomena appeared, but the barbarism of Hitler and the Nazis shows itself, in the years from 1933 to 1939, to be much nastier, more menacing, more insane . . . The last years of peace [from 1937 to 1939] were the most horrible period of my life. As one crisis followed upon another, engineered by Adolf Hitler, one gradually realized that power to determine history and the fate of Europe and all Europeans had slipped into the hands of a sadistic madman.[3]

Even when the danger of our being overwhelmed and enslaved by the forces we had failed to contain seemed likely, there were many who, like Leonard Woolf, had scruples about contact with the Communists:

I was asked by Victor Gollancz, Harold Laski and John Strachey to write a book for the Left Book Club. I wrote a book to which I gave the title *Barbarians at the Gate* . . . I met the critics in Victor's office after dinner. They were upset by my criticism of the Russian Communists and their government. The modifications which they asked for would, I felt, be dishonest, from my point of view, for they would obscure what, in my opinion, was the truth about authoritarianism in the Russia of Stalin.[4]

Leonard was more squeamish than I. The failure of the German Left to unite was to me a terrible precedent. I remember when, in the mid-Thirties, I had to fill in with a speech to a small audience whose political colour I didn't know. I made the point that Germany had been the first country to be overrun by Hitler. The divisions in Germany and in our own country were a crucial point with a lot of people; I mean the kind whom we might call the 'thinking Tories' and also the 'feeling Tories'. They, or some of them, became gradually more uneasy and uncomfortable as they began to see through Mussolini's 'good deeds'. True, he really had drained the Pontine marshes and 'Giovanista' really was a capital marching song, but even before the invasion of Abyssinia other aspects of his Fascist state began to appear; aspects that they, as well as we, saw as unacceptable. The posturings of il Duce began to seem sinister, rather than theatrical and absurd.

Among the thinking and feeling Right there were many academics and other agreeable and not unintelligent men and women who, for quite a while, really did give quite a lot of weight to Hitler's constant assurances that he was not a new Bismarck, but a progressive. They had disliked, just as we did, the harsh, vindictive Versailles Treaty, had thought all along that the Allies' reiterated claims for reparations were sordid. Especially they felt that German culture and scholarship ought once more to be added to the common stock of humanity. For quite a long time these decent innocents supposed that it was this new Adolf Hitler who could do the much needed job, above all that he (with Bismarck and Kaiserism forgotten) could restore Germany's self-respect and bring her back to all she had been in the culture of the West.

As for the mass of the people, the miners in the South Wales valleys shall represent them all here. They were not, I confess, really typical except of other mining communities. Elsewhere, as I have said, it was home economics that were the debating points, but the miners had stayed out after the collapse of the General Strike.

Because of having had a look at the Don coalfields with my brother (still on the editorial board of *The Miner*) I was invited to go round some of the miners' lodges and other gatherings to speak about the miners in Russia and the things that I had seen. Before adopting a point of view, they wanted to know whether Russia was in fact the Fatherland of the Workers, as many propagandists were assuring them, or the graveyard of all idealistic hopes, as progressives such as Leonard Woolf felt sure.

To go to South Wales was doubly interesting to me. For one thing, it was a chance to see something of another kind of Wales. Because I was still, as usual, trying to improve myself in my craft, I kept diary notes, of dialogue, landscape, sights, sounds and streetscapes. I was gathering impressions of an industrial complex that was new to me. On 9 May 1932 I found myself in Tonypandy:

First impression that the Rhondda Valley is not all that black. The Mountain – steep grass sides to the winding valleys. Like the South Downs only that it is lumpy and with rock bones coming through, and of course has the mine buildings and winding gear. All less ugly and much less derelict than was supposed, at least by me. It's not as bad as the Aston division of Birmingham, for example, or Oldham, because you have the sense that it has edges. The urban part never seems to be more than, say, a mile and a half wide. You can look out of it, you can look across it. However, squalor is very apparent if you hunt about a little. Empty shops in the main streets. As in our Blaenau Ffestiniog there are sheep which act as scavengers here, rather as half-wild dogs do in the East. Very dirty – I don't know whether anybody uses their wool or not. The miners' 'rows' cut straight across contours with no concession to the shape of the land at all. Individual houses often very cramped.

I talked with a woman who lived in a three-roomed house with her husband, her sister and her husband, and eleven children. Her daughter of nineteen had an illegitimate child of four. She was a wild kind of girl who laughed and laughed at whatever she said or was being said around her. She had tried service, she said, never kept a place for more than six weeks, some only for one week.

Most of these houses have no drains and, for the most part, only one tap to a terrace. But here and there a house had water laid on. Sanitation, an earth closet, *tŷ bach*, down the path. The people I was billeted with told me a lot of gossip. One tale was about a girl who couldn't get on with her husband. She was a Communist and he a Conservative. There was a baby that died. Her solution was to go into service as a nanny in Cardiff.

Another neighbour was an old lady who had had a stroke. When she was thirty-six she had been left a widow with six children. She married a man of twenty-seven.

'Was he kind to your children?'

'Well, he brought back his money all right.'

Now a married daughter living two streets away talks about his conduct. The old lady is now seventy-five or so. When she had the stroke she fell into the fire and was burnt a bit, but she kept about. He didn't let anyone know what had happened. Then she had another stroke.

'Queenie, that's my sister, has been up four nights with her and I five, and Rene (another sister) three, so you see we've had our hands full. *He* won't let her or us have anything, we must bring even our own milk, sugar and tea, and every night he gets into bed with her, and she can't bear it. I thought if one of us daughters could go and live there, she could do the day and we could manage nights, but *he* says, "I don't want none of you here." My older sister's enormously stout, you know. It isn't money. *He* has got hundreds of pounds saved, but he says that he's going to send my mother to the Union. We must prevent a thing like that. Isn't it awful to have reared nine children and then be treated like that when you're old!'

People talked about the time after the General Strike when the miners were still out, especially a nice little old man – quite sure about the Russians – who walked a four to six hours' round with the *Daily Worker* every day. We were talking in the kitchen with a very hot fire and very bright brass. I was cleaning my teeth at the small sink in the scullery. 'We had a demo here. Ooh, it was fine! Twenty thousand there must have been. We didn't half look the coppers in the face that time! The roads belonged to us that day!'

No. 8 Tyntyla Avenue, Llwynypia, reading the last instalment of one of John's books. Bright sunshine on the parallelograms of the slate roofs of the miners' rows, chickens everywhere underfoot. In the middle of the valley a tall stack and long thin plume of smoke. Sound: ger-lump, ger-lump, from the mineral trains. Now and then a faint, dismal horn. This is the rag-and-bone man and his tired horse. Local version of 'Death and His Pale Horse'. Far away a 'squiffer' in the hands of a convalescent patient from the fever hospital. The sheep as usual coming to tip over garbage pails.

Later in the afternoon at the pit-head, men coming off shift, their lips scarlet in the black faces, eyelids white, eyes shifting nimbly about, squinting a bit in the daylight.

Sunday evening: young people walking on the Mountain; whistling groups of young men passing remarks at groups of girls. The men wearing dashing coloured mufflers; groups of girls with linked arms, giggling. One group of young men start throwing stones at a party of girls. This is taken, and meant, as a compliment, but it seemed to me there was a lot of real sex antagonism. Mining is a dangerous trade and the position of the women is not good, and having this bad position makes them backward and hen-brained, so the men hate them.

This was not, of course, my only visit to South Wales. I went on to look at Cardiff Docks and also at how steel was then made. Going back a year or two later, I remember saying to someone from Tonypandy who happened to be in Cardiff: 'How do you like having a Communist as the miners' leader?' Arthur Horner had just been elected.

'Oh, Arthur's all right,' said he. 'You say "Nice day, Arthur, isn't it?" and blimey, he's got to ring up King Street to know is it!' This was said with an amiable laugh.

Twenty-One

WORDS AND SILENCE

By the mid-1930s, even the most optimistic of those whom we might call the Conservative anti-Fascists had begun to feel a more urgent sense of alarm at the build-up of power the Nazis seemed to be achieving, always in a fog of denials. The typical Hitler saying, 'My patience is exhausted', seemed to be alternating with, 'We have no more territorial ambitions.' Bob Boothby renewed his warnings at Conservative dinner tables, while in the Press the silence began to seem more sinister.

Lady Anglesey told me lately about an incident that concerned her father, Charles Morgan, then one of the least subversive of the serious popular novelists. He was then drama critic of *The Times*. After having been to report the famous Passion Play at Oberammergau, he had sent a despatch to his office describing what he felt to be the dangerous mood among the audience, a very large audience and predominantly German. Disturbingly, as he felt, this part of his critical opinion got an unusual reception: it was not printed. Such reports and impressions of what was going on in Germany, especially from well-known Conservatives, were, as the Berlin Press Corps had found, progressively more often called 'unhelpful'.

Leonard Woolf went on expressing reluctance to work with Communists, but many of us believed that it was ever more urgent to establish a solid anti-Fascist front, but we couldn't do much except write and protest.

The news grew bad and then worse. The Nazis re-armed (contrary to Treaty terms). Hitler introduced conscription (1935), marched an army to the old German frontier of the Rhine (1936), occupied Austria (March 1938), then part of Czech territory (October 1938), and then the whole of that country (March 1939).

When the Spanish Civil War began in 1936, the involvement of the Left became a matter of life and death for individuals. Till then our efforts must often have seemed comically amateurish and futile to our powerful opponents. We realized this and yet we persisted. The part that was played by us who were writers must have seemed especially inadequate and ridiculous to the Nazis, who, as they said openly, didn't give a tinker's cuss for culture. But we, without believing Shelley's charmingly boyish assertion that poets and writers are 'the un-acknowledged legislators of mankind', we yet felt that we must doggedly do what we could in our own line. I agreed to join the editorial board of a new literary monthly, *Left Review*, because not only was Germany surreptitiously arming but also Goering had begun saying such things as, 'When I hear the word "culture" I reach for my six-shooter.'

We wanted to make plain that Goering was talking like a gangster and that for us what he called 'culture' was important. It was in this context that I found myself in Moscow as British delegate at an International Writers' Conference. There were many speeches by the famous and those who were soon to become famous. Some of these speeches were excellent – Ehrenburg's particularly struck me. Most were long and predictable to anyone used to writers' conferences such as those of the PEN Club.

What really seemed absolutely new, and interested me very much about this particular congress, was the way in which the public participated and the way in which readers were encouraged to talk and express their points of view. In the ten days of the conference, dozens of deputations from readers spoke. The first came from an industry about which I already knew a little: a young 'shock brigader' spoke for the coal miners of the Don. Peasants, textile workers, engineers, the army and navy, all, like the miners, said in effect: 'Writers! You should write about us! We are doing something new in the world. We are building a new nation out of the ruins.'

The Russian sense of theatre was strong. The railway workers started their deputation off with a whistle and a green flag, and most brought presents. The Tula factory workers brought a brand new samovar and a sporting gun, peasant groups from the south brought grapes, from central Russia it was grain, from the north furs. Altogether there was country produce only a little more exotic than one would expect at an English harvest festival, so that the conference hall soon began to look countrified.

Nor was this all. One afternoon, towards the end, the whole conference adjourned to Moscow's Park of Rest and Culture. There, in the tradition of most conferences, we visited a big exhibition, and moreover there were speeches. But what was unexpected were the processions and also in the outdoor stadium there was an assembly that seemed to be of at least ten thousand readers, as well as (inevitably in Russia) brass and balalaika bands. But it was the processions that were the most surprising.

People with a sense of satire and who had not suffered 'improving' novels gladly had been at work. We were confronted by pantomime figures, some of them on stilts, all with enormous comic heads. Some were dressed as pioneer komsomols. They had ridiculous simpering faces and large blue eyes lifted to the skies; they carried banners: 'When you write about us boys and girls, don't make us look like this.' Tiny children were also represented by grotesques and again had faces of idiotic naivety: 'We children don't look like this. Don't write as if we did.' The peasants had the same sort of thing to say. A girl in peasant dress with enormous red cheeks and little pig eyes and a loutish boy with a thatch of straw instead of hair and enormous feet carried a banner: 'Writers! We peasants are not a bit like this.' Finally there were critics who danced about on stilts, vicious, bilious grotesques with red noses, dissatisfied expressions and pairs of enormous shears in their hands: 'We are the critics. It is we who will cut up your books in the end.'

It was Maxim Gorky who opened the conference. He spoke, as all Russians do, at length and talked about the Union of Soviet Writers itself and its aims. A point that struck me, however, was a comment he made on children's books. There was still in what they called 'the deaf villages' quite serious belief in magic and sorcery. Returning soldiers had met with accusations of what amounted to possessing the evil eye and of 'overlooking'. Moscow had thus decreed that children were, for the present, to have no more fairy tales; the word went out, 'Animals must not speak.' The great Gorky said this was bureaucratic nonsense. Fairy tales are, he said, everywhere part of a country's cultural heritage and Russian children were not to be deprived.

Two of the best children's writers, Marshak and Chukovsky, read English as easily as Russian and were great admirers of Lear's Nonsense Books and of Lewis Carroll's *Alice* and of his *Hunting of the Snark*, and (agreeing with Gorky) also of our traditional nursery rhymes and fairy tales, and of those of Germany. 'Write the truth for children by all means,' said Marshak over a glass of tea, 'but write it so surprisingly that it will have the element of astonishment and magic. This a child reader demands.'

It turned out that somehow I was the only English delegate at the conference and so it fell to me to write, for *Left Review*, a longish account of the working part, and I included some of those points that had pleased and refreshed me – reader participation, the crowds, and the air of festivity. Back at home there was criticism. This was written much later and marks a depressing change:

In its second number *Left Review* printed a report on the Congress by Amabel Williams-Ellis, who was an editor of the journal and had been the only

British delegate in Moscow. Strangely enough in her report she neither mentioned the concept of Socialist Realism nor gave much space to the other leading theme, the taking-over and critical revaluation of the bourgeois literary tradition. One cannot help wondering whether she fully understood what was on the agenda.[1]

(I didn't.) This was the age when 'Prolit-cult' became powerful. A further comment was that I had said nothing about the 'utter decadence of bourgeois literature'. I remembered with sorrow not so long ago as I read this the carnival figures of the critics in that cheerful park in Moscow, and I reflected that some Communists had more fun than others.

A quite different kind of United Front activity took me out of Britain again.

It seems worthwhile to tell the tale in some detail. This is because I am convinced that its laborious inconclusiveness is typical of half the international missions and newspaper reporters' efforts at investigation that go on all the time but are never recorded, even with a sigh. I don't mean those missions that are conducted at some prestigious summit conference, nor those that end, like Watergate, in a world scandal and a national upheaval. But I firmly believe it is typical, though in my case trains rather than planes were involved. I know for a fact that it was very much like many of the efforts of Amnesty International on behalf of prisoners of conscience or of quite a few sorties by investigative journalists. The run-around and the interviews with big-wigs that don't come off, the wear and tear of shuttle journeys, the unsatisfactory long-distance telephone calls, keeping your temper with odiously ingratiating or uncivil opponents, are all typical. Nor is it altogether unusual for the envoy or for a special correspondent not to have a very clear idea of the scale of what might or might not be achieved, or what is at stake. I did not, for example, realize that Dimitrov, the prisoner I was concerned with, was a big fish. Some say, with hindsight, that he had indeed been the alternative to Stalin.

I have an idea that all those bargainings typical of the Crusades, and Benjamin Franklin's negotiations over the American War of Independence, were often just like this. Remember Stendhal's Fabrice, who wondered whether the boring and apparently aimless days he had spent had really been a battle; it was Waterloo.

I kept a diary of this, to me, new type of activity. On Monday, 15 January 1934 I met Ivor Montagu, the film writer, at dinner. He was, I knew, active on the United Front.

'I suppose you're not free to go abroad?' says he.

'I don't know why not,' says I.

The consequence was that three days afterwards at 8.30 pm I was in the train on the way to Berlin with an introduction to a number of Press men, some of whom happened to be on the same train.

The Bulgarians I was supposed to help were Dimitrov, Popov and Taniev. They had been involved in the trial of van der Lubbe, who had been accused of setting the Reichstag building on fire. The Bulgarians had been acquitted, but nevertheless had been in gaol for a month since this acquittal. Dimitrov's old mother, her elder daughter Baranova, Taniev's wife and their interpreter Bogdan Danovsky were all in Leipzig. The women were allowed to see the men twice a week for a quarter of an hour, and they were said to be taking food in to them every day, though Tanova had not been allowed into the prison for nearly three weeks, on the grounds that she wasn't Taniev's legal wife.

None of the people I was to see were staying at the Central Hotel. I rang Wadsworth and a couple of other newspaper correspondents, and heard that a letter from Dorothy Woodman was at the British Embassy. Wadsworth came round to the Central Hotel to see me, took me round to see other correspondents, and we spent all that evening talking. Gallagher (the sole Communist member of the British Parliament) was supposed to be staying in the hotel, but he was out. On the next day, Friday, I went to Leipzig. The Bulgarians' interpreter Danovsky had been banished from the Free State of Saxony and the three women spoke no German or English. They were not to be found, but I gathered they were just off to the prison. I made contact only by leaving word.

I went back to Berlin to spread the tale, that is to say, tell the correspondents what little more I knew and to emphasize what this meant in human terms. Danovsky joined me in Berlin. I put in, via Voigt, to the People's Propaganda Ministry for an interview with Goebbels, preferably on the afternoon of Friday 19th. Then on Saturday afternoon, after not getting any answer about the interview, Voigt said he would ring up. Again I went off to Leipzig for the weekend. I was to try to get a report on a doctor's visit (this must have been on the prisoners' physical condition). This I got and was busy after that translating it as best I could. It was in German–in German handwriting moreover–I tried to guess at the doctor's attitude.

Next morning I went to the Leipzig Police Praesidium, and had an interview with a small bureaucrat with waxed moustaches–formal, mild and troubled. He kept nervously typing out who I was and what I had come about. The typing was no doubt for someone greater than himself. I also had an interview with Ebbeke, one of their Foreign Office people. This ended in his banging on the table and shouting over and over again, 'We know better than you do! We know better than you do!' He refused to allow the interpreter back into Saxony. I explained in vain how hard this was on the women, told him how they talked nothing but Bulgarian, but it didn't make any difference. Back at the hotel where the women were staying, I telephoned to Berlin, telephoned to London. Then walked to the prison with Tanova. What she took on that occasion was a kettle, shoes, and some hard-boiled eggs.

On Tuesday I went back to Berlin, still trying to get the interview with Goebbels. In between whiles, in Berlin I was inclined to go to the Taverna, where the correspondents gathered, and also tried to get through to London to *Time and Tide*, which was expecting an article. The correspondents seemed keen that I should go to the Taverna as often as I could because they said some of the things I was doing were not too safe.

I said rather haughtily, 'Oh, I'm not afraid. I've got a British passport.'

They laughed and said, 'That won't help you. Don't you know what happens?'

'No, I don't.'

'Well, our advice to you is don't walk too near the kerb.'

'What d'you mean?' I asked.

'Well, the technique is that you get jostled, and there happens to be a big van – a *camion* – coming along just at that moment rather close to the kerb; you stumble and fall under it, and the remains are sent back to London with the most polite apologies for this most unfortunate "street accident".'

I heeded their advice and after that walked more carefully.

On Wednesday, in Berlin, I tried by telephone and personal visit and every sort of effort to find out if I was really going to get the Goebbels interview, as promised. But in the end I was informed by Goebbels' adjutant that, 'Dr Goebbels knows nothing of the way in which the case of the Bulgarians has developed', and that anyhow it was not in his department. 'He will refer you to the Ministry of the Interior.' So then an interview was arranged with the eternal Dr Erbe (I can't think now why I called him 'the eternal Dr Erbe' – I suppose I had been put off by him before).

Well, that interview did take place, at 3.30 at the Ministry of the Interior. Waiting for a while and looking out of the window, what surprised me was to see the Reichstag building standing there apparently perfectly intact. I felt sorry for van der Lubbe. I suppose it really was gutted inside, but it certainly didn't look as if a stone had been so much as scorched.

What happened at the interview I related in the following week's *Time and Tide* and in the *Manchester Guardian* of Tuesday 30 January. The only point I didn't get into either of these articles was Erbe's little aside, when I told him that in England we took a great interest in the case. 'Ah,' said he, 'yes, you in England have always been the ones counting on a little amusement.'

On Friday I made what I hoped would be my last journey to Leipzig, then visited the Taverna, where Bodka took me on this occasion, and then on with some of them to a party. Putzi Hanfstangel was there. Dancing with Putzi: '*Wie hast du schoene blauer augen.*' And then again: 'Your hair, it is *prachtvoll*, splendid!' 'And what political party do you belong to? How many children have you got? So you interest yourself in these three Bulgarians, do you? I wonder why? That is so, isn't it? How strange! But don't you know what we shall do with those Bulgarians?'

'No, I don't,' I said.

'We shall send them back to Bulgaria, of course, you silly thing. That is now my name for you – sweet little *dumchen.*'

Saturday, most unwillingly, to Leipzig again to try, all in vain, to get poor Danovsky his passport and visa to Saxony. Dined one evening with Albion Ross, but forget which evening. Saw Wadsworth and a lot of the other Press people again. A wonderful send-off to the train. Very kind!

It didn't strike me at the time, but it does now, that one reason why the newspaper correspondents were so welcoming when I came and gave me such a splendid send-off when I went was a wistful feeling that as a newcomer I might help to break what I came to call to myself 'the silence'. Nobody was printing the warnings that they were sending back. At the time I attributed my welcome to what Hanfstangel had called my *prachtvoll* Titian hair and blue eyes.

A little later I went to Berlin once again, but this time as part of a delegation. We flew out, a number of us, trying to do something for Thaelmann and von Osietski and other prisoners of conscience. The highlight of the visit was going to the Sports Palatz to one of the big Nazi rallies. It was to hear Goebbels, the Minister of Propaganda, or 'Wotan's Mickey Mouse' as he was nicknamed. It was splendidly produced. The whole place was packed and was decked out with swastikas and the Nazi eagle. The platform party didn't appear from behind the stage but walked right along the whole length of the Sports

Palatz – a very big building – between rows of saluting young SS men. A compact little body of them was surrounding something or somebody, one couldn't see what. Then, when they got up the steps to the platform, tremendous spotlights shone upon them and the tall young men opened out for the audience to see in the middle the little, lame figure of a man in a mackintosh, the effect being, 'Here is all this military pomp, but the real thing is the tribune of the people – Dr Goebbels – a friend of humanity', and all that sort of thing. My German isn't very good but I have heard a lot of public speaking and can affirm that Goebbels was a superb speaker. He used every sort of device: he altered the pitch of his voice, he altered his pace, he looked anxious, he looked inspired, he opened his heart, and, in short, it really was a triumphant performance, with cheering whenever he made a point, and he was excellent at stopping the cheering and then going on with what he had to say.

At the end of it all there was a tremendous cry of 'Heil Hitler!' Everybody stood up. We couldn't bear to stand up and put our arms out and cry 'Heil Hitler', which involved us in a certain amount of discord with our immediate neighbours. However nothing happened, but it was odd – one just couldn't bear to do it.

One of the things that came of that visit was that we looked after Osietski's daughter for some time. Where she went after she left us I don't remember, but we certainly had her in Wales at Brondanw for several weeks. She got on fairly well with my own children. She was a great admirer of Marlene Dietrich. She kept on about '*Ach, die Marlena, die Marlena*', but she was quite a nice child.

There were other efforts far more spectacular than mine. Earlier on it had seemed to a good many people who were less than delighted with the muddle and lack of achievement of the Labour Party, Baldwin or Chamberlain that home affairs and our economic recession must be attended to, and not only was it necessary to present a united front to the Nazis but also to show them an economically viable Britain.

This is not the place to tell at any length the often-told story of what came of one political effort to get an economic basis at home. This was the formation of the New Party.

In this tale my brother John played a prominent part, working hard and hopefully with Mosley and also with the charming Cynthia Mosley. What everyone knows is how wrong this went. Tom was fascinating, as all women (Mrs Sidney Webb and I included) had to agree, but when he made romantic advances I found myself drawing back. He seemed to have all the right views, he was fascinating, he was handsome, he was pressing, but I felt that he had to be resisted. I recall vividly a scene concerning Tom with my brother in the Harcourt Room of the House of Commons. Looking over my shoulder for listeners, I had begged my brother not to resign from the Labour Party. I agreed that it was currently in a disastrous state, but said that this sickness was surely not terminal. It could be cured and a cure should be attempted from within. But my brother, quick and vigorous as he was, had already even at that early epoch felt that there wasn't time. Something very definite had to be done and done quickly. Britain was in such economic disarray that Hitler would feel that what Britain might do didn't matter.

'Tom Mosley is in a hurry too? He feels, like you, Anything to stop the rot?'

'Yes,' said John.

'But couldn't Tom's "anything" include things you couldn't stand? For goodness' sake, do watch out! He might go Fascist on you and take the New Party with him.'

John shook his head, sure that I was wrong. However, he swore that at the least sign of that, without losing a moment, he would leave Tom.

'And be without a party at all?'

He said that it was a time to take risks.

One of Mosley's trusted colleagues in the Labour Party had been Dr Forgan, whom I also knew, not as well as Tom Mosley but well enough to remonstrate when he followed his leader and became a Blackshirt.

'Why have you done it?'

His answer was to speak as a doctor: 'I can't any longer bear to see the nation's health being so shockingly neglected. It's urgent!'

Tom defected spectacularly, going over to the enemy and forming the British Union of Fascists in 1932.

I remember with a cold sense of horror columns of his followers marching through London in their smart black shirts, and for the first time seeing real thuggery. I was walking with my brother. There had been a big Fascist meeting and what I saw were Blackshirts 'doing over' someone who must have heckled at the meeting, or perhaps he was a Jew. He was on the ground, two men held his arms above his head, two held his legs while a fifth pummelled him in the stomach. I think they must have been on a fire escape outside the hall; in my memory the scene is vivid but not exact. I had never seen this kind of vicious malice before and though World War I had taught me not to be easily sickened, I was appalled.

Mosley turned out to be the only credible dictator the British Right has ever produced. Many people believe to this day that he could have led either the Tory or the Labour Parties; he was intelligent, brave and had a strong feeling of leadership. Like John – but to a much greater degree – he was impatient and, also like my brother, he had a sense of timing. Yet it had been a decent man's distaste for the repressions in Ireland that had led him out of the Conservative Party in 1922, and when he and my brother finally parted, he was still a left-winger and Keynesian, and it was in his frustration at the defects of a Labour Party led by Ramsay MacDonald that he reacted so violently.

Twenty-Two

WRITERS, READERS AND IRRELEVANCIES

At some point I joined in a United Front expedition to America. The Reuters correspondent wrote:

New York

Mrs Amabel Williams-Ellis, the English author and journalist, revealed that she has received a note signed with a swastika threatening her if she testified before the American Inquiry Commission, an unofficial body investigating the events in Germany. She gave evidence at today's session, however, declaring that the persecution in Germany was not only towards Jews ... and quoted Dr Franz Hanfstangel, who is now in New York, as having used the words 'swines and traitors' when speaking of the Catholics.

The American Inquiry Commission was using a type of propaganda that was fashionable at the time called a 'mock trial'. Aneurin Bevan was one of several other participants, together with a melancholy German lawyer who spoke only German and for whom, bad as my German was, I had to do my best to translate.

The trial we were recalling had been the one which followed the famous burning of the Reichstag in which the unfortunate fall guy, young van der Lubbe, had been convicted. 'My' Bulgarians, as this very Putzi Hanfstangel had called them, had been acquitted but kept in gaol.

It was July and I recall a hot New York off-duty evening. The need for something new in written propaganda was spoken of. 'The workers' press all over the world suffers from the worst disease from which a press can suffer, a poor circulation,' said someone. The four of us were seated round a table, each from a different country, all part of that fairly successful 'mock trial', and were shaking our heads over the state of the patient in our respective lands.

We each spoke of the usual practical difficulties in our respective countries, such as the refusal of ordinary distributing agents to handle copies of our newspapers, of prejudice and threats to workers by employers if they were seen reading such papers, and about newsagents and street-sellers being interfered with in various ways. 'Yes! And all that wouldn't count', said the American, 'if only we managed to get out a paper that folk wanted to read!' Upon this there was a chorus of agreement. 'The layout is bad, the presentation is not popular.' The American and I agreed that unconvinced English readers were put off by certain catchwords: deviation, victimization, task, mass struggle, ideology.

As I sat there I had that feeling of 'this is where we came in', for I had lately had much the same sort of conversation with scientific friends; in science the jargon words had been different, but the readers' refusal to read had been the same. So in *Left Review* I started competitions for new worker-writers. 'Try a short impression of something familiar,' I suggested. 'It could be a street scene, a shift at work.' Modest prizes and publication were offered. The suggestion of something concrete to write about did, in fact, set quite a lot of people going. At one point there was a paper avalanche. The entries were supposed to be no more than a thousand words long, but I recall an excellent one (it reached us late for the appropriate competition) of over twelve thousand words. I still claim that we were also putting fresh material in front of professional writers.

There was a wild entry from an engineer called Kenneth Bradshaw, which made me reverse a dogma that I had always respected. Accepted wisdom is that if you make an analogy or comparison, it must always be to something that is already known to the reader. Now I had to think again, for Kenneth Bradshaw created exceedingly violent effects by using two unknowns to make us see the inside of his rather old-fashioned machine-shop. He compared the noise inside it to the trumpeting of panic-stricken elephants, and in another place to ten thousand tigers sharpening their claws on sandstone, and yet he managed not to let his wild beasts run away with him, as strong images often do with an author. Somehow he kept us in his dark, old-fashioned machine-shop all the time.

My experience of setting these competitions has always remained with me because I'm often asked to advise young authors, and I think I learned a lot from this. I don't mean just that one example, but from all sorts of people writing about things that they felt strongly about, and trying to get feelings on to paper. We had accounts of industrial shifts at work, street scenes and a day of threshing corn in the country with the rain coming on. One on 'Soap and Clothes' I liked particularly; the woman writing had noticed the way the clothes balloon out in a boiling copper.

The biggest scale on which writers – as writers – protested was the formation of the Left Book Club. Dr John Lewis, chief organizer of the discussion groups that sprang from it, called my brother John (by this time cast out of the Labour Party and, as I had foreseen, a politician without a party): 'Unquestionably the intellectual force behind what became for a year or two almost a political "Open University" of the Left of Centre.'[1]

The backer and organizing chief of the Left Book Club was Victor Gollancz, the publisher, just as Allen Lane, the great paperback innovator, helped with *Left Review*, and the third founder and academic member was Professor Harold Laski. By 1937 a Left Book Club rally could fill the Albert Hall in London and the biggest hall in other cities from Edinburgh to Bristol. Members bought at least one Left Book each month, sometimes more than one when offered a choice, for about half-a-crown a time, and by 1936 there were fifteen hundred study groups. If, as my American colleague said, the Left seldom produced newspapers that folk wanted to read, the Club had succeeded in producing book after book that was read and discussed in every city and in almost every village in Britain.

Though the Left Book Club was the most massive of the concerted moves towards readability, far the oddest was undoubtedly a little sheet called *The Week*. Clough and I were among its most devoted readers. We used to marvel over what seemed its more incredible statements; these were usually prefaced by the phrase 'certain it is . . .'. Physically the object was a roneoed sheet and Claud Cockburn escaped actions for libel, copyright infringement and the wrath of the Press Lords such as Beaverbrook and the rest by the fact that he himself always managed to be somewhere other than in his little office in Victoria Street, and with the entire stock-in-trade of *The Week* being only a duplicating machine.

By 1936 *The Week* was trying to tell thinking and feeling Tories the unpalatable, disreputable fact that there were those in high places who were not really opposing the Fascist powers, because they thought them the lesser of two evils. It was easy to call the little sheet a scaremonger or a muck-raker, and it was called this and much more. How far the Tory big-wigs had misgivings and wondered why on so many occasions *The Times* (for instance) was silent, we are just beginning to find out.

The Week hurt the feelings of a great many decent people, but was a great comfort to us of the Left. Philip Toynbee, then literary critic of the *Observer*, called Claud Cockburn 'the patron saint of the Thirties'. This odd 'saint' wrote of his publication:

This small monstrosity was one of the half-dozen British publications most often quoted in the press of the entire world. It included among its subscribers the foreign ministers of eleven nations, all the embassies and legations in London, all diplomatic correspondents of the principal newspapers in three continents, the foreign correspondents of all the leading newspapers stationed in London, the leading banking and brokerage houses in London, Paris, Amsterdam and New York, a dozen members of the United States Senate, twenty or thirty members of the House of Representatives, about fifty members of the House of Commons, and a hundred or so in the House of Lords, King Edward VIII, the secretaries of the leading trade unions, Charlie Chaplin and the Nizam of Hyderabad. Blum in France read it, and Goebbels read it, and a mysterious war lord in China read it. Senator Borah quoted it repeatedly in the American Senate, and Herr von Ribbentrop, Hitler's Ambassador in London, on two separate occasions demanded its suppression.[2]

Philip Toynbee commented: 'All this sounds like the ravings of paranoia . . . but everything that he says here is certainly true.'[3] Incidently, my brother John was one of those who helped Claud Cockburn.

The stories in *The Week* were not just capitally written, though heaven knows they were that, but as an eminent friend of mine said recently, 'Good heavens, they were part of our life at that time. What should we have done without all those tales, and so many of them turned out to be true.'

Typical of these was an account of the Anschluss, the connivance of the Austrian Army over Hitler's invasion. This was in 1937, and consisted in the main of a report of a private conversation between Goering and one General Krauss, an Austrian. It was a secret conversation which took place, so *The Week* reported, at Obersalzburg in Bavaria. General Krauss had gone to Bavaria with the ostensible object of delivering a lecture on military strategy, and *The Week* prefaced the story by saying that Krauss was one of the least known yet perhaps the most influential and original of all the theoreticians of Nazi foreign policy.

On arrival in Berlin to give his lecture, *The Week* continued, he was given a motor car and an aeroplane and an officer of the Reich there as his personal ADC. In response to an urgent invitation he flew to Munich and motored thence to Obersalzburg, near Berchtesgaden, and it was there that he was received by Hitler in an interview that lasted for four hours. The conversation with Goering was apparently even more grotesquely improbable, as was also an interview with Neurath, the German Foreign Minister.

At one point in his interview with Hitler, Krauss apparently asked bluntly whether Hitler really trusted his ally Mussolini. In language which was subsequently translated into rather more elegant form, Hitler replied that he was not so foolish as ever to forget a previous double treachery by Italy.

In his interview with Goering, both parties were fairly blunt. 'If, sir, an invasion should be undertaken in the not too distant future, should we or should we not have to anticipate serious resistance by your armed forces?' asked Goering. Krauss gave an assurance that the Austrian Army would offer no resistance at all: 'After all, Hitler is an Austrian, just as much our Hitler as he is yours.'

Goering, telling the story, shook with laughter when he gave his version of the interview, saying that Krauss had actually saluted and clicked his heels as he gave this patriotic assurance.

The Week went on to remark that there were naturally no written records of all this but that Krauss had repeated the story to several people when he got back to Vienna, and much of it had been told by Goering. Krauss added that in the interview with Hitler he had given Hitler information that was in his possession as to Mussolini's determination to prevent the Anschluss, while it was Goering who decorated the story with the saluting and heel-clicking. All this seemed to us readers of *The Week* just a little too good to be true, and yet, and yet, confirmation seemed to come from various quarters of one such story after another.

When *The Week* had anything special to report, Claud Cockburn was in the habit, so we thought, of prefacing that particular story with the words, 'Though it is not clear that . . . it certain is that . . .' and then went on to some tale whose provenance seemed very dubious indeed but which often turned out to be perfectly factual.

This tale is typical and explained why we all read *The Week*, and why Philip Toynbee remarked that, by the end of the Thirties, Claud Cockburn's claims were not the ravings of a maniac but were probably true. Its relevance to us is that his wife, writing in *The Years of The Week*, used a funny caricature of John whispering in Claud Cockburn's ear.

As to the real complicity of the Foreign Office, the Bank of England and others in helping Hitler, I remember a much later conversation on quite another issue. I asked my brother John what he felt was the chief difference for a Member of Parliament between being on the Front Bench in opposition and being in office.

'In office, you know so much more,' he answered without hesitation.

How much was known by the Cabinet of what was really going on? I fancy that Lord Boothby's honest, vigorous opposition to his own party's neutrality in the Spanish Civil War was so unpopular because he, Boothby, knew, and they knew, and he knew that they knew, that in fact the Axis Powers were being far from neutral.

To me the moral of all this is that whatever brilliant new media are invented, children must all be taught to read and write, because a 'Big Brother' of one type or another has nearly always throughout European history been able to manage the other media, usually through the power of money, and while it may be too dangerous to demonstrate or to speak your mind, it is often possible to spread the written word. There is an interesting story told by a doctor, when later the Germans occupied Holland, of how his patients got better when a clandestine newspaper was started.

Meantime all through these years, all sorts of irrelevancies kept breaking in. One was a purely personal one.

On a snowy day in March I got knocked down by a small Hillman car. It had been a day of untimely snow and slush. I had been staying with my mother. The result for the car was a badly dented bonnet. The result for me was concussion and a broken right arm. Concussion is dreadful: for weeks I behaved like a cheap, tiresome version of a Chekhov character. I took offence, became depressed about small things, said that nobody showed any consideration and yet was very dependent, felt sure that all sorts of things ought to be done and yet did none of them. This was all a most unfortunate blend, and bewildered both me and my family.

Back in Wales, Dr Edward Morris, our amiable and observant GP, explained what happens when you get a severe bang on the head. Imagine, he said, a jelly in its mould; then imagine a violent blow on the mould. All manner of little rifts and fissures appear in the jelly. With the brain there will also surely be minute internal bleeding from minor blood vessels. So the sufferer has lack of co-ordination, double vision (I had that) and damage to the sensory nerves (I had complained of what I called the 'ghost pain') and so on. By then I had come to believe strongly in the effects of body on mind. At least, though humiliating and unpleasant, this concussion was a good, drastic, practical confirmation. 'Don't work!' Dr Morris added.

I had just finished the draft of a novel that ultimately was published as *The Big Firm*. I got quite a good advance for it, but the publisher had only had it in draft state before I was knocked down, and I wasn't in a very good way for finishing it. It was Margaret Storm Jameson who went over it with really friendly care, reading it three times. Thus I was, by her kindness, able to send off a typescript, not merely to cry over it.

The other thing I had been trying to do, in collaboration with our three teenage children, was what we then called 'The Children's Weekend Book'. This was ultimately called *In and Out of Doors*. That, too, was somehow achieved and proved a success. Moreover, when the Germans began to bomb Britain, this was a book that parents have told me they would take among the pillows, the sleeping-bags and the biscuits to the cellars, the Underground or the Anderson shelter, for it had games and poems and tales for big and little children.

Another irrelevance was much more fun than having a broken arm and concussion. It was the forming of a small, mildly private and slightly conspiratorial literary committee which we called the Civil Liberties Press Bureau. This committee met at our Hampstead house.

We protesters had a bad habit of writing long letters to national newspapers, signed by a predictable 'stage army of the just', protesting now against what was not in the papers, or next time against what was, or the banning of some book. These letters, signed by all these famous names, were usually printed, but we could not be sure they were read. What our small committee did was to try to co-ordinate these almost professional signers.

If what we wanted to protest about was scientific or medical, we had more than one scientist and doctor. If it was about the environment, very likely Professor Reilly would sign. He was a terrific character, looked like one of Edward Lear's little roundish characters, so eager that they stood on their toes and looked as if they might take off. We had more than one lawyer; if we couldn't get hold of Bertrand Russell because he was abroad, Cyril Joad would often take on a philosophic question. On the whole, however, we were writers or historians, but we had Victor Gollancz and Jonathan Cape as publishers.

A lot of what we did was done on the telephone or by post, but there was an active secretarial group that used to meet at our Hampstead house. These meetings were usually entertaining. I especially remember when we were defending a bore of a book which was banned as indecent. One of us, having reluctantly read it, said mildly, 'Awful, but surely not pornographic?'

'Yes, it is pornographic,' said Rose Macaulay, looking even more donnish than usual. ' "*Graphos*," I write, "*pornè*", that is a hired woman. This dreadfully boring book is exactly that, a writing about a hired woman,' she said.

Rose again, on another occasion: 'We must be clear! Are we talking about virgins or are we talking about spinsters?'

Rose was, incidentally, an expert on Christian heresies, a topic that she made fascinating. Much of what she said is to be found in her *Towers of Trebizond*, apropos the young men who went to Istanbul (Constantinople) and beyond 'to write their Turkey books'.

But the greatest irrelevance of all was very public indeed. This was the Abdication in 1936 of the young King of England, Edward VIII. The Continent had been fascinated long before he succeeded or we were allowed to know anything about his Mrs Simpson, by tales of her and of the heir to the British throne. I (not as a rule one for more than mild feelings about Royals) took an interest in the whole controversy because earlier, as Prince of Wales, I had met him when he had stayed at Portmeirion. It had seemed to me that here was a sensitive and slightly unsure young man whom fate had put in a very extraordinary situation, one only bearable to a stalwart extrovert.

He had just come back from a tour of South America when he stayed at Portmeirion. I knew that he was interested in poetry and, after dinner, I did what is, I believe, not proper to do to Royals, and I drew him out on the subject of Spanish and Portuguese poetry. I asked him how much Brazilian and Argentinian verse differed from the literature of their home countries. He didn't resent this breach of protocol, indeed seemed glad to be asked, to know quite a lot of verse by heart, and to be pleased that somebody would listen.

Just back from Nazi Germany, I tried in turn to interest him in a particularly horrible racist issue of *Der Stürmer*, a popular political periodical equivalent perhaps to our *Reveille*. This issue contained a comic article on grammar – 'The Jews are unwanted, unpleasant, unreliable, unclean . . .' and so on, with all the abusive negatives that the writer could imagine. The Prince looked unhappy but said nothing. This was just before his celebrated visit to the out-of-work miners in the South Wales valleys when he, as I thought, so admirably insisted on what in the 1970s became known as a 'walk-about'.

When we knew about the Mrs Simpson affair I applauded a satirical rhyme that went the rounds. To anyone who doesn't know much about the Anglican Church it should be explained that an Archbishop of Canterbury signs himself 'Cantuar':

> My Lord Archbishop, what a scold you are,
> > And when your man is down how very bold you are,
> Of Christian Charity how very scant you are,
> > Oh Lang! How very full of cant you are!

A new and more acceptable king, with a charming and highly acceptable wife, was immediately conscripted. The irrelevance was over, and we of the United Front went on for another couple of years trying to prevent World War II. Thyssen in Germany and, according to

Claud Cockburn and Bob Boothby among many others, Montague Norman of the Bank of England continued to grow more powerful. These, most of the Press Barons, and who else let the war happen? Unfortunately a great many other people else.

Let it never be forgotten that villains or the noblest of human kind are no good whatever if they haven't got followers. This is such an obvious truth that it seems always to have been overlooked by the people and academics alike of all nations.

In the Twenties and Thirties, too many 'good' Germans followed Hitler; indeed three million of them voted for him. They voted for him, it has to be remembered, before he was in a position to slaughter them if they didn't.

In France, also, too many Frenchmen chose to believe in the Maginot Line. In Britain, cheering crowds greeted Neville Chamberlain when he came back from Berchtesgaden with his false peace and his scrap of paper.

Such were the events that much later caused many of us, all over Europe and the world, to doubt if the innocent rock-and-roll song 'Power to the People' is enough. The sinister fact is that 'the people' (and this includes you and me) can be manipulated.

Millions of us paid, heaven knows, for our failure to choose better leaders, for our exclusive involvement in our own affairs, or our willingness to scoff at cheapjacks and to identify and to restrain scoundrels and madmen. Having said which . . .

Having said which (a 1980s' politician's favourite preface to contradicting himself flat), I still claim that brave and excellent things as well as trivial or irrelevant things were done. Consider that with all the efforts that the Dark Powers made to bamboozle, bewilder and overwhelm us, we did, for those long years, continue to bestir ourselves. But the leaders of the Axis powers had many followers. Towards the end of the war in Spain, when Franco's rebel forces had captured Madrid, he was reported as declaring that it was not so much his four columns of besiegers that had brought him victory, as a fifth column inside the city. As it was with France, so it was with Britain. The fifth column – the collaborationists of Madrid, Paris and London – were very nearly too much for us. But for them, Hitler could have been stopped. It could have been done, but nobody wanted to know. The newsmen couldn't break 'the silence'.

I suppose that many surviving men and women of my own generation (we are not all that numerous) who were adults in the Thirties continue to puzzle over the question of how it came about that Hitler wasn't stopped in 1932. No simple explanations, from the

Materialist Conception of History to any of religious creeds, seem sufficient. Perhaps our children, now parents themselves, will ten years hence be puzzling how it came about that in 1982 several opinion polls and most of the media – we the people – reacted as they seem to have done. We/they were not apparently against 'if necessary' killing and being killed in a shooting war with, of all people, of all irrelevant and unpleasant people, the Argentine junta.

I know that for me, and especially of course in the context of experiencing two world wars, I know that such are the Sphinx questions that have become paramount in my own mind. I believe that they are both moral questions and questions of survival, and that they are not insoluble, and I know that they have not been solved. But I also believe that the sort of diagnosis that has to precede their solution might well be in sight.

I think, too, that in this story, in my attempt to bring my own past to the surface, it has been the events that seem relevant to such questions that have mostly come to the surface, so that in one picture and another an unconscious impulse has put forward one rather than another where either would have seemed appropriate. But in 1939 the tempest of hate was upon us. A desolating sense of regret must not be permitted to weaken our resolve that Fascism must not be allowed to win. We did not at that stage know about the tortures and the death camps – the Holocaust – but we knew enough to be sure that we were threatened by coarse, implacable gangsters, technically our superiors, intent on enslaving us and the rest of Europe, and who must not be allowed to win.

Twenty-Three

WAR FACTORIES AND BORROWED CHILDREN

Hitler's unprecedented march across Europe was most oddly and eerily preceded by what I called Operation Kindergarten. My mother wrote a book about it, which she called *Borrowed Children*, the first actual happening being that on 1 September, two days before our ultimatum to Germany expired, the children came out of the industrial towns to those of us who lived in safe areas.

Earlier that summer, when we saw that the war was coming, Clough and I were indeed heavy-hearted. Clough wanted to have what might well be a farewell look at Europe. It would still be safe this summer, we reckoned, safe for getting home if we went no further than France. On our way back I got food poisoning. We had decided before we left that we had better try to let our old and delightful Hampstead house. Clough thought that he could somehow run the practice from Brondanw. Our part of North Wales had been scheduled as a safety area, which meant that the moment war was officially declared we should be due to receive quite a lot of evacuees, either school-children or mothers and babies, at Brondanw. As I was bedfast for days on end with my food poisoning, the business of the displacement of the London end all fell upon Clough.

Our Hampstead house had once belonged to Romney the painter, who built it with a gallery when he quarrelled with the Royal Academy. In this gallery – Clough's office – there must once have hung pictures of Emma Hamilton, for Romney painted the lovely creature over and over again.

Clough reported that he had had much less trouble than he had expected in finding a tenant. He wrote:

I let it quickly though to a very odd person – a mysterious foreigner who turned out to be the leader of some curious religious sect that revered him as their mahatma. Though he claimed to be able to reincarnate himself in any part of the world at will, London was his and his movement's headquarters, and our gallery and big rooms were, so he said, just what were needed for the ceremonies of his 'Temple of Service'. It all sounded so exceedingly bogus to me and, in the circumstances, so suspicious that I went to see the appropriate person at Scotland Yard, suggesting that investigation of my tenant by MI5 might prove rewarding. However, though I had had private warnings and hints of pro-Nazi activities, he was cleared by the authorities.[1]

We ourselves felt oddly resigned. It was our inability to spare the children from the consequences of the catastrophe that made our hearts so heavy. I kept repeating to myself the seventeenth-century saying, 'He that hath Friends hath given Hostages to Fortune.' How well tyrants and all the Dark Powers understand that to have children is to be still more at the mercy of 'that strumpet' as Shakespeare called Fortune.

Back at Brondanw and having joined the WVS (Women's Voluntary Services), I was still only convalescent and I remember driving a small but sufficiently noisy car along the only bit of straight road near home; being alone and realizing that no-one could hear me so that it would do no harm, for the length of the road I screamed my despair, wept, sobbed, howled like a wolf, and then drew into the side of the road, composed myself, and drove on and did my errand, whatever it was.

But the War, after all, had become a necessity, the time to halt the Axis powers had gone, the chance had been lost. True, we didn't at the time know much about the slaughter by Hitler of his own Brown Shirts in 'the Night of the Long Knives', and nothing about the plans for extermination camps, but we knew enough. This was not an ordinary war. Forced labour began to be hinted at, and with the invasion of Poland more details came out. Soon even *The Times* – not *The Week* – was to write this sort of thing:

> There is no reason to suppose that the Nazis, once they had us in their power, would not formally enslave us, as they have formally enslaved the Polish people . . . Himmler, the German Chief of Police, has declared that all Poles in the Reich must now wear a badge consisting of a yellow diamond edged with a lilac-coloured band and bearing a large letter P, so that they may be distinguished from the rest of the population . . . A circular issued by the *Verein für das Deutschtum in Ausland* (Association for Germandom Abroad) explains that decent Poles do not exist, any more than decent Jews. All Germans must see that the Poles in their employment wear this distinguishing mark. Circumstances have necessitated the employment of Poles in the Reich for the duration of the war, but no German must ever forget that he is a member of the *Herrenvolk* (master-race).[2]

My brother was also writing of the horrors that would come with defeat:

We are engaged in a total war. Defeat in such a war is total defeat. And total defeat equals slavery . . . In spite of the desperately narrow margin which separated us this summer from such total defeat . . . when we talk of the Nazis desiring to subjugate and enslave us, we are not using some figure of speech . . . There are today a dozen subtle economic devices by means of which a whole people can be enslaved. Enslavement means, precisely, the taking from a man, or a people, of everything which they produce over and above what is necessary to keep them alive.

The bewildered children, heaven knows, were not bathetic but the gas masks which encumbered them were. Evacuation was by schools with their teachers. We had not been told when they were coming, but Susan and Charlotte and a teenage cousin, and my house staff, Laura and Mrs Bowden, began to get Brondanw ready. Christopher was still in America visiting his godfather, Joe Brewer.

I knew that my mother was in the same pickle, but it wasn't possible to do more than telephone, and I realized that she was still as capable an organizer as she had always been. I was glad that her house was smaller so that she was not down to take very many, and she told me that she had specified that they were to be little girls.

She described the day's events, and her account can stand for the experience of tens of thousands of old ladies:

1 September 1939
We had been on the alert all day. An abrupt message had been left at the door early that the children were expected, and that nobody could possibly find time to telephone what time they would arrive. The house had been unoccupied till late on the previous Tuesday (29th August) and the preparations for the six children expected had been necessarily hasty. The hours passed quickly. Even tea-time was over when at last there was a shout. 'Here are the cars!' I had asked for and been promised a helper, no boys, and six girls of about nine 'plus' which is the slang of the London County Council for 'and upwards'. I ran downstairs. Two cars drew up. The doors opened on both sides and out of them tumbled eight little beings, none of them more than knee-high and half of them boys.[3]

We in North Wales had Liverpool or Birkenhead schools. On the first evening there were seventeen little girls round the table, and so many mattresses on the floor that next day you could hardly sweep the rooms. All right while the fine weather lasted, we thought. About six of them wetted their beds that night. At the end of a week the mother of two sisters found a billet three miles away. These were two we were rather glad to part with for, as we carried in the dinner, one of them would say aloud, amid an interested silence, 'Oh, *I hate* boiled mutton!' or 'I wish it was jelly instead!' The others, of course, joined in.

The first score to the grown-ups was due to one of my daughters. She discovered that two birthdays were coming up. Out of the continuing confusion we conjured two cakes, iced them, and wrote names and ages in pink sugar. The children decided that we were all right.

Parents came, and we had our first tears. Then the novelty wore off. Children who had never left home before, even for a single night, now felt very far away. After the two faddy little sisters had been so providentially removed, we were able to deal much better with likes and dislikes in the way of food. There was the sum of 8s 6d (42½p) per head, per week, to consider. 'If you really don't like it, I'll only give you a doll's helping, but you must eat it!' Gradually the plan worked, especially when praise was given to those who were not faddy. Soon the child whose turn it was to be waitress would say: 'Doll's of vegetables for Jean, but elephant's when it comes to me!'

On the first day, one little girl, whom I had driven to another billet, had been full of what she wanted.

'Oh, I do hope it's a farm. I do hope there's a pig. Would there be a calf, d'you think?' After a silence, as if all this had been perhaps too much to ask, 'Well, I do hope, anyhow, I go to a lady with a kitten.'

Boasting competitions natural to all children were usually about animals: 'We've got a *huge* dog, Rover, at home. I *think* he's a retriever.' 'Our cat's had kittens and Mum says I can keep four of the next lot.' Then a sad voice, 'I've only got a goldfish!'

A very tall, well-behaved boy of about nine with an angelic expression pleased his hostess very much at first, but later she was dreadfully upset. He told a neighbour that she could drink more beer than his own mother! This was in a closely integrated village and the hostess was a teetotaller and terrified of her neighbours' criticisms. He thought he had been paying her a compliment.

Like the rest of the host-houses in all the safe areas, Brondanw had a fluctuating population. When there was less persistent bombing of Liverpool and Birkenhead, parents or big sisters would appear and children would go back. This happened often in spite of all sorts of official warnings and prohibitions, or threats of withdrawal of billeting allowances if and when the bombing hotted up again.

In fact 'Operation Kindergarten' felt to the participants, official and unofficial, like all wars – a matter of 'Hurry up there – get ready to hang about!' When another wave burst out of the harassed cities, it always seemed to consist of new, different children. Again, as is typical of war, far too little organized wisdom was drawn from this massive opportunity for child study. For years I do know that we got welcome visits, often from an apparent stranger, someone with a child or several children, who said, 'Don't you remember me? I'm Shirley (or Maureen). Can I take the children to see . . .' (some special hiding hole in the garden or the room where Shirley's bed had been). 'You see, I've so often told them . . . So I wanted them to see . . .' To this day we get an occasional visit from former evacuees.

There were weeks or sometimes months in the long frightening years when a receding wave of evacuees left Brondanw empty. Christopher, back from America, was at Cambridge, his conscription postponed; Charlotte at Oxford, Susan teaching art at Dartington or, clever creature, in a most unexpected little cottage she had found almost in Trafalgar Square, to which Clough and the rest of us all occasionally resorted. The Blitz taught us a lot about shelters as time went on.

In Wales at Brondanw the whole village had, of course, helped with the evacuees, and especially my Laura, but every now and then when there was a pause in the bombing of our cities, the tide of children would recede, they would go back to their families. It was during these pauses that, anxious and restless like the rest, I thought up an occupation for myself that would be compatible with going back to Brondanw if there was warning of new evacuees from the billeting officer via my efficient helper Laura, and compatible also with visiting my mother, who was still in Surrey. Her evacuee waves had, of course, a different timing to mine as her children were snatched away from Home Counties towns and cities.

I decided to do a little journalism and find out what part of this strange mobilization for war that we were experiencing had been neglected. There was a good deal about women in the forces, for instance, in the media, but we knew that for every WAAF or WREN or ATS girl, at least ten conscripted girls and women were working in munitions. There they were on day-shift, night-shift, slogging away on assembly lines, doing men's jobs, mostly in engineering works, and all at risk of course for it was the industrial towns that were being blitzed. They were certainly at risk, for their places of work and their homes were the prime targets of German night-raiding aeroplanes, north, south, east or west, at all points of the compass. So, with slightly lukewarm support from the Ministry of Information, I began touring round a number of factories to talk with the girls and women, conscripted or volunteer, who were manning them. Housewives, often with husbands in the same factory, had shifts more or less arranged so that the house should not be entirely deserted for the children coming

home from school. Often there were lone women and young girls living
in hostels far from home. Some of what came out of this was published
in a 'quickie' pamphlet, published by Gollancz, which we called
'Women in War Factories'. Much of it was used by the Ministry as
short articles in local papers in various parts of the country.

The dangerous Royal Ordnance Factories where explosives were
made impressed me with their special passes, handing in of contraband, and many guards. Such factories were usually enormous,
impressive and alarming to a newcomer. Cigarettes and matches
became 'contraband'; no outsiders might go in, sometimes the
workers might not go from one department to the next without going
through a 'shifting room' where clothes and shoes must be changed.
Thick walls, many small low buildings, work which came through a
hatch a little at a time, and a dozen other things were reminders
that here was something not to be trifled with. Slow, niggling, exact
work in such surroundings affected some women's nerves, but not it
seemed Miss Janet McFarlane. She wore the regulation white coif and
overall as she checked the goings out and comings in, and looked like
a recording angel, stern and dignified. She told me that, having as a
stewardess at sea been torpedoed a couple of times, she was now en-
joying 'a nice shore job'.

'Funny to choose an explosives factory?' I asked.

'Ach! There's nae danger here!' and added thoughtfully, 'Being
torpedoed was pairfectly straightforward. What a didnae like was our
lifeboat being wrecked by the rescuing ship and being eight hours in
water that was nane too warm. But it's cosy here – we're at the richt end
o' th' explosives!'

I saw no young girls at any ROF. But in engineering things were
different. Imagine a grand piano built for a giant out of steel. Now
imagine this piano standing up on the keyboard side; then turn it inside
out and, for good measure, add extra pipes from racing cars and some
stops like those of an organ. Big planing machines looked rather like
that, and there was often a row of them set up on platforms down one
side of the long aisle of an engineering shop. At each there stood or
perched a girl in a blue-boiler suit, her hair tucked under a smart
peaked cap. Each girl was up on this platform and, with one hand near
the controls, was watching the one bit of the whole big complicated
machine that was obviously moving. This was a chisel, which moved
backwards and forwards, scoring and shaping a bulged piece of steel
that looked as if it might be going to be the door of an outsize fuse-box.
As the tool moved back and forth, a soapy waterfall jetted over
chisel-edge and steel – a cooling lubricant.

Kath, intent most of the time on this, glanced up. Like the others in the row, she was not long out of training, and felt the machine would be up to its tricks if it got half a chance. When she began to talk, she had to lean down from her perch to be heard through the noise.

'If you make a mistake in that other work' – she nodded towards the girls doing die-sinking on the other side of the long shop – 'it's only drawing on the steel from the blueprints, and you can just rub it out. But not with this one. There's a lot of work gone into this already, but if you make a mistake – why, it's scrap.'

'What happened to Agnes?' asked my companion from Welfare. 'The one that cried the first time she saw the planing machines?'

Kath said that Agnes had been transferred to an ordinary lathe and was all right now.

'I don't wonder, you know – nervous type – these things do seem terribly big after the ones you get at the training centre.'

She patted her machine and repeated with satisfaction, 'This is a job where you mustn't make mistakes. The fellows rubbed that in.' She added that Agnes hadn't ever done much before, hadn't even been in business.

'Were you frightened yourself?' I asked.

'Me? Good gracious, no! I've been in hairdressing.' She saw that I didn't follow, and added, 'If you've put a customer under the drier and given perms, there's nothing here to be afraid of.'

Jean in Hot Pressing had been in ladies' wholesale mantles; Beryl had been on the stage as a showgirl. At most factories, some of the younger girls larked about; two of them, learning to be hammer-drivers, were caught by one of the sourer male exponents of Welfare both going to fetch one bottle of water for their machines and running a three-legged race back with it.

'If it'd been two lads, I'd have warmed their backs for them . . . !' This foreman disliked the women workers. Perhaps workers of any sort seemed a disagreeable necessity to him – and he spoke of women and girls as 'a very expensive form of labour and a darned nuisance', adding that they didn't give a hoot about the war and were bad time-keepers.

Not all wore uniform overalls. Somewhere I noted a dark bib-and-brace boiler-suit over a pink satin blouse. For the newspaper pieces I stressed how odd this all was and that to study the past was to realize that never before in our history had the whole nation made such an effort. There had never been anything like it. To read what contemporary writers had to say about what went on when we were threatened by the Armada, or when Napoleon, like Hitler, had his great army camped just across the Channel, was to realize that most people's lives went on just the same then. 'We have never mobilized as we are mobilized today. This is the heroic age.'

As usual we idealized past ages and underestimated the greatness of events when they were happening under our noses. Most of all we noticed the seamy side. In one Scottish factory the manager was telling me how well a group of girls were working and how quick they were. There was a casting job, which women had never tackled before, and to which he had set them because he could get no more men. It was not heavy, but it was tricky. Two men working a normal shift could produce seven of the castings in question. This management trained girls for seven or eight weeks and put them on the work. The girls' production figures crawled up and up; soon they had beaten the men; in a little while more they were producing twice as much as the men, and finally, instead of seven castings per shift, they made over forty.

'That sounds almost impossible. Perhaps you broke down the job and made the work easier or quicker in some way?'

'I assure you we didn't,' answered the manager.

I digested this for a while. Presently I asked, 'How do the girls get paid for it? If it's piecework, they must be the ones who are really coining it?'

'Oh, we don't pay them as much as we used to pay the men,' was the answer.

Twenty-Four

'AND TURNETH NOT HIS HEAD'

It was when France's Maginot Line had been so effortlessly turned, when France had been overrun, when the British and French armies had suffered that alarming defeat at Dunkirk, that the bombs began to rain down. Hitler declared that he would 'wring Britain's neck like a chicken', and with little except a heartening gift for repartee Churchill answered, 'Some chicken! Some neck!' It was only then, when the bombs began to rain down, that it really occurred to everyone that the War wasn't happening to someone else, it was happening here. Hitler's invasion barges lay at Boulogne, with a short crossing, and we could hear the guns from across the Channel, while all night and sometimes all day the bombs rained down, shattering a dozen cities – Bristol, Hull and Glasgow, Swansea, Coventry . . .

The ensuing tale of resolution, confidence and confusion has been told a hundred times. Just how Britons managed at that time to eat and even occasionally to sleep in our cities during the raging of the blitz is hard to understand. What is certain is that there was an odd, almost hypnotic mixture of fear and of painful fascination about being in an air attack that kept many people in the cities who didn't have to stay there; kept them even out in the streets, hearing the guns, watching the flak. There was a feeling that it was all unreal, we didn't want to think that Europe had been overrun and that we were alone:

> As one who walks a lonely road and turneth not his head
> Because he knows a frightful fiend doth close behind him tread.

There seemed no doubt that this was a case of 'a frightful fiend'. Watching the strange geometry of a sky battle or the sinister shape of some unusually low-flying enemy plane pursued by our flak, we civilians felt a strange sort of participation and an almost sporting instinct. The flak was often ineffective. 'Behind the birds again,' as a sporting county lady remarked.

For reasons that were grotesque but explicable, for some months of the London blitz my brother John had the most lowly job in Civil Defence as an assistant air raid warden. He wasn't trusted with a proper job. Post D was the name he gave in a book to the Chelsea air raid post to which he found himself attached. I doubt if anyone wrote a better account of what the Civil Defence volunteers in Britain's bigger and more vulnerable cities experienced. I was at intervals near enough in the course of some factory visits to vouch for what he wrote. Episodes came out in the *New Yorker*, the American version being called *Digging For Mrs Miller*.

To Post D would come by telephone or runner word of another 'incident', news which the wailing of sirens, the roar of our barrage, the crash of high explosives, and the glare of incendiaries confirmed or outran. Each branch of Civil Defence had its task. Victims, living and dead, were dug out of the ruins by the rescue men. The ambulance drivers were mostly women; wardens might be either. The rescue men were in immediate command of digging operations, wardens co-ordinating:

> The harsh rank raw smell of a high explosive attack was characteristic. Its basis certainly came from the torn, wounded, dismembered houses; from the gritty dust of dissolved brickwork, masonry and joinery. But there was an acrid overtone from the high explosives which the bomb itself had contained; a fiery constituent . . . Almost invariably, too, there was the mean little stink of domestic gas . . . But the whole . . . was the smell of violent death itself. It was as if death was a toad that had come and squatted down at the bottom of the bomb craters of London.[1]

Waiting one day at Post D with two or three ambulance girls and some other wardens, the talk ran on what seemed the worst part of their respective jobs:

> We agreed that corpses were quite all right as long as one had an official relationship with them. It would have been intolerable unless there had been definite things which had to be done, such as digging them out, covering them with blankets, putting them on to stretchers, taking them away . . .
>
> In the darkness, under a mound of rubble a certain Mrs Wells was probably buried. Others also perhaps? Every now and then the gunfire would get heavier, and the rescue men would hear an enemy plane apparently directly overhead. Then they would all shout 'Lights!' 'Put that light out!' and insist on every torch, even the most carefully masked, being put out, so that they had to work in total darkness. They were extremely fussy and particular about this. An hour of labour, scrabbling in the gritty rubble and brickwork, now turning slimy in the rain, went by. About every ten minutes the rescue men would shout for silence. Everyone would stop dead. The rescue men who had burrowed deepest would ask for the buried people to give their position. These

listening silences seemed eerie. At first there seemed to be two other faint voices as well as Mrs Wells's. But the last time there was only one other answering voice. Gradually the outlines of an unshattered floor, the boards still holding to the joists, began to be revealed in the mound. They all guessed at once that this floor must be held up, if only a foot or so, by something. Only this could account for the fact that there were still people alive underneath, for there were many tons of debris on top. Human beings could only have survived if at least one end of this floor was being held up off them. They dug on . . . It turned out that Mrs Wells was still alive, the others not.[2]

My unfortunate brother was distrusted both by the Establishment and by his former left-wing readers. The trouble, as Professor Galbraith put it, was that John's books of this period were 'so well written'. His *Coming Struggle for Power*, for example, as John once told Galbraith, had sold over a hundred thousand copies in hard-cover in the United States alone. 'It was influential because it was the work not of a party hack but of a Strachey, and therein was the danger.'

That is one of the reasons why the Establishment distrusted him and would not give him any sort of job. Marxists were equally unforgiving because he had said that there might be capitalist remedies for the massive unemployment – America's 'New Deal' and Keynesian economics. 'Strachey submitted his *Programme for Progress* to the "Keepers of the Communist Scrolls", and they didn't like it at all.'[3]

Slow learner that I am, tied up and anxious for my family (the girls in the blitz fire-watching, one in London, one in Oxford, Christopher's call-up now certain), I did not properly realize what my brother was going through during this period of double rejection. I merely thought he was ill, which is what he said. Having been parted from his wife and children, who had gone to Canada, he found himself officially distrusted to the extent of having his letters opened by MI5, of being howled down by people who had been colleagues (on one memorable occasion by 'the Hampstead Reds') and, worst of all, being for long entrusted with no responsible war work.

At last, things began to happen. Someone on high noticed, I suppose, that there had perhaps been, to put it mildly, no particular reason for suspecting John of being a Nazi. Anyhow, the embargo was lifted and John joined the RAF in a lowly position. Looking back, Patrick Blackett remarked, 'It is probably several hundred years since anyone except a Royal has advanced more quickly up the ladder of service promotion.'

I expect that other people who write memoirs find that it gives them an uncanny feeling of reliving the past to an unexpected degree. For me this has been a strange sort of pleasure, a sense of being alive all over again. The experience has been of fresh life, regained vitality, even including some painful episodes such as the anxious, frustrating years of World War I or, in a different way, the unpleasant feeling of behaving like a hysteric after I had concussion and thus incurring a painful sort of disbelief that almost amounted to coldness from my immediate and usually loving family. In a sense the writer is calling up a real past, including elusive things that, often for lack of skill, don't get on to the paper. But this often vivid second living is something that I completely refuse to do for the next event in my life. This was Christopher's death in action when the Second Front in Italy was launched. He died at a place called Monte Purgatorio. Nobody should ask me to relive this and, as I say, that is what writing about one's own past so often amounts to. So let oblivion cover it for the reader, if never for the writer.

The misery was prolonged because at first he was posted as missing. It seemed to me that there was a simple choice for myself – to be alive or dead (one of the few cases where moderation is out of place). But I had to think of my family: two daughters, one of them just married and the other fairly obviously courting. One of them was married in London at St Martin-in-the-Fields, a wedding that was peacefully accomplished though Hitler's rockets were still falling on London every day. The other wedding was not long after in Wales.

These V1 and V2 rockets were Hitler's last attempt at winning the war. His armies in the east were in full retreat and now those from the west. At last there came a time when both German armies, east and west, were in full retreat. Paris and then all France was liberated.

I managed to go to Paris on a press card and indeed was one of the journalists who got there early. The man I particularly wanted to see was Jean-Paul Sartre. In general I had long admired him as a playwright, but now I had a curious reason for wanting to see him.

Earlier in the war, Arthur Koestler, who had a cottage at Blaenau Ffestiniog about ten miles away, being unable to get home one night, stayed at our house and left behind him a play of Sartre's called *Les Mouches*. I turned it over, meaning of course to return it to Arthur, and then noted curious things about it. It was obviously an anti-Pétainist tract in the guise of a bit of classical tragedy, and it had apparently (according to the printed version) been produced in Paris during the German occupation. This seemed to me a very strange circumstance and I longed to know how it had come about.

I suppose I stayed with John's friend Yvette and with her sister Micia, now Madame Benda. What stands out in my memory is two conversations with Sartre and a curious emotional feeling in Paris then. Asking Yvette, for example, about some mutual acquaintance, she would shake her head, '*Non, elle a collaboré*' – 'She collaborated, we don't speak of her.' And then at half a dozen places, usually where one street crossed another, there would be a little shrine – not a religious shrine but a little bunch of flowers in water and a cross. This signified that someone had been killed or arrested there by the Germans.

Sartre and Simone de Beauvoir were to be found, as so many French writers then were, not at home but in a café. Was it at the Flore or was it Les Deux Magots? Anyhow, one of the two great famous cafés. He was affable, ready to talk, indeed the whole atmosphere was extremely emotional and electric. I told him that we had lost our only son in the fighting. He asked how old he had been. I said twenty-one. 'Oh, well at least he knew what it was to be a man,' said Sartre. 'It's better than being killed as a child.'

I told him how much I admired his plays – I have never greatly admired his novels – and asked particularly about *Les Mouches*. How had it been possible that such a play had been publicly acted during the German occupation of Paris? He smiled behind his strong spectacles, the frog-like mouth expressing pleasure at my surprise, but said nothing. 'I suppose the Germans felt that the French were always producing classical plays and thought nothing of it?' I said. He nodded. 'But didn't people begin to understand what you were at? That it wasn't so much perhaps an attack on the Germans but a satire on Pétainism?' He shook his head, but in such a way that it was clear that he didn't mind being cross-questioned, so I persisted. 'Didn't the cast understand?' He said, 'Oh, actors, you know what they are.'

I can't remember now whether we were talking French or English, but I think a judicious mixture of the two. 'No, they didn't understand what it was all about, they just said their lines, said them well too.'

'Did no-one understand – none of them?'

'Yes,' he said, 'the girl who played Electra understood, and I told her to keep her mouth shut. Gradually, however, the Germans did begin to see that there was something in the packed houses that were playing, something that wasn't just a tribute to the excellence of the drama or their interest in the classical theme, and they began to post representatives in the house, plain-clothes-men, women, anybody that was likely to pass as a genuine playgoer, but we got wind of this and passed the word round that nobody was to applaud, nobody was to express any particular feelings. So you had the extraordinary sensation of a play being acted in complete silence on the part of the audience, a little tepid hand-clapping at the end of the act, that was all, not a single speech applauded or made much of.'

'What did the actors think of that?'

He shrugged his shoulders. 'I think we consoled them and told them that it was no reflection on them. During the occupation we'd all got used to peculiar precautions, you understand.'

We talked further on a second or third occasion, I suppose, and at one point he showed me a photograph. We had got on to the subject of atrocities. I had asked about this. It was a picture of two young German soldiers sitting on a wall and stretched across the knees of the two of them was the naked body of a young woman. She had been eviscerated. I don't think I expressed my sense of the blasphemy – it was hardly necessary.

He said, 'The worst of it was, you see, that these were not particular villains. These same young men would burn down a church full of people who had taken refuge there, and then the next day they would be helping some old woman draw the water from the well, or playing with the children. What was so horrible was that apparently normal human beings did these things. These young fellows don't look particularly like devils, do they?'

At the time he and Albert Camus were working together closely on a newspaper, and Camus published a book on the Absurd, a book that expressed his pain at the irrationality of the human predicament.

'But why?' I asked. 'We English can't understand this feeling that Camus has. Why does he worry so much about the absurdity of human life? We've been brought up on Edward Lear and *Alice in Wonderland*, we know, we've known from infancy that life isn't rational.'

Sartre shrugged his shoulders and said, '*Eh bien, le pauvre Albert, il est tellement meridional.*' I don't quite know how to translate the word *meridional* but I think that what he meant was that Camus was such a rational Latin. Sartre himself, I felt, was very much the Northern French type, apt to be Protestant in feeling if not precisely in faith, and I knew he had read our nursery classics.

I have noticed that such conversations, moments of truth I suppose some people would call them, are not uncommon when there is crisis and a general emotional situation is created, but I shall never forget the peculiar feeling of Sartre, that of a very intelligent man who had allowed himself to be faced not just by the absurd but by the horror of human life, and had come up with acceptance or forgiveness, or at any rate one of the positive feelings. I admired him for it. I feel this is right in the old-fashioned, moral sense of that word.

Twenty-Five

EMINENCES AND ECHOES

At last, on 7 May 1945, there was an end to the War in Europe. This time demobilization was comparatively quick and efficient. To the general astonishment an immediate General Election brought a landslide victory for the Labour Party. For me this meant that, as when I was a child, many of the people in the House and in power were friends of ours, so that MPs and Cabinet Ministers were not unusual apparitions.

My brother John was shortly made Minister of Air. This meant that he was now in charge of the service in which, as Patrick Blackett had commented, he had experienced jet-propelled promotion. There was again some re-shuffling under Attlee so that next he was Minister of Food. The change was no doubt prestigious but the job was thorny, since there was still food rationing, of which we were all heartily tired. It proved so thorny that my poor sister-in-law, Celia (back from Canada with the children), hardly dared show her face in any kind of provision shop because of the mob of angry and well-organized Tory housewives who blamed the horrible Labour Minister for rationing.

But mostly, and for most people in Britain, this was a time of euphoria. For the Labour Party it was a time when it seemed possible actually to achieve some of the proposals of the Beveridge Report. In this harvest time many trifles seemed enjoyable. Beautiful red official boxes were circulated by messenger, and there were special telephones with scramblers for priority calls.

A small contented picture comes to my mind. A party of us are in the drawing-room at Plâs Brondanw. Our daughter Susan and her husband Euan are there and also one of their little girls; the child, a toddler, sits on the floor by Sir Stafford Cripps, an old friend and now Chancellor of the Exchequer. As he talks, Stafford dangles a bunch of keys on a chain over the arm of his chair; the child, pleased, plays with them and Stafford remarks, 'The keys of the Treasury'.

Another old friend, Aneurin Bevan, was at the combined Ministry of Health and Housing. Some of us trembled a little for him. He hadn't been good at getting up in the morning. He was an open-hearted South

Walian and a witty, companionable fellow, and a first-rate House of Commons hand, but how would he get on with his civil servants, would he be at his desk at nine, would he know how to organize?

He was at his desk at nine; he got on capitally with his civil servants, and the Beveridge Report came to life: the National Health Service was founded. What a relief! However, he had to fight a lot of people, especially the Establishment doctors. But founding a National Health Service was a wonderfully appropriate job for him. As a teenager he had worked down the mines and, like many miners, had developed shoulder muscles which later resented the change to sedentary life. As trade union official and an MP he knew what the lack of proper medical care and medical precautions can do to a miner's lungs, for his father had died of pneumoconiosis.

As for the top civil servants, it was said that Sir William Douglas, Permanent Secretary at Health and Housing, had declared, when he heard which ministry Nye had been given, that he would never serve under 'a loud-mouthed demagogue'. But Sir Douglas gave it a try and was soon heard to report that he had never had a better Minister.

Labour Ministers who had never held office before had anticipated some initial coolness. However they found that, if they themselves were competent, they were not just served with disgusted integrity but were supported and even befriended. It often seemed to my brother only right to pay tribute to the way he was treated in successive Ministries. Later, those who have had the pleasure of watching and hearing *Yes, Minister* (that well-acted, incomparably witty and entertaining BBC television series) saw a true picture. But it was a picture of what an incompetent Minister sometimes had to suffer. Competent newcomers were very differently treated.

But, alas, there was something that we in Britain and many people on the Continent, as they tried to rebuild Europe, had almost forgotten. This was that in the Pacific there was still war. The Americans hadn't forgotten or forgiven Pearl Harbor. Attlee, as Prime Minister, announced to us on the radio a piece of news that stunned us. It was news that once more turned interesting theological and moral speculations into a series of urgent Sphinx questions. These are questions which it was, and still is, death not to answer. What he told us that day over the radio was that America had dropped two bombs of an entirely new kind and of unexampled destructive power onto two populous Japanese cities, Hiroshima and Nagasaki, on 6 and 9 August 1945.

Slowly we began to take in what it was that had been done. We realized the truth about the blasts, and even more slowly the truth about fall-out.

It was years rather than months before two or three further points came out. One was that the young airman who had flown the plane and had dropped the first atomic bomb was said, on learning more, to have gone off his head; another was that the American Government had known, before ordering the bombing, that the Japanese were on the point of surrendering. The third thing we realized was that America had been warned in the most moving terms by some of the eminent physicists whose research work had contributed to the discovery of how to set free atomic power. They had implored the Government not to use it in warfare because of the long, irreversible effects on human tissue.

There is no need here to enlarge on this theme, but it is as well to remember that each bomb of the 1980s is of the order of ten times more destructive than the bomb that seared Hiroshima, and that at one firing Trident delivers ten such mega-bombs.

So the Frightful Fiend still treads close behind us all. But I feel bound to point out that at last there does seem to be a revulsion among quite a few million people, mostly young and in most countries. A faint feeling seems to stir even in some otherwise lion-hearted bosoms. But, as I have said before, I am a slow learner, so that like the majority of the human race who were not actually guilty of promoting two world wars, I only listened with half an ear to the agonizing of those whose researches made them feel guilty about the Bomb. It wasn't for several years that I began to wonder if, since neither religion nor common sense seemed to outlaw war, we could look for its causes in some new way. Meantime, as usual, I wrote, mostly for children.

I imagine myself standing before a bookshelf, but a bookshelf that carries a strange collection of books. What is so odd is that some of them are quite solid, either hardbacks or paperbacks as you would expect, and can be taken down in the usual way and looked over. With others this is impossible. I imagine that most prose writers have just such an imaginary bookshelf and that they, like me, visit it from time to time. As the author passes a hand along their backs, some of the books will get patted on the head, some will get ignored and some, poor despised things, will have their faces turned to the wall. Perhaps very few of us have felt able to say like Dean Swift, as we take down and open some substantial volume, 'Good God, what a genius I had when I wrote that book!' However, as Virginia Woolf remarked (and her bookshelf was a large one), 'Very few books come out and get published as their author meant.'

In my own phantom bookshelf I suppose that *The Pleasures of Architecture* (only half mine), *Noah's Ark, The Tragedy of John Ruskin, The*

Big Firm, and *Darwin's Moon* are the five that I should pat on the head.
Yes, and of the many books for children, *How You Began*.

But there really is something strange about such bookshelves, for
interspersed among these tangible volumes there are apt to be quite a
lot of others. These are books that we didn't write and – a sadder lot
these – also books that we did write but were never published. Some of
the most wraith-like still often seem fascinating; I mean the books that
never did get written.

On my shelf there is one such called *Prolegomena to a History of
World Nonsense*, and another which I very much wish I had written, a
children's book, is *An Outline of Ignorance*. That would be very agreeable
reading. Children do so hate to think that grown-up people know
everything; they are quite right: it's a lie. About the wraith that
would have been called *Introduction to World Nonsense*, I once said to
Arthur Waley that the trouble was that nearly all the best nonsense
was either English or at any rate written in English. There is a little
German, scarcely any French, so it would be terribly chauvinistic.

'Not at all,' said he. 'At this moment I'm translating a splendid long
nonsense novel from the Chinese.'

This turned out to be his version of *Monkey*, an incomparable piece of
work. Next time we met, I shook my head.

'*Monkey*,' I said, 'magnificent! But it's not nonsense. Charming
satire, chaff about Buddhism, a fairy tale. I'm a purist. Surely it's no
more nonsense that *Gulliver's Travels*.'

But Waley wouldn't have it: no, it wasn't satire or a fairy tale. So
then we passed back to the savagery of Swift and to remind each other
of the contemporary bishop who declared of Gulliver that for his part
he 'didn't believe the half of it'.

A surprising proportion of my own books were published in the
1950s and 1960s. There was at the time, and there has to some extent
persisted, a revulsion against science. There was a muttering that it
had been the physicists who had made the Bomb possible. In most
tribes praise for culture heroes such as Prometheus have alternated
with disapproval of knowing too much, for instance Dr Faustus, who
trafficked with the Dark Powers. But I no longer felt so simply that the
methods of science provided a causeway that led the way that humans
should travel. I was, and am, convinced that the rigours of scientific
proof and in general the scientific virtues are irreplaceable stepping
stones in the shifting sands of conjecture, prejudice and propaganda.
These stepping stones would be needed by our children. But in this
second post-war period, as when I wrote *How You Began*, there were
again hardly any accounts for children of recent scientific 'marvels' let

alone good stories of how these marvels had been achieved. Children's arms were jabbed or scratched to prevent them from dying of smallpox or choking with whooping-cough, but their minds were deprived, for instance, of the riveting tale of how the secret of antibiotics was so nearly missed.

I enjoyed telling these stories for children. For grown-ups I wrote *Darwin's Moon*, a life of Alfred Russell Wallace. He was the self-taught collector for museums who was Charles Darwin's runner-up, a gentle Owenite socialist. Quite independently he worked out the very same principles of the workings of evolution as Charles Darwin, and then generously conceded priority. Writing the book was enthralling because, as well as the usual vicissitudes of research, his story involved enormous butterflies, fires at sea, birds of paradise and all sorts of invigorating adventure story props as well as the opportunity of studying an exceptionally endearing human being.

Also on my shelf there is a row of fat, handsome volumes of the substantial sort, and paperbacks, with the general title *The Enchanted World*. Children are as invigorated as I am by hearing about dragons, princesses, enchanters, magic castles, mermaids and lake-ladies. Anyone who has ever heard of me seems to suppose that these traditional tales are the only books I have ever produced. They were a success, so that I soon got type-cast, to my annoyance, as a children's writer.

There was a real need for authentic re-tellings of traditional tales if Disney and Enid Blyton were not to reign supreme. The war seemed to have driven out of print even the best known magic for children, such as *The Arabian Nights*, while there was nothing like the Andrew Lang Coloured Fairy Books to be had, still less J. J. Jacobs's versions.

My son-in-law, Euan Cooper-Willis, having a family and being in charge of Blackie's publishing house, we set to work to amend the situation. But this is obviously an insufficient cause for five or six comely collections of golden princesses, winged horses and dark towers. I enjoyed collecting tales direct from narrators, or rescuing them from entombment in scholarly tomes, or from entanglement in the meshes of the *Jakata* or the *Mabinogion*.

'But why', said a proud Marxist Nigerian student scornfully to me one day, 'why do you ask me to tell you the foolish and childish untrue legends of my people?'

'Maxim Gorky', I was able to remind him, 'says that the old tales are part of every child's cultural heritage.' The upshot was that he told me a couple of capital African tales. I fancy he was a born and secretly practised story-teller.

It seemed to me that the same kind of need was being met by a very different type of book and author for a different audience. What I found to be very much to my taste was science fiction. This initially was written for adults but I soon realized it was read by teenagers. So, working with two different colleagues, first a schoolmaster and then a biologist, we produced a dozen *Out of this World* anthologies. There were tales in which humans were able to share the consciousness of other familiar life-forms, such as white mice and guinea pigs. There was the moral dilemma of the board of directors who had got an anti-social, obnoxious and dangerous chairman to go voluntarily into cold storage, and who suffered pangs of remorse about not having thawed him out for forty years. There was the bulldozer that became possessed by a minute but malignant life-form and went berserk. There was the dentist who, having been shanghaied by extra-terrestrials, had to try to stop the toothache of not only Leviathan but of sundry snappish life-forms, and the hospital in space where a hysterical dinosaur had to be treated, and the tale of the beautiful sentient diamond trees, of the young lung-fish whose uncle refused to leave the water, and of course many a tale invoking the immensities of space and time.

Of phantom books – the unwritten and the unpublished – there are a good many.

But enough of what actually got written and printed. One book for grown-ups that I like started life as a well-acted broadcast series. This was *The Art of Being a Woman*, and it was followed by *The Art of Being a Parent*. Another was a novel that I still like, *The Big Firm*, which has in it the only portrait that I ever tried. It is of Miss Hilda Greaves, Clough's engaging, peppery, cultivated, maiden aunt who inhabited the house in whose beech woods Shelley once shot at an intruder.

Of wraiths there are more than just the *Prolegomena* and the *Outline of Ignorance*. There was a novel that Margaret Storm Jameson urged me to write and that never took shape; and in the sadder category of the written but, alas, unpublished, two full-length novels, a one-act play, and a book that I called *Pills to Cure Melancholy*. About this one, on which I worked on and off for several years, and about which I thought for much of the time when I was editing SF and re-telling those fairy tales, I feel thoroughly wistful. I still want to say what I think I managed to say in that one.

Twenty-Six

THINGS DIDN'T STOP
HAPPENING

During the 1950s and 1960s, when I was so diligently writing many of the books on my imaginary shelf, we did all sorts of things and all sorts of things happened to us; some of these happenings were very awkward and some agreeable.

In 1955, for instance, Clough and I went for a holiday to the Caribbean. I was partly collecting tales about Anansi, but why it comes vividly to mind is because it was on that holiday that I learned the joys of snorkelling. The blues, reds, yellows and silvers of the little fish, the sight of which and, later, the recollections have never ceased to delight me – a whole miniature living world as strange as the big imaginary worlds of science fiction.

We enjoyed going to PEN conferences abroad. Clough never joined the club but always chose to come as my guest. The side-effects were often extraordinarily pleasant, seeing foreign capitals, being invited to parties in some palazzo or castle, and attending special concerts, plays or ballets.

We sailed, too, in home waters and abroad, including the Caribbean.

But matters of much more consequence for us was the fact that our daughters both married and that our first grandchild was born at Plâs Brondanw, just as my two younger children had been born in my parents' house. Charlotte had married Lin Wallace, a fellow biologist from New Zealand.

Politically, the Labour landslide had, as I have already said, brought back the days when there had always been MPs and a Cabinet Minister or two about. John was a minister in Attlee's government, while Clough was soon appointed Chairman of Stevenage New Town, the first of those fresh starts in regional planning for which Britain became famous. Then something on this job went wrong for him. I was, by the way, completely on his side when he resigned.

It was about then that Charlotte reported from New Zealand that twins were imminent, and Clough being unexpectedly free and needing a change, we took ship first for Australia (impressive) and then for New Zealand, a country which I liked at first sight and continue to like very

much indeed. What the newcomer feels about it has been very well put
by Dr W. J. M. Mackenzie in a preface to his *Biological Ideas in Politics*:

I suppose that Scots, rugby footballers, political scientists, naturalists,
mountaineers, foresters and farmers idealize New Zealand a little too much.
But only a little: to many strangers New Zealand is a mythological place [the
scene of] the crossing of the mountains in Samuel Butler's *Erewhon*; of
Macaulay's image of the 'traveller from New Zealand, in the midst of a vast
solitude, taking his stand on a broken arch of London Bridge, to sketch the
ruins of St Paul's'; of John Wyndham's vision of New Zealand in his novel *The
Chrysalids*, as the guardian of the future in a world scorched by nuclear
catastrophe . . .[1]

All through these years the hotel at Portmeirion was lively, that is it
was lively as soon as the war damage had been put right. The damage
was partly a result of being taken over by the military, and partly
because all building materials were strictly rationed, with no materials
for repairs, and no manpower to use them. However, Clough was
always a great contriver.

The hotel under Jim Wyllie's direction had become very comfortable
indeed. Actors and actresses from the Royal Shakespeare Company
often came over from Stratford-on-Avon; Noël Coward wrote his
Blithe Spirit there in a fortnight; Bernard Shaw, having forgotten to book
his first intended visit, had most reluctantly to be refused (he was one of
Clough's favourite authors); Bertrand Russell made his headquarters
in the Castle annexe, while town planners and fellow architects, grim
with the new Bauhaus ideas, came with dubious minds: the place was
frivolous – no 'machines for living' here! Not unnaturally, Clough
sometimes felt apprehensive about what they would think.

On the occasion of a frightful hydro-electric scheme being proposed
in which all the rills and waterfalls of Snowdonia would have been
imprisoned in steel and concrete, we wrote a satirical squib, *Headlong
Down The Years*, in the manner of Thomas Love Peacock. 'Squire
Headlong' in the story is, of course, Clough, and the Manager is James
Wyllie. In the story he asks the manager about how the austere
functionalist architect Sir Stylytes Post has reacted to his first sight of
the place:

'Is he drawing cubes and straight lines? Is he exorcising you?' asked the
Manager.

'On the contrary,' replied Squire Headlong. 'When I looked at his
drawing-board it seemed to me that I myself could hardly have combined such
a crowd of nereids, tritons, conches, drips, dolphins and sea-horses into a

single fountain in a week. Has he really done all that drawing this morning?'

'Yes, he has, but then I suppose he had never run wild before?'

'Unfortunate man,' mused the Squire. 'He must have had all that bottled up inside him for years – tridents and all. Terribly bad for the system!'[2]

Miss Sebastiana Tempest was a disguise for my dear, amiable Margaret Storm Jameson, and I called her a novelist whose compositions were noted for their deep melancholy, who commonly slept in a hair shirt with a volume of Kierkegaard as a pillow, and I noted that her conversation was usually in marked contrast to all this. Bertrand Russell figures in the tale, wearing as a button-hole a plant with a square root, which some called 'Bishop's-bane'. He (in real life) had remarked that Portmeirion or the Croesor Valley could be compared with the Place de l'Opéra in Paris; if you sat there, sooner or later everyone you knew was sure to pass by.

Politicians appear frequently in the book: 'How their ideas whirl about! It's a remarkable little turn-coterie.'

'Last time', remarks a disgruntled local up the valley, 'I counted a couple of ex-Communists, three neo-Catholics, and some assorted neo-mystics – and a number of Freudians who had managed some grave deviations.'

'What about moral rearmament?' asked another local in a tone of reproof.

'We mustn't exaggerate,' was the answer.

A lot of us had a hand in this tale: Richard Hughes wrote the preface and an epilogue for instance, and our daughter Susan designed a witty jacket.

We experienced one most unpleasant and unwelcome event. Very early one December morning in 1951, our cherished Plâs Brondanw was gutted by fire. While it was thrilling in a dreadful way to see the flames fly out like curtains when the windows burst with the heat and to hear the crashing of the glass, the effect was alarming as well as splendid. The thick old granite walls stood firm, even when half the roof had fallen in, but the few dark winter hours that had been so dramatic had extremely awkward consequences.

Luckily we had been alone in the house when it happened. We found shelter first with Susan half a mile away, and then here and there. Clough had quite a few burns, and most of the furniture had gone. Then, before Clough, tormented by post-war building restrictions, could heal the house's wounds, there came the realization that our daughter Charlotte was ill in New Zealand, had been ill for some uncomplaining time. She had tried to get and I had tried to send her domestic help, but all in vain.

By the time of the fire the decision had, I think, already been taken that she, and her five little creatures under five, had better come home for some mothering, not only from me but also half the village. Clough got a roof on the house and we just managed to make the top storey habitable as an adequate flat.

Our going to New Zealand and the five grandchildren coming here grew into a series of happy interchanges, but both families felt it a pity that New Zealand was exactly on the other side of the world. However, one by one or two by two at different stages, Charlotte's children came back to Wales for enjoyment or bits of their education. It was to them in New Zealand, when Clough died in 1978, that I fled, alone, and took refuge for a while. I fled in the passionate desire to get away that so often follows bereavement.

With Susan, Euan and their young family, as with Charlotte, the long story of mutual help and support went on as roles exchanged and supporters needed support.

The grandchildren grew up and I contemplate nearly all their doings with pleasure and often hilarity. It would be fun to chronicle expeditions that I did with one or other of them to foreign parts, including Zambia and Malawi, but there were and are travels in the interior world, the world of my own head, that I want to follow up.

There was, of course, all through the Fifties and Sixties the continuo of public affairs which affected us all. The morality of the Bomb, the Cold War and the truth about the death camps impinged even on those who were ostensibly not interested in public affairs. Fancy religions flourished, drug-taking, the Nuremberg trials, Albert Speer's book, the unspeakable secrets of the Holocaust, and discreditable doings at home and abroad, posed all the old inscrutable questions over again.

Whenever the music stopped, this anxious continuo kept reasserting itself. Had science or religion got answers to pass on to 'a fair posterity'? 'He that hath friends hath given hostages to fortune' – now it was our grandchildren. Love is the most terrible of the passions, for we are mortal.

I tried to think out (and managed perhaps to set down something of my thoughts in the book that for the time being I call *Pills to Cure Melancholy*) some way to take the debate further. I began to muse once more over a train of thought that I had begun to follow when I wrote *Noah's Ark*. Looking back, I can see that I have never quite abandoned this search. I was, in the sailing sense, tacking – often facing first one way and then another – but I believe I was never completely off course, and now I had come to the time of life just before old age when some sort of harvesting of ideas is very usual.

This business about the age at which my sort of speculation is usual is actually classical in the structure of society in many Eastern civilizations: it is the done thing to go on a pilgrimage; it is proper for a man and, in some cases, for a woman to turn over their worldly affairs to their heirs and to take up whole-time what is sometimes called the making of their souls.

Looking back, what seems peculiar is that such a search never engaged Clough in the least; such speculations seemed never to cross his mind. He was perhaps like Wordsworth's 'happy warrior' who even into old age relies 'upon a genial sense of youth'. I walked shoulder to shoulder with him; we were married for sixty-three years.

Twenty-Seven

LAMAS IN KATHMANDU

Said a granddaughter who was 'into' Buddhism, 'You know far too little about any religion except Christianity to be able to say anything about the subject.' When I protested that I had read a good deal, she declared that reading was very thin stuff. With this, of course, I had to agree.

The upshot was that I arranged to meet her in Kathmandu and learn to meditate from Tibetan lamas. This being decided, her parting shot was a shake of her head and the remark that she feared I was undertaking this expedition mostly 'for that book of yours' and not 'for your own improvement', the implication being that improvement was something that my character could well do with. I had to admit both her allegations.

It has always seemed to me that one of the advantages enjoyed by those who have faith in creeds and religions is that they have at hand words such as 'triumphalism' for the absurd inflation that follows a new insight and also a vocabulary of actions, such as prostrations and processions, in which Sphinx questions can be brought into consciousness, often without the distortion of being formulated.

On BBC Radio 4 a listener seeking clarification asked a question to which a bishop answered briskly, 'Do you mean God Imminent or God Transcendent?' I was startled, but I could see that the discussion was being advanced and clarified. Religious technical language, actions and attitudes, from simple actions like kneeling to kiss an icon, really are expressive. So, of course, is the creation of great works of religious art (such as composing *The Messiah* or painting the Sistine Chapel) and they do body forth feelings that are commonly incommunicable.

Going to Kathmandu seemed a chance of sharing in the communication of one important form of religion belonging to another civilization. After all, no single religion has a monopoly of mankind's reflections on Good and Evil, and 'Time, Death and Judgement'. I kept a diary and tried, and still try, to evaluate any long-term effects of my brief contact with the lamas.

The scene is a lamasery or *gompa* six or seven miles out of Kathmandu and much higher. The time, 6.30 am on a Sunday in March 1973. A lovely morning, the sun rising through mists and the air full of the sound of cuckoos and woodpeckers. There are about a hundred of us, men and women in about equal numbers; most are drop-outs of between eighteen and twenty years old – quite a few are couples with small children. I am the only one of grandparent age.

When the young lama comes in – Rimpoche Zopa – everybody stands. This is quite difficult because everyone had been sitting cross-legged, and the meditation hall – a square room – is so packed that they have been elbow to elbow and knee to knee. I am the exception; I have been given the only chair.

Having greeted us, the lama explains that he is in charge of the meditation course, arranges yellow drapery over his dark-red monk's robes, and then sits cross-legged on a little raised seat with a low table-cum-altar in front of him. The robes do not cover his right arm, which is bare in token of poverty. His voice is soft. You would guess him to be a tenor when speaking normally, but when chanting he is a bass. He does very little chanting but, if he does so, he often manipulates a small bell and also something pointed which I took at first to be a ritual dagger. Later I found that (rather charmingly in his delicate right hand with its bare arm and fluid gestures) it represents a thunderbolt for use against evil influences such as negative thoughts. He speaks rather quickly and his English is not always easy to follow, but a good deal of what he tells us has been summarized on roneoed sheets.

He quotes various Buddhist scriptures and begins to explain the form of meditation that he is proposing. It differs from thinking something out and also from the Zen meditation technique of just sitting and making your mind receptive. A meditation, he says, should benefit people other than the person meditating.

As he enlarges on this point, some of us are reminded of the way in which many Christians – Catholics, for instance – pray and meditate with a 'special intention' for someone or something. In the Litany of the Church of England, the congregation prays, for example, for 'all prisoners and captives, and all women labouring with child'. Our 'intention' could, the Lama says, be for personal friends or for souls struggling to get out of either a 'cold hell' or a 'hot hell' (in the Buddhist faith there is no eternal punishment). Or the meditation might help someone out of an inconvenient reincarnation. A useful technique, he explains, is trying to visualize some particular aspect of the Gautama Buddha:

At the height of your forehead and facing you, try to see the throne of the Gautama Buddha, a square platform adorned with jewels and supported by

eight snow lions, two for each side. This is all made of pure light. The snow
lions are visualized as alive and made of light like the throne . . . and the whole
is supported on a lotus. The Buddha's aspect is very peaceful. Then imagine
that the vision of the throne, and all except the Buddha, is absorbed into the
emblems that adorn it, those of the sun, moon and stars. Finally, only the
shining figure of the Buddha himself is left. Speech comes to me from him,
while his mind comes to my mind and I am filled with happiness . . .

A point that he emphasizes is how fortunate we all are to have been
'nobly born' – that is born as humans – each of us seems to have had 'a
perfect human birth'. Many other incarnations into other worlds or as
animals give less opportunity for reaching enlightenment. He soon
comes to the doctrine of reincarnation. It is, he several times implies,
one of the few specific tenets that is fundamental to Buddhism. He does
not, for example, say specifically that Buddhism does not postulate a
Creator, but he does emphasize that our minds and also to a great
extent the phenomenal world as we experience it are constructs, that is
concepts – interpretations of reality created in our own minds.

This idea of the subjectiveness of all things that we see, hear and
experience, was emphasized by the Dalai Lama, head of the Tibetan
School of Mahayana, when I heard him speak in London in July 1981,
eight years later. Reality, he said, is not something that is 'analytically
findable'. The most satisfactory way of interpreting what we experience is something that has to be learned, and leads to the
cultivation of the 'altruistic mind' – that is to say unselfishness – and
especially to love and compassion.

For the individual the goal is necessarily happiness, satisfaction and
the avoidance of suffering, and in this he will be wise to engage in the
search for wisdom. Wisdom is the understanding of 'non-inherent
existence'. In this context this phrase referred not so much to material
objects (that is, not the Bishop Berkeley philosophy), but more to our
own beliefs in the inherent 'goodness' or 'badness' of events. What he
was expressing here, I thought, was the fact that in our comprehension
of a concept, there was so much interpretation and so much depends, as
the English proverb says, on 'the eye of the beholder'.

But to go back to the meditation course in Kathmandu, it was some
time during the second day that Lama Zopa began to explain the
general Buddhist concept of karma. Karma seemed, as he explained it,
not to be exactly conscience as Christians interpret it, but something a
little more public. I found myself comparing it with what in some
modern schools replaces examinations – continuous assessment.

To keep your karma in a good state, he said, includes receiving as well as giving. It is essential, he went on, to let other people help you; you must often allow yourself to be under an obligation. This is not only for your own benefit but because you must let yourself be useful to others who want to give otherwise you are selfishly depriving them of opportunities for improving their own karma.

'But how', someone asked at one point, 'am I to atone for a slip, let's say an unfriendly act, when actual reparation happens to be impossible?'

The answer was that then one should try doing good elsewhere, try adding to the general stock of karma, as it were, by increasing loving kindness in general. I remember that the Jesuits are said to hold that remorse is bad, and this way of thinking of karma certainly seemed a good way of dealing with guilty feelings.

Lama Zopa never spoke of sin or guilt or wickedness, only of ignorance and the advantages of happiness and 'positive' in contrast to 'negative' thought.

This emphasis on love is, of course, common to practically all the meditative types of religion. The general absence of resentment among the Tibetan 'clergy' I have met was striking. The Dalai Lama and those at Kathmandu were all exiles, refugees, who had seen their way of life denied and destroyed. Their attitude certainly compared very strikingly to that of other refugees with whom World War II brought me in contact.

Perhaps the Buddhist emphasis on non-attachment helped. In personal relations, the combination of love and this non-attachment emphasised in Kathmandu and also by the Dalai Lama in London, was something that we, in Kathmandu, thought about a great deal, and some of us could see that in personal relations this non-attachment was very difficult to combine with love, for love nearly always has a protective element in it. And yet, since we were many of us parents and there were young couples among us, many of us knew only too well the misery that possessiveness can cause in a family or in love affairs, and in fact in all human relations. It can wreck the relations of parents and children, and that between spouse and spouse. Learning how to combine love with non-attachment, it was implied, was part of the wisdom into which we were trying to inquire.

One evening towards the end of the first week, as dusk came on, Lama Zopa began to ask questions and to encourage us to talk. Feeling perhaps that we might be getting too smug and cosy, or feeling disposed for mild fun at the expense of Western science, he started us off on a little cosmic jaunt through space and time, hoping I thought (and with success) to trap us into what I believe philosophers call infinite regress.

'You believe that all life stems from other life, and that life that we see in turn had parents?'

Yes, we do.

'And the same about matter? Or don't you know how matter came to be?'

Someone murmured something about steady state or big bang.

'In fact you don't know?'

No, we don't.

'But with life? Living things? Do you trace it back in an endless line?'

Yes, we suppose that we do.

'But you think it must have had a beginning?'

Some of us tried to conjure up Professor Oparin's conjectural primal soup or Hoyle's galactic viruses, but most of us felt that it would take too long. Check mate.

After a pause, we saw that Lama Zopa had a perfect right to his amiable smile and to his remark that the Buddhist concept of the origins of life had at least the advantage of being short. 'Beginningless,' he murmured in the by now almost dark room, and added 'Isn't it also possible to think of time not so much as a line or as a stream, but as a wheel? Why not?'

We talked among ourselves, of course, and among various Christians the old discussions about the respective merits of contemplatives and activists came up. The New Testament was invoked: Jesus and his disciples, says St Luke, are received into her house by Martha. Martha, 'cumbered by much serving', asks Jesus to tell her sister Mary to help, but Mary is listening to Jesus's teaching. 'Martha, Martha,' answers Jesus, 'thou art anxious and troubled about many things', and goes on to say that Mary, the contemplative, has chosen well.

Someone recalled the famous commentary on this in *The Cloud of Unknowing* by an unidentified author in about 1350:

> Mary regarded not the business of her sister, although her business was full good and full Holy. From Jesus's side Mary would not move for nothing . . . she sat full still and answered not one word . . . And right as Martha complained thus on Mary her sister, right so unto this day all actives complain of contemplatives . . . for be it man or woman in any company of this world – I except none – the which man or woman feeleth himself stunned through Grace to forsake all outward business and to live through Grace a contemplative life, as fast their own brethren and their own sisters and all their nearest friends, with a great complaining spirit shall rise up on them and say that it is naught that they do.

Later, following up with a few books on Buddhism, particularly

Tibetan Buddhism, and what Westerners have had to say about it, I came upon Jung's praise of *The Tibetan Book of the Dead*, which he calls 'The Bardo of The Dying', and this indeed made me see the greatness as well as the charm of some of their teaching. Their tolerance seems unmatched in any other religious teaching, and some of their concepts are Miltonic. This is how the dying man is to be reassured and supported by a priest or, if no priest is available, by some other friend or comforter:

A known and venerated being is to be invoked and visualized. To appeal to a Shivite devotee, the form of Shiva is visualized; to a Buddhist, the form of the Gautama Buddha; to a Christian, the form of Jesus; to a Moslem, the form of the Prophet; and so on, for other religious devotees, and for all manners and conditions of mankind.[1]

Because he is human, the dying man is, whatever his condition, to be addressed as 'the nobly born':

Oh! Nobly born, that which is called death being come to thee now, resolve thus: This is now the hour of death. By taking advantage of this my death, I will so act, for the good of all sentient beings which people the illimitable expanse of the heavens. This I do by resolving on love and compassion for them.[2]

Bodily death should be and can be the path to liberation:

Oh! Nobly born, when thy body and mind are separating, thou will experience a glimpse of the Pure Truth, subtle, sparkling, bright, dazzling, glorious, radiant, awe-inspiring like a mirage moving across a landscape . . . Be not daunted thereby, nor terrified, nor awed. That is the radiance of thine own true nature. Recognise it. From the midst of that radiance, the natural sound of Reality, reverberating like a thousand thunders simultaneously sounding, will come. That is the natural sound of thine own self. Be not daunted thereby, nor terrified, nor awed.[3]

Twenty-Eight

WHAT NEXT?

I came back from Kathmandu grateful to the lamas and quite a lot wiser, ready to follow up what I had learned from them, but no more convinced of the ability of the followers of Buddha to solve the Sphinx questions than of the efficacy of the doctrines of Hindus or Christians. 'What is truth?' asked the Roman governor rhetorically, feeling fairly sure that the rabbis would not be able to answer.

So far it seemed to me that every form of organized religion (and this goes for Marx-Leninism as well) has had growing in it the seeds of regression, or else has been hampered or destroyed by built-in obsolescence. In the case of Buddhism, for instance, there seems to be an almost endearing tendency to revert to magic, say to take note of astrology rather than astronomy. Recent as well as ancient history indicates that, alas, a succession of Christians, Moslems and Hindus have not managed to answer the great inscrutable questions. Milton's statement of one of them is:

> What makes a Nation happy, what keeps it so?
> What ruins Empires and lays cities flat?

Having lived through the end of an Empire and witnessed the flattening of cities, I am convinced that on the whole mayhem isn't the work of plagues or earthquakes, but of humans.

The religious, as I could see, have been right when they have all along seen large Sphinx questions as intertwined with puzzles on a different scale: what had better be the individual's moral values? Christians have summarized this in a single question: 'What shall we do to be saved?' Yes, indeed.

Like other living species, we have evolved in such a way that most of us spend most of our lives in efforts to live out these lives: 'What shall we do to survive?' At this point I seemed to notice the use of a plural – 'we'. The laws and usages of human societies have commonly acknowledged this in-built general passion, acknowledging in various degrees the individual's passionate, often self-thwarted, insistent desire for 'Life, Liberty and the Pursuit of Happiness', and condoning what would otherwise be crimes if done in self-defence.

I began to think (facing a few such paradoxes) about trying a method

of thinking and acting that has proved so fruitful in a great many lesser
puzzles – science. True, it has never been much good trying to analyse
those old brutes, the good, the true, and the beautiful. A much more
basic approach could show that a few well-tried scientific procedures
can be used on the conceiver rather than on the concepts. Our
questions might be not about abstractions but about humans.

This creature has a purpose; it wants to survive, uses a plural when it
chances to think about the matter and, like all other organisms that
appear to be purposive (especially those that have become extinct), the
creature often blunders.

This isn't the place to tell at any length about my one-woman,
untaught attempts to come upon some fruitful way of coming to terms
with all this. But so many cities having been laid flat, even in my
lifetime, these Sphinx questions had as usual a certain urgency.

Metaphorically and indeed sometimes literally, I took out the little
looking-glass in my handbag and persistently held it up to nature. My
own face turned out to be instructive, for it was quite typical of my age
and sub-species: fair colouring, roundish, flattish. The jaws were clearly
not much good for aggression or even cracking nuts. I had binocular
vision, like my cat Lucy, but ears that couldn't be pricked like hers or a
dog's, and a nose that I couldn't wiffle about to catch what was faintly
on the wind, nor could it be put to the ground to warn of the approach of
prey or predator. My hands (front paws) I could see directly; they were
holding the looking-glass in a way that only a primate could have held
it. The fingers had only vestigial claws, no good for defence or attack,
but, like a primate's, my hands were a creator's or evolution's rash
venture. Much, but not all, of the general outline of the rest of this
creature I could also see by direct observation. (In Russian fairy tales,
the impossible is stated as, 'You will as soon see your own ears . . .')

One of the things that the looking-glass couldn't tell me, but that
being a mother and a grandmother could and did emphasize, was what
a long infancy and juvenile stage we had, and about our particularly
helpless infancy. A little fawn or a foal will stagger up on to its knobbly
legs after a few hours; a kitten after a few weeks; a human baby will take
over a year and perhaps a leisurely two to be able to walk. A real ape,
male or female, will be adult in six or ten years; a boy or girl, even if
born into a simple pre-literate tribe, will not count as fully adult till
twelve or fifteen. In what we call 'the developed world' the process may
take twenty years or more.

So I began to read books on the behaviour of organisms in their
native habitats. There was Konrad Lorenz's delightful *King Solomon's
Ring*, Desmond Morris's best-seller *The Naked Ape*, and Elaine

Morgan's *The Descent of Woman*. All this has acquired the convenient name of Ethology, as contrasted with the earlier Animal Behaviour. The newer word was coined I think (or anyhow fortified) by Professor E. O. Wilson, the excellent researcher and synthesizer.

And then, at last, it occurred to this slow learner that what I had been reading was, as the vulgar phrase goes, 'spot on' to what I had been trying to think out for myself. This exhilarating feeling of not being alone, of having far better equipped fellow-workers and leaders, I have found most invigorating. Perhaps a fruitful way really has been discovered for diagnosing the nature of the old questions.

Mary Midgley in her *Beast and Man*, John Maddox in conversation on the radio with Professor Richard Gregory and Dr Donald Broad-bent, and going even further – further than I want to go – Francis Crick in his *Life Itself* and Sir Fred Hoyle with their conjectures about outer space, Attenborough and Bronowski with their incomparable cameramen – they have all made splendid company for me.

And then, after all that, I began to wonder if there could be anything that I myself, using my own musings or experience, could possibly contrive to add to this vital discussion. I have come to the conclusion that there is something that has not been formulated. The point on which nearly all are agreed is the absolute need for communication among the members of any social species, from the rabbit with its white scut onward. With humans the emphasis is usually on language. All the refinements of scientific converse help us to understand each other, but I believe the arts are also essential.

This unique ability of the arts to express and communicate is something that the religious have always understood. I think of the splendours of a sung mass, of the beautiful phrases in *The Tibetan Book of the Dead* and of the great serene, enigmatic carved triptych in Bombay's Caves of Elephanta.

A picture rises insistently in my mind, a picture as imaginary as Bunyan's dream. I am sitting by a swimming-pool. It has a diving-board at each end. On one stands a young man in the minimum of clothing. It is possible to think of him as a specimen of large, hairless, carnivorous ground ape. It is also possible to think of him as a very handsome fellow. It is again possible to think of him as a creature that can only keep alive under certain quite restrictive circumstances; keep the oxygen from his brain for ten minutes and his spark of life has gone.

Someone has switched off the news and now a popular record is being played. I know most of the words, having been instructed by a fifteen-year-old. It is a song by David Bowie: 'I don't know what I was waiting for/And my time was running wild . . ./I turned myself to face me/But I've never caught a glimpse . . .'

On the other diving-board stands a young woman. You can see her also as a predator or as suffering the same restrictions as the boy and, in addition, another anatomical hazard. Like the boy, she is full of life. I think how she won't pass her finals unless she gives her mind to them, and may miss her PhD if she gets carried through the open doors of Noah's Ark. But she isn't thinking about that, and the boy is watching her. She dives, he dives too. They meet in the middle of the pool. Will their heads bump? Do they know how dangerous the primal urges can be? They don't care. Their heads do not bump and they come up laughing, her long hair over her eyes. I just hope they know that it isn't chess they are going to play, but a game more like gin-rummy, when you are dealt a hand and then keep picking up unseen cards. But all the same, my dears, you can use skill.

Time is like a wheel, said the Lama, so that I see another picture. I am sitting not exactly as I sat once so long ago by gaslight with my back to a good coal fire. Someone has switched off the news and it is very quiet. As before, I've got something in my lap. It isn't a doll this time but a sleeping child, one of my great-grandchildren. What, I muse, will her parents tell the sweet-breathing, confiding little creature? That life can be well worth living, I hope.

BOOKS

Year Published	Title
1919	*The Tank Corps* (with Clough Williams-Ellis)
1922	*An Anatomy of Poetry*
1923	*The Pleasures of Architecture* (with Clough Williams-Ellis)
1925	*Noah's Ark*
1926	*But We Know Better*
1927	*The Wall of Glass*
1928	*How You Began*
1928	*The Tragedy of John Ruskin*
1929	*Men Who Found Out*
1930	*HMS Beagle in South America*
1931	*Volcano*
1932	*How You Are Made*
1933	*What Shall I Be?*
1933	*To Tell the Truth*
1936	*The History of English Life* (with F. J. Fisher)
1937	*In and Out of Doors*
1938	*The Big Firm*
1938	*Good Citizens*
1939	*Learn to Love First*
1939	*Ottik's Book of Stories*
1943	*Women in War Factories*
1950	*Princesses and Trolls*
1951	*A Food and People Geography*
1951	*The Art of Being a Woman*
1951	*Headlong Down The Years* (with Clough Williams-Ellis)
1951	*Laughing Gas and Safety Lamp* (with Euan Cooper-Willis)
1952	*The Art of Being a Parent*
1953–8	*Seekers and Finders*
1957	*The Arabian Nights*
1959	*Grimm's Fairy Tales*
1960–73	*Out of this World* (10 vols SF anthologies with Mably Owen)
1960	*Fairy Tales from the British Isles*

1961	*Modern Scientists at Work*
1963	*Round the World Fairy Tales*
1965	*Russian Fairy Tales* (with Moura Budberg)
1966	*Old World and New World Fairy Tales*
1966	*Darwin's Moon*
1966	*Worlds Apart* (with Mably Owen)
1968–70	*Life in England* (illustrated by William Stobbs)
1973	*Gypsy Folk Tales*
1973	*Tales from the Galaxies*
1975	*Strange Universe*
1976	*Strange Orbits*
1977	*Strange Planets*
1977	*The Rain-God's Daughter*
1980	*The Story Spirits*

SOURCE NOTES

One: LITTLE GIRL

1 Reprinted in *The First Cuckoo 1900–80*, Times Books, 1981.

Two: POWER OF THE PRESS

1 *St Loe Strachey and His Paper*, Amy Strachey, 1930.
2 Preface to *Spectatorial Essays*, Lytton Strachey, 1964.
3 *John Strachey*, Hugh Thomas, 1973.
4 *Spectatorial Essays*, Lytton Strachey, 1964.

Three: OVER THE BANISTERS

1 *The Scarlet Tree*, Osbert Sitwell, 1946.
2 *Memoirs of a Dutiful Daughter*, Simone de Beauvoir, 1959.

Five: THE RITUAL CHANGE

1 *All Change Here*, Naomi Mitchison, 1975.
2 *The Scarlet Tree*, Osbert Sitwell, 1946.

Eight: TRENCH WARFARE

1, 2, 3 *The Tank Corps*, Clough and Amabel Williams-Ellis, 1919.
4 'Strange Meeting', Wilfred Owen.

Nine: THE BELLS RANG OUT

1, 2 *Architect Errant*, Clough Williams-Ellis, 1971.

Thirteen: THE POLITICS I WAS TRYING TO AVOID

1 *John Strachey*, Hugh Thomas, 1973.
2 *Inside the Left*, Fenner Brockway,

Fifteen: CLOUGH AND PORTMEIRION

1 *Architect Errant*, Clough Williams-Ellis, 1971.
2 *The Pleasures of Architecture*, Clough and Amabel Williams-Ellis, 1924.
3 *The Architect*, Clough Williams-Ellis, 1929.

Sixteen: MICROSCOPE AND TELESCOPE

1 *Antic Hay*, Aldous Huxley, 1949.
2 *The Life and Work of J. B. S. Haldane*, Ronald Clark, 1968.
3 *Antic Hay*, Aldous Huxley, 1949.

Seventeen: VENICE AND RUSKIN
1, 2, 3   *A Toccata of Galuppi's*, Robert Browning.
4   *The Tragedy of John Ruskin*, Amabel Williams-Ellis, 1928.

Eighteen: RUSSIAN JOURNEY
1   *Workers' Control in the Russian Mining Industry*, John Strachey, 1928.
2, 3   *Volcano*, Amabel Williams-Ellis, 1928.

Nineteen: SAILING
1, 2, 3   *Riddle of the Sands*, Erskine Childers, 1903.
4   *Architect Errant*, Clough Williams-Ellis, 1971.

Twenty: THE THIRTIES BEGIN
1   *Recollections of a Rebel*, Robert Boothby, 1978.
2   *Architect Errant*, Clough Williams-Ellis, 1971.
3, 4   *An Autobiography*, Leonard Woolf, 1980.

Twenty-One: WORDS AND SILENCE
1   *The 1930s: A Challenge to Orthodoxy*, edited by John Lucas, 1978.

Twenty-Two: WRITERS, READERS AND IRRELEVANCIES
1   *The Left Book Club:* An Historical Record, Dr John Lewis, 1970.
2   *Cockburn Sums Up*, Claud Cockburn, 1981.
3   *The Years of The Week*, Patricia Cockburn, 1968.

Twenty-Three: WAR FACTORIES AND BORROWED CHILDREN
1   *Architect Errant*, Clough Williams-Ellis, 1971.
2   *The Times*, 20 September 1940.
3   *Borrowed Children*, Amy St Loe Strachey, 1940.

Twenty-Four: 'AND TURNETH NOT HIS HEAD'
1, 2   *Post D*, John Strachey, 1941.
3   Prof. J. K. Galbraith writing in *Encounter*, September 1963.

Twenty-Six: THINGS DIDN'T STOP HAPPENING
1   *Biological Ideas in Politics*, Dr W. J. M. Mackenzie, 1978.
2   *Headlong Down The Years*, Amabel and Clough Williams-Ellis, 1951.

Twenty-Seven: LAMAS IN KATHMANDU
1, 2, 3   *The Tibetan Book Of The Dead*, W. Y. Evans-Wentz, 1960.

INDEX

Carroll, Lewis, 139
Casson, Sir Hugh, 111
Chamberlain, Neville, 127, 144, 155
Childers, Erskine, 118
Chrysalids, The (Wyndham), 178
Chukovsky, Kornei, 139
Churchill, Clementine, 7
Churchill, Winston, 7, 126, 165
Civil Liberties Press Bureau, 153
Clandon (Surrey), 23, 47
Clark, Ronald, 105
Cloud of Unknowing, The, 186
Cockburn, Claud, 149–50, 151, 155
Colefax, Lady Sibyl, 129
Coloured Fairy Books, 29, 175
Coming Struggle for Power, The (Strachey), 167
Communists, 132, 133, 137–40
Coniston, 111
Conrad, Joseph, 88
Conservative Party, 81, 84, 106, 130, 132, 137, 146
Constant, Benjamin, 75
Cook, A. J., 108
Cooper-Willis, Euan (son-in-law), 107, 171, 175, 180
Cooper-Willis, Susan, *see* Williams-Ellis, Susan
Corbusier, Le, 68
Cornhill Magazine, 110
Corridors of Power (Snow), 104
Country Life, 62
Coward, Noël, 178
Crick, Francis, 190
Cripps, Sir Stafford, 171
Cromer, Evelyn Baring, Lord, 7
Cromwell, Oliver, 18, 20, 83
Cunard, Lady, 130
Cunard, Nancy, 107
Curry, Bill, 100

Daily Mail, 20, 41, 63, 65
Daily Telegraph, 62
Dalai Lama, 184, 185
Danovsky, Bogdan, 141, 143
Dartington Hall, 100
Darwin, Charles, 175
Deeds That Won The Empire (Fitchett), 19

Descent of Woman, The (Morgan), 190
Diggers, 20
Digging for Mrs Miller (Strachey), 166
Dimitrov, Georgi, 140, 141
Dr Zhivago (Pasternak), 89, 113
Don Basin coalfield, 112–15
Douglas, Sir William, 172
Draper, Ruth, 107

Easton Lodge (Essex), 130
Edward VIII, 154
Ehrenburg, Ilya, 158
Einstein, Albert, 69
Elizabeth, the Queen Mother, 154
Elles, General, 61–2
Engels, Friedrich, 82, 108
Erbe, Dr, 142, 143
Erewhon (Butler), 178
Esher, Lionel, Lord, 119
Esher, Lady, 119

Fabians, 127, 132
Faraday, Michael, 103
Fascists, 133, 137, 145
Fisher, F. J., 127
'Flower People', 72
Forgan, Dr, 145
Forster, E. M., 126
Fox in the Attic, The (Hughes), 87, 88
Franklin, Benjamin, 103, 104, 140
Frazer, Sir James, 99–100
Fry, Roger, 58

Galbraith, J. K., 107, 167
Gallagher, Willie, 141
Garvin, J. L., 19, 20, 83
General Strike, 106, 126, 134, 135
Genji, Prince, 48
George VI, 154
Glasfryn, 63, 92
Goebbels, Josef, 141, 142, 143–4
Goering, Hermann, 138, 150, 151
Golden Bough, The (Frazer), 99
Gollancz, Victor, 133, 149, 153, 162
Gordon, General, 7
Gorky, Maxim, 139, 175
Grant, Duncan, 6, 58
Graves, Robert, 88